Everything but Money

Everything but Money

The Hidden Barriers Between You and Financial Freedom

Jessica Moorhouse

Collins

Everything but Money
Copyright © 2024 by Jessica Moorhouse.
All rights reserved.

Published by Collins, an imprint of HarperCollins Publishers Ltd

FIRST EDITION

HarperCollins books may be purchased for educational, business, or sales promotional use through our Special Markets Department.

HarperCollins Publishers Ltd
Bay Adelaide Centre, East Tower
22 Adelaide Street West, 41st Floor
Toronto, Ontario, Canada
M5H 4E3

www.harpercollins.ca

Designed by Renata DiBiase

Library and Archives Canada Cataloguing in Publication

Title: Everything but money : the hidden barriers between you and financial freedom / Jessica Moorhouse.
Names: Moorhouse, Jessica, author.
Description: First edition. | Includes bibliographical references.
Identifiers: Canadiana (print) 20240495802 | Canadiana (ebook) 20240495810 |
ISBN 9781443472173 (softcover) | ISBN 9781443472180 (ebook)
Subjects: LCSH: Finance, Personal. | LCSH: Finance, Personal—Psychological aspects.
Classification: LCC HG179 .M66 2024 | DDC 332.024—dc23

Printed and bound in the United States of America

24 25 26 27 28 LBC 5 4 3 2 1

To my loving husband, Josh. If it weren't for you,
I don't know if I would have ever gone to therapy.
I mean that as a compliment.

Contents

PART III

Stacked Against You: The Invisible Barriers Holding You Back

Everything but Money

Introduction

Is it just me or do you ever get low on New Year's Day? Because I do. Every. Single. Year. For whatever reason, at the stroke of midnight on December 31, something triggers my body to deflate like a grounded hot air balloon. My limbs get heavy, it becomes hard to move, and the only place that's safe is under the covers. At the same time as my body turns to stone, my mind starts to race, bringing to the surface all my failures from the past 12 months.

You sure didn't earn as much as you thought you would this year. Ouch, that's embarrassing.

You bought a house at the peak of a seller's market and now it's worth $100,000 less than when you bought it a year ago? That's just downright dumb. You call yourself a money expert?

Wait, you're telling me you didn't pay off six figures in debt in only eight months and didn't become a millionaire by 30? So . . . what have you done that's so special to warrant any kind of attention? Nothing. That's what I thought.

That's some next-level unhealthy negative self-talk going on. I know. I'm working on it. Nevertheless, things took a turn at the end of 2022. The week before I was supposed to fly back to my hometown of Vancouver, British Columbia, for Christmas, I got COVID. That meant spending the holidays at home alone with my husband, with no presents to exchange (they had all been shipped to my parents) and a socially distanced pre-made turkey dinner from the grocery store. Considering the previous two Christmases had been ruined by the pandemic and government-mandated lockdowns, I'd built up this visit to look like a full-blown Hallmark movie in my mind. So, when it didn't happen as I'd imagined, a dark cloud came rushing over me.

Everything I saw on TV and social media was triggering. Everything was a reminder of how I wasn't rich enough, successful enough, or young enough. *I* wasn't enough. But it was one particular post I saw on social media that made me snap. Irate, I started venting my frustrations to my husband as I normally would, but instead of sympathizing with me, he looked at me with concern.

"Why do you care so much?"

I paused.

"Umm . . ."

I didn't have a good answer.

Why did I care so much about what was going on in someone else's life or career? Why did I waste so much energy comparing myself to someone else's accomplishments that have nothing to do with me? Why was I so hard on myself? This line of questioning continued for hours until I hit a very vulnerable point. I was faced head-on with a question that I had avoided like, well, COVID, for years: What am I running away from?

When I Finally Stopped Running

Ever since high school, I've been extremely ambitious. Get straight As, get a degree, get an impressive job, earn good money, become successful, and live a wonderful life. That was the plan I set for myself, and I'd been working toward it with the determination of a racehorse with blinders on ever since. But at 36, not once had I slowed down in my self-imposed race to the top to acknowledge the truth about why I wanted any of it in the first place. It wasn't my desire for comfort and financial stability. It wasn't to realize my potential. And it certainly wasn't to smash the glass ceiling for future generations of women.

No. Deep down, it was much more basic than that. The real reason I wanted wealth and success was to be seen and loved. What I discovered during my year of introspection while writing this book was that from childhood to young adulthood, I entered a variety of unhealthy friendships that made me believe I was invisible and unlovable. And because I was young and naive, I didn't know how to get out of the cycle. So, when a friendship ended, I would jump right into a new one that was familiar and similarly toxic. After years of compounding hurt, my coping mechanism of choice was to put all my walls up and vow to become so rich and successful that no one would dare ignore, reject, or abandon me. No one would ever cause me the same hurt I experienced in my formative years. I would finally be enough. And hopefully one day, those same people who caused all that hurt would see my name on bookstands and feel a twinge of jealousy (which I know is petty, but hey, I'm human).

In addition to that, I'm the middle child in my family. As much as I once dismissed the idea of middle child syndrome—the idea that middle children feel generally excluded, neglected, and like they are given less attention than their siblings—I've got to admit that, after some extensive therapy, for me, it rings true. I've always been competing for my parents' attention, either consciously or subconsciously. It's a big part of why I pursued a degree in film at university, because my dad and I had a special bond when it came to classic movies, and strived for top marks in school, since there was no better feeling than when my mom expressed her pride after reading my report card. Nevertheless, whatever I achieved, it always felt like it came up short, forcing me to once again move up the goalpost to an even bigger achievement to get their attention.

I was running toward money and prestige so I could run away from the pain and insecurities of my past. This was the real reason why I became obsessed with personal finance in my early 20s and ultimately made it my career. It's also the reason why throughout my adult life, I've worked myself to the bone and prioritized making money and career advancement over what's really important in life: human connection and real-life experiences. Once I realized this hard-to-swallow truth, I started to breathe again. Like *really* breathe.

The thing about money and success, as I've heard countless times interviewing wealthy and successful guests on my podcast over the years, is that they're never enough. No matter what you achieve or how many millions you have in the bank, it will never be enough to fill that deep, dark void you're trying to fill inside you. Why do you think there are so many miserable millionaires and billionaires out there? Why do you think suicide is so prevalent among celebrities and famous influencers? Why do you think Prince Harry—a literal prince—ditched being a royal even though he seemingly had everything we could only dream of?

Because money and success aren't the solutions to your problems. Don't get me wrong; money can help meet all of your basic needs, but beyond that, it can serve only as a temporary bandage for your psychological and emotional wounds. You can accumulate swimming pools of cash and rooms full of trophies, but your problems will be right there where you left them when you're alone at night in your mansion with only your thoughts to keep you company.

There's this old meme that's been circulating for years that reads: "They say money can't buy happiness, but I'd rather cry on a yacht." Well, sure, if your options are to cry on a yacht or cry on a bus, I think we'd all choose the yacht. But why are you crying in the first place? And can you get to the root cause of your pain without having to spend the rest of your life fighting your way to the top like everyone on *Succession?* Is it possible to fix your toxic relationship with money and find peace to enjoy your life?

The answer is YES.

It's about Everything but Money

If you were to go to any bookstore right now, you would find a multitude of books about how to pay off debt, budget, and invest, all with the promise that if you follow through with their simple steps, you'll live a better life. And for some people, that may be enough. Some people may just be looking for a guide on how to pay off their debt, and once debt-free, they'll be content with their money. Some people may just be looking for an easy-to-follow budget template outlining how best to organize their finances. Some people may not know the first thing about investing and are just looking for some actionable steps on how to get started.

But for the rest of us, we need more than that. Part of the reason

I decided to become an accredited financial counsellor was because I wanted to learn how to dig deep with my clients. Having entered the personal finance landscape in 2011, I'd gotten used to talking with people from all backgrounds and income levels about their money issues. But conversation after conversation, one thing was always clear: Their problems weren't just about money. They were actually about everything *but* money.

I remember one of my early clients, Raya, came to me for help with her spending problem. She'd racked up a bunch of debt, was living paycheque to paycheque, and couldn't figure out how to stop the cycle. I looked at her numbers and gave her some specific steps to pay off her debt over time, cut some expenses to free up cash flow, and start saving for future emergencies to get her on the right path. But the real point of our sessions wasn't to go through the numbers (that part was easy). It was to find out how she got there in the first place.

Ultimately, we discovered that she made most of her financial decisions based on what others wanted, not what she wanted. Due to past conditioning and trauma, she had become the perfect people-pleaser, putting everyone but herself first to attract attention and love. That's why she would regularly lend money to friends even though they rarely paid her back. That's why she would succumb to peer pressure and spend money on eating out at expensive restaurants with friends even though it wasn't something she valued spending her money on. That's why she would go shopping every time she felt low about herself, so she could have something to show off to her friends to gain their admiration. That's also why, just like me, she often fell into a cycle of negative self-talk without recognizing how unhealthy it was to think that way.

Luckily, over time, she was able to overcome a lot of what was holding her back from a better, more fulfilling life, and develop healthier habits with her money. She started practising positive self-talk and advocating for herself so her spending aligned more with her personal values. This helped her build a stronger sense of self-confidence, which bred stronger motivation to pay off all of her debt, find a better-paying job, and save up enough to buy her first home. This transformation happened over years. If you want to create lasting change and discover what it means to live your authentic life, it takes hard work, vulnerability, and patience. Just like there's no legitimate way to get rich quick, there are no shortcuts when you are fixing a broken relationship with money.

Let's Turn the Page
(Figuratively and Literally)

The good news is that you *can* fix it. Whatever money story you've been telling yourself up until now, it's never too late to turn the page and start a brand-new chapter. This book will serve as your guide to uncovering the real reason behind your internal and external struggles with money and provide you with the tools you need to overcome them. Once you do this, you'll be able to finally live out the true meaning of financial freedom, or as I prefer to call it, financial fulfillment.

Because the truth is, you're not bad at money and you are enough, no matter how much you earn or what your current net worth is. You just have some unresolved trauma you need to process. And some human behaviour you need to rewire. And then don't forget the fact that we live in a society whose structures protect and reward the already privileged and suppress the marginalized. In other words, you didn't end up here just because you made a few poor choices or don't have a natural talent for finance. There are a whole lot of things working against you, making it hard to see the forest for the trees.

But if I didn't truly believe these obstacles are surmountable, I would have abandoned this career long ago. Call me an optimist, but that's exactly what you need to be to take your first step into the rest of your life. Life is hard. The world is unfair. Money and everything it touches is complicated and can make you want to give up before you ever really get started. These are undeniable truths. Nevertheless, we're going to push through and write that damn next chapter no matter what your darkest negative thought inside your head tells you.

Are you ready?

PART I

Express Yourself: Unlocking Your Feelings about Money

1.

We're All Doing the Same Thing

The only true wisdom is in knowing you know nothing.
—Socrates

One of my favourite things in life is meeting someone new and seeing their reaction when I share what I do for a living. The interaction usually goes something like this:

"What do you do for a living?"

"I run a financial education business and teach people about money."

To which they usually respond one of three ways:

"Cool. I don't know the first thing about money," followed by some nervous laughter, shifting of feet, and a quick scan of the room to see if there's someone else they can talk to.

"That's nice," followed by an abrupt change in topic to avoid any talk of money whatsoever.

"Oh, really?" followed by them leaning in, eyes darting from left to right to ensure no one else is listening, and their voice lowering to whisper, "Can I ask you something?"

I've talked to hundreds of people about money over the years, and the one undeniable truth that we all share is that *everyone* finds talking about money uncomfortable. Research even shows that people are more comfortable talking about sex, race, mental illness, and drug addiction than they are talking about money.[1] Even I feel uncomfortable talking about money sometimes, and I've been immersed in the personal finance world for over 13 years!

Still, despite money making most of us uncomfortable, we can find some solace in knowing that we're not the only ones who feel that way. It's oddly reassuring knowing that we're all just doing the same thing, nervously laughing at how little we know about money or whispering to someone we just met about how we've never told a soul about our financial problems or insecurities. Once you realize that you're not alone and we've all got similar struggles with this pretty major part of our lives that's still considered taboo or rude to talk about, it's actually a lot easier to take that first step in uncovering what your relationship with money is so you can change it for the better.

Let's start by taking a big step back in time.

Where It All Started

What is your first childhood memory of money, and how did it make you feel? Take a moment to think about that (we'll come back to it in the next chapter). In the meantime, I'll share mine from when I was four years old to show you how our deep-rooted feelings about money start developing at a very young age.

For me, these feelings started on one of my mom's regular visits to the grocery store. I can still remember it so clearly. I was at the Save-On-Foods on Pinetree Way in Coquitlam, British Columbia. I loved grocery shopping with my mom, mostly because if I behaved, she'd treat me to a chocolate-glazed long john. But also because I loved walking through all the aisles and checking out the different types of food. My favourite was the bulk aisle, with all of those containers full of nuts, dried fruit, chocolate, and candy. I used to pretend I'd landed in Candyland and was walking through Candy Cane Forest and Gumdrop Mountain. But one day, instead of just looking at all the treats in my imaginary paradise, I decided to have a taste.

There was so much there, no one would mind me taking one little thing. Plus, I saw adults pop a sample into their mouths all the time. *What's the harm in having one little gumball?* I thought. Well, first, it wasn't so little. It was so big and hard to chew that all I could do was keep it in my mouth like a squirrel hoarding nuts for later. It was also bright blue and, being a typical sticky-handed kid, my mouth and hands quickly changed colour as if I were girl-turned-blueberry Violet Beauregarde from *Charlie and the Chocolate Factory*. Nevertheless, I thought I'd gotten away with it as we walked our cart to the parking lot without a word from my mom.

Until we got to the car. Just as my mom popped the trunk to start loading the groceries, she saw my guilty-looking blue face with a big, marble-sized ball protruding from my cheek. She was furious. Recognizing what I'd just done, she made me spit the gumball onto the ground, grabbed my hand, and dragged me back inside the grocery store, to the bulk aisle. She then looked me straight in the eyes and told me, "We don't steal things! These are things we have to pay for. Never do this again!" Or something to that effect (I was four, remember). I bawled my eyes out and felt ashamed the whole car ride home and for the 30-plus years that followed.

That was the first time I started to associate money, or the lack of it, with something shameful. Though not for the reason you may think. Although I did steal that gumball and stealing is generally wrong, that's not where the feeling of shame came from. Instead, it came from the overall undertone of what my mom was saying. Although her words told me that stealing was bad and not to repeat that behaviour in the future, what she was also communicating through her worried eyes and uneasy body language was her own shame at having our family appear as though we couldn't afford something and had to resort to stealing to get it.

In other words, I didn't just steal a gumball; I made my family look poor in front of all of our peers through my thoughtless, though innocent, actions. This would have been a serious faux pas in the early 1990s, when everyone was trying so desperately to keep up with the Joneses because nothing was worse than your neighbours, and greater society for that matter, thinking you didn't have money. Because if you didn't have money, the consensus was that you'd done something wrong to end up there. You were lazy and didn't work hard enough. You were stupid and made some bad financial decisions. You didn't pull yourself up by the bootstraps like your forefathers who immigrated to this country with only the clothes on their backs and $10 in their pockets, and therefore it was your own fault for being poor and you deserved the struggles that came with it. In essence, any hint that you weren't on the same financial footing as everyone else could result in your being perceived as a less valuable and respected member of society.

No wonder my mom was furious. The stakes were incredibly high, and being labelled less than middle class was the modern age's equivalent of the scarlet letter. Sadly, nothing really changed in the three decades that followed. Many of these firmly held beliefs about why people are poor or have less than others still exist today largely due to the toxic messaging of hustle culture, the explosion of social media, and some curmudgeons with microphones.

Don't Ever Let Them Know

To give you some context about my family's financial background, throughout my childhood, my family would have been considered low-to-middle income. I don't deny I grew up with ample privilege (a topic to be discussed later in this book), but in terms of what my parents earned and our family-of-five's cost of living, it was clear that for many years, balancing the budget and trying to keep up appearances in our suburb of Port Coquitlam was a skilled tightrope act my mom had to perform every single month. Even though I've never experienced poverty like so many others I've talked to over the years, like going to school hungry or having the heat shut off because a bill went unpaid, I was still hyper-aware that we had less than others and could also easily point out which families had more, which inevitably informed my understanding of money as a child.

Because of this, I used to view money as a negative. Money was the number one reason why my parents argued when they thought my sisters and I were asleep at night, and why they more often than not said no to things that seemed par for the course for other families, like new clothes every school year instead of hand-me-downs, eating chicken for dinner instead of ground beef, or buying name brand items at full price instead of waiting for them to go on sale or buying the off-brand equivalent.

A common phrase in my family was "We can't afford it." That phrase is still so ingrained in me that to this day, it's still the first thing that pops into my head when I contemplate making a purchase, even if it's not true. It's also the reason I struggle with guilt whenever I do buy something that's not on sale or choose not to order the cheapest item on a restaurant's menu. I've still never purchased anything from the hotel mini-bar because as one hilarious tweet so aptly put it, I'm "deeply terrified that consuming anything from the hotel room mini-bar will bankrupt my entire family."[2]

The complicated thing about this is that a lot of the skills I developed from mimicking my mom's shopping habits, like discount shopping, couponing, and making sure I don't spend more than I can afford, have come in very handy as an adult. But these habits aren't the issue here. It's the associated negative feelings that linger afterwards that are the problem. Not only that, it's the fact that although I, and likely you, have these kinds of negative feelings, we keep them private. We don't talk about them because it's one thing to feel something about money, but it's quite another to be vulnerable and speak about it publicly.

It's like that song from *The Book of Mormon* about turning off your feelings just like a light switch. I'm not Mormon, but I was raised Roman Catholic and, oh boy, did that song hit a little too close to home when I saw the musical. What this song perfectly illustrates is what so many of us do with our most vulnerable feelings, especially our feelings about money. Whenever we feel something, we instinctively try to turn it off, push it down, and lock it away in a vault deep inside ourselves, because the worst thing that could happen would be someone discovering it and perceiving us as weak or a failure.

You're Not an Ostrich

Confronting and sharing our feelings about money can feel like standing on a soapbox naked in the centre of town, proclaiming, "My life is a mess and I have no idea what I'm doing!" No wonder most of us would rather bury our heads in the sand than address our feelings. When your head is buried, you can't see any of your deep-rooted issues with money. And if you can't see them, do they even exist?

YES. They still exist. Just like if a tree falls in a forest, even if you weren't there to hear it, that doesn't negate the fact that it made a thunderous sound on its way down. Burying your head in the sand, also known as the ostrich problem, is simply a cognitive bias that causes people to "avoid information to avoid the unpleasant emotional impact that they expect it to lead to . . . even if this avoidance will lead to a greater emotional cost later on."[3] This is why so many people avoid their true feelings about money and go decades without making any headway with their finances, even if this avoidance results in bigger financial problems and could potentially exacerbate those negative feelings down the road. It's a coping mechanism to ward off negative emotions temporarily, but it usually causes greater suffering over the long term.

But that's not you, is it? There's a reason you chose this book, and there's a reason I needed to write it. You don't want to be an ostrich anymore. You want to try something new because it's not fun having tiny grains of sand make their way into your eyes, mouth, and nose. You want to dig your head out and breathe again!

Well, to do that you're going to have to get comfortable being uncomfortable. You're going to have to embrace being vulnerable. The only way to detach your negative feelings from money and thus create a healthier relationship with it is to acknowledge those feelings and put them into words.

Putting It into Words

It can be easier said than done, putting your feelings into words (pun intended). Most of us don't know what our feelings are in the first place because we've pushed them deep down for so long. It can be difficult to recall those feelings when you finally want to, but they're still in there somewhere. This is where starting a mindfulness practice comes in (for which I'll share some exercises in the next chapter). Before you roll your eyes because the term *mindfulness* has become a buzzword in recent years, let me share what it is and how it can help. I'll also tell you straight up that I'm the furthest thing from a "woo-woo guru" or an early adopter of any kind of trend (just ask my wardrobe). But more importantly, mindfulness is backed by science.

Too often, we're either looking back or looking forward, instead of sitting still and looking at the present moment. Not only that, even when we think we are in the present moment, we're actually spending most of our brain power reliving the past or pre-living the future.[4] That's where integrating a mindfulness practice into your daily life can make all the difference. It can help you become aware and pay extended attention to how you really feel in the moment, both internally and externally.

A typical mindfulness practice could involve activities like meditation, journaling, yoga, and tai chi to help your body and mind focus on the present and your place in it. A similar practice for money mindfulness can be used to help you identify your feelings about money and connect them to words. When feelings and words connect, it can be a powerful thing. Not only can it help you describe that feeling and validate it, but ultimately, it can help you change how you think and behave with money in general.

In *The Dictionary of Obscure Sorrows*, John Koenig describes the importance of words this way: "Whenever life feels chaotic and uncertain and everything runs together, words offer us a sense of clarity and definition, with clean lines that separate one thing from another. . . . Just the act of putting something into words can give you the impression that everything is under control."[5]

If you can name it, you can better control it. It's when you keep your feelings hidden from yourself, and from others for that matter, that they maintain a firm hold over you instead of the other way around. In order to start healing and rewiring old patterns, you first need to acknowledge and define the problem.

A 2007 brain image study from the University of California, Los Angeles confirmed just as much. Neuroscientist Matthew D. Lieberman and his team of psychologists at UCLA analyzed the brain activity of research participants using functional magnetic resonance imaging while showing them pictures of individuals making different emotional expressions. Below the images, participants were either shown words to describe the individuals' expressions, like "angry" or "fearful," or a name like "Harry" or "Sally." What the team discovered was that the participants who were shown emotional labels beneath the pictures had a decreased response in their amygdala (the part of the brain that affects emotions like fear and pleasure) and increased activity in the right ventrolateral prefrontal cortex (the part of the brain involved in inhibiting behaviour and processing emotions).

What they learned from this discovery was that labelling your emotions "turns down the amygdala alarm centre response in the brain that triggers negative feelings." In effect, by putting your feelings about money into words, you can dampen the intensity of those feelings and thus control your emotional responses to money more effectively. Or as Lieberman so aptly put it: "Putting our feelings into words helps us heal better."[6] When you put your feelings about money into words, you'll be better equipped to unearth the deep-rooted reasons behind your self-harming money behaviours, so you can heal your wounds and eventually move forward.

To find out what those feelings are and put labels on them, I think it's important to know what those labels are in the first place. Often, when feelings come into play, it can be hard to find the right words or any words at all. Let me help you with that.

2.

And How Does That Make You Feel?

The best way out is always through.
—Robert Frost

If I were to ask you right now how money makes you feel, you'd likely say, "Not good," because there's a reason you're reading this book. But "Not good" isn't very specific and words matter. To get to the root of how money makes you feel, you need to dig deeper.

I had a pretty good idea of how most people felt about money from my years as a financial counsellor and educator, but I wanted to see if there were specific words people used that came up more often than others. So, I ran a short survey, and here are examples of responses that came up over and over:

"I sometimes feel **ashamed** when I'm in social settings because I didn't come from money, but it seems like everyone else did."

"Because I had so little growing up, I feel a bit **guilty** whenever I spend money now."

"Even though I'm in a good financial situation today, I'm always waiting for the other shoe to drop, and I'm **afraid** of something bad happening to derail all the progress I've made."

"I'm **anxious** that I'll never have enough and worried that I'll make a big financial mistake to ruin it all."

"I can't help but be **envious** of others who graduated with
no debt, were able to find a good paying job right away,
and are miles ahead of me financially. It feels unfair."

"Defeated, oppressed, hopeless, and just general **despair**.
Like no matter what I do, it's never enough, so what's the
point in even trying to get ahead and catch up to my peers?"

Shame. Guilt. Fear. Anxiety. Envy. Despair. These words kept coming
up in the survey responses, and unsurprisingly, they're the same words
people have used when sharing their feelings about money with me over
the years. It goes without saying that none of these feel good, so where
do we start? Based on my own experience and the stories from many
others, shame is a common undertone, so it's a good place to jump in.

Shame

What is shame exactly? Ever since watching *Game of Thrones*, I can't help
but visualize Cersei Lannister's walk of shame through the streets of
King's Landing for having an affair with her twin brother. Hopefully,
none of us will have to experience shame on that level, though sometimes it can feel just as torturous in our minds. *Shame* is defined as "a
self-conscious emotion arising from the sense that something is fundamentally wrong about oneself."[1] Or as Brené Brown describes it in her
book *Daring Greatly*, "Shame is the intensely painful feeling or experience of believing that we are flawed and therefore unworthy of love and
belonging."[2]

This definition is important, because often shame gets confused
with guilt, but they are distinctly different feelings. Guilt is the negative feeling resulting from doing something wrong. Another way to remember the difference is that shame is feeling like "I'm a bad person,"
whereas guilt is feeling like "I did a bad thing." Since guilt has to do
with something we have done, you can see how that feeling is easier to
overcome than the feeling that you are fundamentally flawed in some

way. Fortunately, it is possible to step out of shame or develop shame resilience, as Brown discusses in her book. To do that, however, you must first identify what types of shame you're dealing with.

THE SHAME OF GROWING UP WITH LESS

My first experience with shame and money was when I was four at the grocery store, but that certainly wasn't my last experience with it. Growing up with less had always been a big source of shame that I kept private until I discovered the world of personal finance blogs in 2010, where people openly shared stories of similar upbringings.

Growing up with less had a profound impact on me. I still have flashbacks of being ridiculed in school for wearing my sister's hand-me-downs or being judged for what was in my lunch box. Most painfully, though, I remember not being able to participate in the latest toy trends, which made the difference between being invited to the inner circle or pushed to the fringes in the schoolyard. Remember Tamagotchis, Furbies, and Super Nintendo from the 1990s? I sure do. Not because I ever owned any of these toys, but because I made strategic friendships with kids who did, which was my only way to experience them. Looking at it now, I feel guilty about befriending kids because they had the trendiest toys, but at the time, it was my survival tactic to distract others from discovering that I wasn't a financial equal. And as a child, you don't have control over what impacts you; you deal with the situation you're in with the tools you have.

As I got older, the stakes got higher and my shame intensified as social circles started to form based on family income level. I never got an allowance like most of my peers because there was no extra money to spare for me and my two sisters, which was a huge roadblock when trying to keep up with everyone my age. If I wanted something that wasn't considered a necessity, I had to find a way to buy it myself. Before I became legal working age, my only options were to hoard any Christmas and birthday money I was gifted and babysit the neighbours' kids. I did both until I turned 15, but that also likely kick-started my habit of hoarding cash in a savings account, which lasted until my 30s.

Once I was finally hirable, I began my almost decade-long part-time career in the fast-food and retail industries. This was both freeing as I got my first taste of financial independence and a source of shame in itself. I can recall several times when I worked the drive-through window at A&W, in my brown visor and grease-stained uniform, seeing a classmate pull up in the new car their parents bought them and pretend that I was a complete stranger, despite us sitting near each other in class. The shame of having less and thus feeling like I was less is a big reason why I've worked so hard to break out of that cycle in adulthood.

Reading the origin story of my shame with money may have stirred up some feelings inside you that I want to discuss before moving on.

THERE ARE NO WRONG FEELINGS

Perhaps you read my story and thought to yourself:

"I had to wear hand-me-downs, too, and
you don't see me complaining."

"You didn't get a Tamagotchi when you were a kid? Eye roll."

"Boo-hoo, you didn't get an allowance and had to work a fast-food job? I had it *way* worse than you. Quit your whining!"

You're not wrong for feeling that way. Although I grew up with less than my peers, I recognize that I also grew up with privilege as a white kid in suburbia and I had more than some others, too. For me, growing up with less meant growing up with less than others, which had a big impact on me and my personal relationship with money. For others, it means growing up with less than you needed, for example, lacking food, clean water, shelter, clothing, stability, or safety at any point in your life, which is a very different experience. It's important to remember that everyone's backstory is different, and that as children, you don't have control over that or how it affects you. What's important is figuring that out now, whatever your backstory.

I questioned how much of my own story I wanted to share before writing this book, because while I knew some readers would be able to see themselves in it, others wouldn't and that could be alienating. From time to time, I even find myself rolling my eyes to the back of my head when I hear someone with obvious privilege bemoan the challenges they had to endure when those challenges seem insignificant compared to my own life experiences. We're all human. That's why I will be including stories of others from a variety of backgrounds to provide a broader experience than my own.

Your feelings are completely valid. And so are mine. That's the thing with feelings. We all have them, and they are all equally valid. There are no wrong answers when it comes to how someone feels. Ultimately, we all need to learn to better accept how others feel, especially when we can't understand or don't share those feelings. We need to identify our feelings and put labels on them to heal, and we need to allow the same courtesy to others. Not only that, but when you're playing the who-had-it-worse game, no one wins. In the end, everyone will leave with their shame exacerbated, and no one will feel safe to dig into their feelings and share them with others for fear of judgment, making healing even harder.

EMPATHY IS THE MISSING PUZZLE PIECE

I've been in the personal finance space for over a decade, and what I've come to know is how cold, hostile, prejudiced, and negative it can be. On the surface, it can look like a welcoming environment where people are cheering you on to better your financial situation, but there are rabbit holes where it can get really dark and ugly. There's a reason that, even with my years of experience, credentials, and hundreds of stints as a money expert on the news, I actively avoid going on finance subreddits or reading the comments on any news website I'm featured on. People can be cruel and judgmental, and that's not going to motivate you to make any progress with your finances. That type of negativity will just make you want to slam your laptop shut and bury your head in the sand again.

What the personal finance space truly needs is more empathy. Empathy is an important yet often overlooked piece of the puzzle. As described by psychologist Carl Rogers, empathy is "seeing the world through the eyes of the other, not seeing your world reflected in their eyes."[3] Empathy bridges the gap between people, allowing you to understand what someone else is experiencing, connect with others, and ultimately feel seen and supported.

That can be really difficult to do when you've built armour to protect yourself throughout your life, like the blinders I used to wear, which I talked about in the introduction. When I went to university and left behind traumatic childhood relationships, I vowed to become a different person. I'd no longer be that naive weakling who let people walk all over her. I pushed my emotions to the side to become tough, and I turned inward to put the focus on me and my journey instead of giving everything I had to others, which had left me with nothing so many times before. I felt that if I didn't close myself off to other people's feelings, I would be vulnerable. I couldn't risk having all the armour I'd worked so hard to piece together fall to the ground and leave me exposed to being hurt again.

I hope you can see how unhealthy that kind of mindset is and why I've spent all of my 30s unlearning those tactics that I used to protect myself when I didn't know any better. Life can be really lonely and angry when there's no place for empathy. So, if you're like me and have had a hard time seeing the world through other people's eyes because you've kept your blinders on for too long, just know that it is a skill you can develop over time and it does get easier. And once you do allow empathy a place in your life, it doesn't make you weak. It makes you stronger. My life is so much fuller now that I've invited empathy back in. And my relationship with money and how I teach others about money have improved tenfold by integrating empathy as a key element.

For this reason, throughout this book, especially as I continue to share my story and the stories of others, I challenge you to practise empathy when your gut reaction is to judge, dismiss, or compare it to your own situation. Take a moment, sit with it, and then reread the story, trying to view it through that person's eyes. See if you can take away something new from doing so. Maybe you can relate to the heart of the story, if not the context. The more we actively listen and truly see someone else's perspective, the easier it will become to show ourselves compassion, too, be vulnerable and open to change, and ultimately break free from what has been holding us back from a better relationship with money.

ANDREW

Andrew has been a long-time listener of my podcast since its launch in 2015, and although we've exchanged many messages over the years, this was the first time I got to dive deep into his personal story of money shame. The first money memory he can recall is crying in the back seat of his parents' car when they told him they'd bought him a bike for his birthday. You'd think he was shedding tears of joy (what kid doesn't want a bike?), but they were actually tears of shame for causing his parents further financial strain. Throughout Andrew's childhood, his dad had a tendency to blame his children for the cost of raising them, often complaining that kids were so expensive and that life would be a lot easier without them.

So, when he got a bike for his birthday, it didn't just come with a bow and a "Happy birthday!" It also came with a "And that cost us $100, so you'd better be grateful." Andrew knew from an early age that his family didn't have much compared to other families, but being led to believe that he was one of the main causes for this understandably left a mark on him. What he ended up discovering later on was that the real causes of the family's financial troubles were his father's poor choices. He racked up consumer debt left and right, he bought a house that was too big and expensive for them, and as Andrew put it, "He was every salesman's dream customer."

As a reaction to the messaging he received growing up, Andrew studied finance and worked in banking for a large part of his career before transitioning to teaching business. If he was such a financial burden growing up, he was going to make sure he was as financially independent as he could be as an adult. However, it took him a while to unlearn some of the unhealthy financial habits he'd adopted along the way, such as overworking, being fearful of debt, judging others' financial decisions, and living uncomfortably below his means. He also did what many of us do as a coping mechanism for childhood trauma and began parenting the parent by helping his dad stick to a budget and making sure he set him on a better financial path.

When Andrew turned 40, he started going to therapy to finally start letting go of the baggage he'd been carrying around since childhood. Since then, he's been able to make huge strides in his financial life, too. We'll talk more about how therapy can help in Chapter 8.

THE SHAME OF GROWING UP WITH MORE

Shame isn't exclusive to those who grew up with less. It also exists in those who grew up with more than others or more than they needed. This is a difficult type of shame to tackle because, honestly, most people find it pretty hard to have empathy for those who have more than they do, no matter if they are simply part of the comfortable middle class or the ultra-wealthy. And it makes perfect sense why. When you've grown up with less, the obvious solution to all of your problems would be to obtain what you grew up lacking: more. So, if lack of money was never an issue, why would anyone who grew up with more struggle with shame, too? One reason may have to do with how most of us perceive wealth and the wealthy in the first place. As family wealth advisor Kristin Keffeler wrote in her book *The Myth of the Silver Spoon*: "Culturally, we have a tangled relationship with wealth and with those who have it. We can admire the gritty entrepreneur and celebrate how he or she represents 'the American Way.' And we can just as quickly despise the wealthy and assume that only those who are willing to be ruthless or unscrupulous get to the top. We can envy the lifestyles we assume the wealthy have and just as quickly dismiss those lifestyles as self-indulgent and wasteful."[4]

We want what they have, but we hate that they have it and we don't.

We don't want them to have more than we do, but our own happiness improves when we know we have more than others.[5] How can all of these conflicting feelings be true? And if the majority of society feels this way, how does it affect those who do come from wealth? This is where empathy comes in.

THE RICH OUTSIDER

I can tell you right now, I wouldn't want to be on the receiving end of hate or criticism for having grown up with more. Because at the end of the day, no matter how much (or little) money we have, we humans all want the same thing: to be liked and valued by our peers and to feel a true sense of belonging. But if you grew up with more than your peers, you're automatically an outsider. Not just because you can't relate to their life experiences and struggles (and vice versa), but also because your peers may envy you for not being financial equals or believe some of the stereotypes they learned from their parents, like wealthy people are greedy and corrupt (which feels especially unfair when you're a kid and likely had nothing to do with however that wealth was accumulated in the first place).

It reminds me of the 1994 film *Richie Rich*, starring Macaulay Culkin. It was one of my favourite movies when I was growing up, because it was a feast for a young kid's eyes. Richie had every luxury a kid could dream of, like an in-house McDonald's, Jet Skis at his private lake, and, of course, a roller coaster in his backyard. But the main theme of the film is how, despite these luxuries, Richie grew up isolated and alone. His parents were always away working, so he was predominantly raised by his butler. His private school classmates were often too busy to hang out with him and could offer only surface-level friendships. Further, the lower-income kids he finds playing baseball in the dirt field nearby refuse to play with him because of his wealth and make fun of him, assuming he's unskilled and weak. It's only when he proves his baseball-hitting skill and brings the kids to his mansion to hang out that they start to treat him as an equal and include him in their friendship group.

When I used to watch the movie, all I could think about was how Richie had won the birth lottery, and I wished I could pull off a *Freaky Friday* with him (my other favourite childhood film). He had every comfort in the world, never had to worry about his parents saying, "We can't afford it," and his main struggle of feeling lonely and lacking friends was resolved fairly easily. I wished I had Richie Rich's problems! But many real people who come from wealth never experience that kind of resolution and carry the shame of having more than others throughout their entire lives. That's why you hear stories of people who inherit wealth and give most or all of it away,[6] try to prove that they've earned it in some way, or do everything they can to hide their financial status from others so they can assimilate and avoid judgment.

THE POOREST RICH KID

But what if you didn't grow up as the wealthiest kid in class? What if your experience growing up was less *Richie Rich* and more *Gossip Girl*, in which your peer group was wealthy, too? Would that thwart any possibility of shame? Unfortunately not. What often happens in this scenario is you get caught up in comparing your family's wealth to that of your peers. If you're not at the top of the food chain in terms of wealth and status, you may even grapple with a similar type of shame as growing up with less. As Brooke Harrington, professor of economic sociology at Dartmouth College, shared with *The Atlantic*: "The sensation of 'being well-off' is not about fulfilling a childhood dream of buying a sailboat or something; feeling wealthy is about comparison with others in your reference group. So the question is not what individuals want to buy, but what they feel they must buy in order to keep up their status."[7]

If your family has a net worth of $10 million, to most people, you'd be considered well-off and could live an incredibly luxurious life. But if you live in a community in which everyone's net worth is $100 million, you might not be able to keep up with their level of spending and feel shame in comparison. You may be a multi-millionaire, but you can still feel inadequate and lesser than in your social circle. It's all relative. And how you feel about money doesn't come from external logic or arbitrary income levels—it comes from how *you* experience it. It's not about the facts; it's about your feelings.

THE NEPO BABY

And then there's the shame of not having actually earned your wealth. If you grew up with wealth and weren't a working child actor, for example, it's likely you fell into one of two categories: your parents amassed wealth themselves through work, starting a business, or unexpected inheritance and thus were able to elevate the family's financial status from having less to having more; or you are part of a legacy family in which wealth has passed down from generation to generation. In either case, you didn't "earn" your wealth in the sense that you personally didn't generate it. We might fantasize about winning the lottery or discovering we have a long-lost relative who gifted us part of their estate upon their death, but we often judge others with wealth for not being "self-made," which means that if you're on that side of the equation, you could feel shame about it. A commonly held societal value is making it on your own and turning your rags into riches in the land of opportunity. And yet, if we discover that someone's great-grandfather did just that and then set up a plan to maintain his earned wealth so future family generations could experience it, too, we're dismissive and hypercritical.

Just take the Hiltons as an example. Conrad Hilton, the man who propelled his family into fame and fortune, was born in New Mexico in 1887 to immigrant parents originally from Norway. He was one of seven children who grew up very humbly, with his father owning a grocery store and renting out rooms in their house to earn extra income to support the family. After serving in the First World War and saving up $5,000, a significant amount at the time, a 32-year-old Hilton used that money to invest in his first hotel. Over time, he built one of the most successful hotel chains in the world and consequently became extremely wealthy. He's the perfect example of the self-made man, and it's a rags-to-riches story we so love to hear. But the admiration stops with him.

Once we learn that his wealth was passed down to his descendants, any admiration for his lineage quickly fades. It doesn't matter that his great-granddaughter Paris Hilton built a successful career and brand of her own. What most people focus on is that she started on third base, so her achievements don't count.[8]

So, you might feel shame for not having earned your wealth. There's also the shame of not being able to replicate the rags-to-riches or self-made achievements of your parents or ancestors. One benchmark we use as adults to ensure we're on the right path and are successful is whether we're doing the same or better than our parents, financially and career-wise. This is likely when you've come from less, but if your parents are multi-millionaires or the Hiltons, it may feel like no matter how many degrees you get, followers you have on social media, or dollars you earn yourself, your achievements will always pale in comparison. This can be a recipe for shame and despair if you feel nothing you do will ever be good enough.

THE SHAME OF FALLING BEHIND

Have you ever been out with your friends and thought to yourself, *Wait . . . is everyone doing better than I am?* It's normal to compare yourself to your circle, but it can also cause a lot of shame if you realize your peers are miles ahead of you financially. Just take Clarissa's story as an example.

CLARISSA

Clarissa Moore, now a prominent money expert and coach under the moniker *Clarissa Explains Money*, felt a deep sense of shame for falling behind her peer group for years. Most undergrads take four to five years to graduate with their degree in hand. Clarissa took 10. She was just one semester shy of graduating with her psychology degree after five years when she and her husband at the time had to relocate from New Jersey to Pennsylvania for their jobs at the same telecom company. Thinking she could start at a new school where she'd left off at the previous one, she discovered that not all of her credits were transferable, and she had to take two more years of classes to obtain her diploma.

As she continued her education, her company decided to close the office and move it down to Florida. Wanting stability for her two kids, she chose to remain in Pennsylvania and find a new job to support her family. Unfortunately, the job she got required her to work weekdays, the same hours that all of her classes were being held. Needing the income, she had to switch schools yet again, to one that offered classes at night and on weekends. Unfortunately, this also set her back several semesters, because the school didn't recognize all of her previous education either. Ultimately, these changes meant it took Clarissa 10 years to finally finish her degree. She felt immense shame for not being able to hit certain financial and career milestones as soon as all of her friends who had been able to graduate years earlier.

On the bright side, the shame of falling behind led her to the world of personal finance, so she could figure out how to play catch-up. Because of that, she was able to hit the accelerator and now finds herself in a much better financial situation. It's like the story of the tortoise and the hare. No matter what setbacks or delays you may experience, you win the race not with speed but with endurance.

Falling behind can take several forms and mean something different to everyone. It can look like not earning as much as your peers, or it can look like not reaching financial milestones within certain timelines, such as paying off your student loan, buying your first home, or reaching a six-figure net worth by the time you hit a particular age. It could also look like not getting raises and promotions at work, switching careers and starting at the bottom again, or simply blinking and realizing you're 50 with no retirement savings. The good news is that it's never too late to catch up or reach your goals.

THE SHAME OF TRANSITIONING FROM LESS TO MORE

For the first four years of being a financial content creator, I didn't make any money. At the start, I just saw blogging as my creative outlet and a way to teach myself more about personal finance. Plus, at that time, no one was monetizing these types of things and the term *influencer* hadn't been coined yet. But since running a blog and then eventually starting a podcast cost me money every month, when I finally started to get interest from brands, I was over the moon. Finally, I could break even or perhaps even make a profit!

And then everything came crashing down. In 2017, when I decided to quit my job to try to make a go of being a full-time financial counsellor and content creator, one of my biggest fears happened on one of the most public stages—Twitter. I had negotiated a podcast sponsorship with a brand to promote its free credit-scoring tool on my podcast, and I was super excited about it. Since I started my blog at a time when no one was monetizing anything, in 2017 there was still some lingering criticism toward anyone who did. *Sellout* and *money-grubber* were terms frequently tossed around. I was hyperconscious of that criticism, and I wanted to be able to fully stand behind anything I was putting forward, so I chose sponsors for my podcast very carefully (and still do).

The ads aired, and then I saw one tweet that made my heart stop. It was from a public figure I had looked up to most of my adult life, and they were publicly shaming me for being a shill only interested in making money, not helping people. I was devastated. Their followers started attacking me and characterizing me as someone I knew to my core I was not. Knowing that there was no way I could win a Twitter battle (not that I even wanted to attempt one), I tried contacting the instigator to have a rational conversation about the situation, but never received a response. In the end, all I could do was send a tweet back saying, "Sorry you feel that way," hit the block button, then ugly cry for the rest of the day. Even though this took place over eight years ago, it still hurts when I think about it.

The whole episode made me reconsider trying to run my own business and ultimately led me to seek help from a therapist to learn how to manage not just my overwhelming imposter syndrome but also online negativity that was beyond my control. All I was trying to do was make a living.

What's even more hurtful is that this condemnation didn't just shame me for trying to transition from a place of less to more; it also shamed others who were attempting to do the same thing. I received a lot of messages from other content creators at the time who expressed worry about getting similar backlash for monetizing their platforms, even though, like me, they'd been producing valuable content for free for years and were paying costs out of their personal savings.

What I realize now is the criticism that you're greedy if you want to earn more money than you're currently making or you're a hypocrite for wanting to make money from something that is meant to help people comes from a place of privilege and prejudice. Only someone who has enough money could find it hard to understand why someone would want to make more for themselves, and surmise that it must be for selfish reasons. Since I knew I was neither greedy nor a hypocrite but did, in fact, need the money to cover my business and living expenses, I pushed forward anyway and, as they say, made my haters my motivators.

Thankfully, we're seeing a big shift in sentiment online. Not only is making money online being normalized, but content creators and influencers are even admired for working with brands or using platforms like OnlyFans to elevate their financial status. I think it's great and shows that real progress is being made in levelling the playing field. No one should feel shame for earning a legitimate living, being compensated for what they do, or raising their income level, no matter whether they're an influencer, a sex worker, or an Uber driver. We should all be encouraging each other to go from less to more by any legal and ethical means we have. Shame just keeps us all down, and we need to rise up and lift each other up in the process.

I've explored the most common kinds of money shame here, but if I haven't covered your particular money shame, it is valid, too. Remember, feelings can't be wrong, and it's important that you identify them to start the process of healing. For now, I want to move on to the feeling of guilt.

Guilt

As I shared earlier, guilt is different from shame because it is a negative mix of feelings about something wrong you've done. However, there are actually two types of guilt: rational guilt and irrational guilt.[9] Rational guilt is a good thing because it makes us feel remorse and helps prevent bad behaviour or encourage better behaviour in the future. In other words, rational guilt is essential for our personal growth and self-improvement. For example, you may feel rational guilt if you put a non-essential purchase on your credit card when you know you already have a high balance you need to pay off first. It's completely rational to feel guilt for putting an impulse want ahead of an important goal like getting out of credit card debt. You're going against your own intentions, hence the guilt.

Irrational guilt, on the other hand, doesn't have the same helpful function. We feel irrational guilt when we take over-responsibility for a situation or overestimate the suffering or consequences of our actions. In effect, irrational guilt is unreasonable and unwarranted.[10] For example, something I've been trying to unlearn for years is the guilt of practising self-care and relaxing instead of working 24/7. Because I got used to working extra jobs on nights and weekends in my past career and got sucked into "hustle culture" when I became newly self-employed, there's still this voice inside my head that pipes up on a lazy Sunday afternoon when I'm binge-watching *Bridgerton* that asks, *Shouldn't you be working?* Even though my rational mind knows that working all the time can lead to burnout and decompressing is important for my physical and mental health, that irrational guilt is still very loud and present. As you might guess, irrational guilt is something we need to control and minimize, because research shows it could lead to bigger issues like anxiety, low self-esteem, and depression.[11]

To help you pinpoint some of your own feelings, here are some examples of how rational or irrational guilt may show up when managing your money.

RATIONAL GUILT

- spending more than you're earning
- consistently going over your budget
- spending money to self-soothe because you're exhausted, hungry, stressed, sad, jealous, or angry

- not saving up for your retirement or other personal financial goals
- spending money on a want when it's earmarked for a need
- not taking action when you receive helpful financial advice

IRRATIONAL GUILT

- spending money on things you can comfortably afford as an adult when you couldn't afford them growing up
- taking money out of your emergency fund when a legitimate emergency arises
- earning more than your parents, siblings, or friends
- receiving a financial gift or inheritance from your family
- using social programs like employment insurance or social assistance when you need financial aid
- not being able to afford a vacation or gifts for your kids due to a reduction in income

Now that we've covered how guilt can either help or harm your finances, let's discuss another big barrier to finding financial fulfillment: fear.

Fear

Besides shame and guilt, fear is one of the most powerful feelings when it comes to money. Fear can be a big deterrent in making any forward movement with your finances and can also influence you to make financial decisions you may later regret. But what exactly is it? Put simply, fear is the feeling you get when you believe you're being threatened, leading to avoidant or coping behaviour to manage that threat.[12] Fear can stem from negative experiences that left a mark, events you've witnessed or been told about, or anxieties and insecurity born out of poor mental health. As with guilt, we've all got rational and irrational fears. Rational fears can be good because they can motivate you to change and make better choices. Irrational fears can be disruptive and paralyzing and could lead you to make some costly mistakes. By identifying the difference between these two types of fear, you can either transform it into helpful feedback or recognize that these are thoughts you need to let go of.

For example, a rational fear of mine is that I won't have enough money for anything beyond a humble retirement, unlike all the wealth management advertisements featuring seniors on yachts or clinking champagne flutes at the country club. This fear largely stems from the frugal lifestyles I've witnessed my grandparents living in retirement, so it's completely rational to feel that that might become my reality, too, because it's all I've seen up close.

An irrational fear of mine, however, is that all my clients and work opportunities will dry up one day, I'll stop earning a living and won't be able to afford my mortgage payments, and my husband and I will be forced to sell our house and move in with my parents. This is completely irrational because not only have I proven over the last eight years that I can consistently earn an income working for myself, but if something were to happen to my business, I know how resourceful I can be. I can switch careers (it wouldn't be the first time) or find a traditional job with an employer again. Nevertheless, whenever there's a slow period in my business, which happens every summer like clockwork, this fear creeps in and I have to work really hard to push it back into its box.

To help you reflect on your own feelings about money, here are some actions that can lead to fear, both rational and irrational.

RATIONAL FEAR

- making a simple mistake with your money, like transferring money into the wrong account or confusing the ticker symbols of two stocks and buying the wrong one
- getting scammed and losing some (or all) of your savings
- being a burden to friends and family
- experiencing a bank failure
- losing your job or having a job offer rescinded
- being rejected for a raise or promotion

IRRATIONAL FEAR

- talking about money with friends and family
- never having enough money, no matter how much you save
- living with debt for the rest of your life
- spending money you've purposefully saved up
- being mocked or chastised for using the wrong financial term or not understanding a particular concept
- losing your life savings by investing it in the stock market

Anxiety

I've watched every season of *Keeping Up with the Kardashians*. Reality TV is my guilty pleasure and mental escape, and although most of it is just fluff, you'd be surprised at how much they talk about money on these shows (and it gives me life whenever they do). One thing I've been doing to de-stress while writing this book is rewatching old episodes of the show, and the number of times they talk about anxiety is shocking. I don't think I've watched one episode where someone doesn't proclaim, "This gives me so much anxiety" at least once. At one point, Kendall had it so bad she was getting sleep paralysis.

I bring up this example because you may feel like everyone either has anxiety or has at least been talking about it more than ever. According to the American Psychiatric Association, anxiety "affects nearly 30% of adults at some point in their lives."[13] Similarly, a 2014 survey found that 11.6% of Canadians over the age of 18 reported having a mood or anxiety disorder,[14] and the World Health Organization said anxiety disorders are the world's biggest mental health problem with around 4% (275 million) of the global population suffering from it, 62% of those people being women.[15]

For a clear definition, anxiety is "a normal reaction to many different kinds of events and situations in our lives [and] is one of our internal warning systems that alerts us to danger or other threats and prepares our bodies to fight back or get out of a dangerous situation."[16] Just like rational guilt and rational fear, anxiety has a useful purpose and can motivate us to find safety or resolve a threat. But there's a big difference between experiencing anxiety and having an anxiety disorder. Normal anxiety is a rational response to a specific situation and is generally short-lived. An anxiety disorder can cause anxiety to be felt unexpectedly or without reason (as if it's something uncontrollable), is often a much stronger sensation (as if it will overwhelm you), and may last for a significantly longer period of time (and feel as if it will never end).

This difference is important, because when you do an inventory of your money feelings, you can gauge whether you're experiencing normal anxiety or if there's a bigger issue at play. For example, normal anxiety around money could be like feeling concerned about your higher mortgage payments when interest rates go up or worrying about your income when you hear rumours that your company may be cutting jobs soon.

Having an anxiety disorder can have a much more harmful impact on your relationship with money. It can look like losing sleep over upcoming bills, avoiding looking at your bank accounts, leaving financial statements to pile up unopened, getting irritable when someone wants to talk about money, and just having a general obsession with money in a negative way.[17] This can propel you into a vicious cycle that will damage both your finances and your mental health and can be difficult to break out of.[18] The good news is that normal anxiety and anxiety disorders are treatable, and we'll dive into solutions later on in this book.

Envy

In this age of social media, how can you *not* feel envy when everyone on the entire planet is snapping pics and publicizing how great their life is, tempting you to compare yours? I'd say the only way to avoid feeling envy completely would be to live alone and off the grid. But for those of us who can't quit everything and leave our cellphones behind à la Christopher McCandless in *Into the Wild*, envy remains an everyday experience. It may be ubiquitous because of the internet, but envy can be such an energy-sucking, time-consuming, and self-destructive feeling that it's crucial to address it head on if you want to improve your relationship with money. As defined by the American Psychological Association, envy is "a negative emotion of discontent and resentment generated by desire for the possessions, attributes, qualities, or achievements of another (the target of the envy)."[19] Or as late humour columnist Harold Coffin was quoted as saying, "Envy is the art of counting the other fellow's blessings instead of your own."

Envy is what I experienced the Christmas I got COVID and was scrolling through social media. It was a familiar yet monstrous feeling that would sneak up on me, making me irritable, angry, resentful, and hostile. I hated feeling that way. And in a two-for-one nobody would want, I'd usually feel extreme guilt afterwards, partly because growing up Catholic had hammered into me that envy is one of the seven deadly sins.

Nevertheless, envy is a natural feeling based on social comparison, and just like all the other feelings I've discussed, it can be useful depending on which category it falls into: benign envy or malicious envy. Benign envy is when you compare yourself to someone else in a better position than you and it motivates you to take action to improve your own situation. Malicious envy involves the same comparison, but instead of wanting to move upward, you strive to pull the person you envy down.

There are a ton of content creators who publicly share their age and net worth online, many of whom garner media attention for achieving a high net worth by a young age, for example, $1 million by age 30. In this case, you might compare yourself to this high achiever and feel motivated to increase your own net worth by cutting back on spending, increasing your income, and investing more wisely. Or you might compare yourself to them and think, *That's not fair. That's unrealistic. I bet they're hiding something or lying. They probably started earning six figures right out of college and just banked it all while living at their parents' rent-free. If I was that lucky, I could've done that, too.* Not only does this way of thinking not motivate you to change your actions or behaviours to elevate yourself, but it may instead push you to try to take that person down by leaving a negative comment on their account, gossiping about them in online forums, and generally rejecting their achievements. If you feel this way about someone you know personally, malicious envy could lead you to be rude or cruel to them.

Benign envy has elements of positivity embedded in it, since it can influence you to improve yourself in the future by using the success of someone you admire as an example or template. Malicious envy is rooted in negativity and overrides empathy completely, which helps no one, least of all you.[20] In other words, although envy is a primal feeling that we all experience, you can't let it run rampant inside you. It can lead you down a dangerous road, so it's important to identify it and get a handle on it.

Despair

The last feeling we're going to cover is despair. You may have heard the phrase "compare and despair" before, which describes when you get trapped in a social comparison loop where no matter what you do, you'll never be good enough compared to that person. Despair is envy's evil sidekick.

Originally deriving from the Latin term *desperare*, which means "down from hope,"[21] despair is a feeling of hopelessness and the belief that everything is wrong and it will never get better.[22] It can also be the feeling of having no purpose in life or the world in general, expressed as "What's even the point anymore?" Despair is not a feeling you want to spend much or any time in, largely because of what it could lead to if untreated—the diseases or deaths of despair.

Research has shown that despair is strongly linked to an increase in depression, alcohol dependency, substance abuse, suicidal thoughts and behaviours, as well as death by alcohol-related liver disease, drug overdose, and suicide.[23] Research has also found that people who suffer from financial instability and insecurity, and who are most vulnerable to job loss or financial downturns, are the most susceptible to despair.[24] In other words, if you're in a precarious financial situation, you are statistically more likely to fall into despair's clutches.

With that said, there are different levels of despair. You can feel true despair, which is the ultimate feeling of hopelessness and dissociation from the world and your place in it. Or you can feel situational despair, which is a feeling of despair for a particular life situation, such as your job or financial prospects. True despair can best be treated with the help of a mental health professional, but situational despair is something you can overcome yourself with tools I'll share later in this book.

But until then, let's circle back to a question I asked you in the previous chapter so we can start to unlock your true feelings about money.

Your First Money Memories

Whether we consciously know it or not, money begins to have a major presence in our lives starting in early childhood, and our first memories with money can set the stage for how we feel and behave in adulthood. To improve our relationship with money, we need to go back in time, find those early money memories, and see how they connect to our present-day feelings about it. You already know what my first money memory is and what it led to (gumball → stealing → scolding → shame), so go through the following exercise to unpack yours.

If you're like many people who are able to recall only a few (if any) childhood memories and are already thinking of skipping this section because it makes you anxious or uncomfortable, that's completely understandable. See if any memories come up, even if you're not sure they're the "first." For some, the lack of early-life memories could be due to childhood trauma, which can be safely explored by working with a therapist. With that said, I encourage you to read through the following exercise even if you aren't able to carry it out just yet.* Listen to cues from your body and remember you are safe, and you can always put this book down and come back to it later.

---

* The "Your First Money Memory" exercise was developed in collaboration with Nadine Salz, MScOT, OT Reg. (Ont.), The Mindful Way.

EXERCISE

In this exercise, you are going to use mindfulness to elicit a memory. Remember, mindfulness is a kind of meditation that focuses on being in the present moment, in our bodies, without judgments or distractions. So, find a comfortable and quiet space to sit and have a piece of paper or journal at the ready to write down your thoughts.

Step 1: Pick an anchor, something to bring your attention back to when your thoughts inevitably drift to a to-do list, judgments, or critical thoughts. Your goal throughout is to stay present, grounded, and in your body. When you are thinking of what you need to do tomorrow, you are no longer present. For this exercise, your breath can be your anchor. When you feel yourself drifting away from the present moment, bring your attention back to your breath. Practise inhaling and exhaling using the prompts below.

Breathe in through your nose, feel the air come through your nose as your belly expands. Breathe out through your mouth, feel the air leave your mouth as your belly empties.

Step 2: Practise five breaths as described above. As your mind drifts, remember to bring it back to your breath.

Step 3: Now practise eliciting a memory. What did you eat for dinner last night? Okay, now you know how to elicit a memory. Do not judge the memory—we cannot change the memory. The memory just *is*.

Step 4: As you continue to sit, grounded, start breathing intentionally, through your nose and out your mouth. If it feels right for you, close your eyes. I'm going to ask you to think pretty far back now—do not worry if it takes some time, or multiple attempts, to do so.

Step 5: Now think back to your first experience with money. Be patient as memories surface. Observe the memory without judgment. Use your five senses to elicit more details about the memory. What do you see, taste, feel, hear, smell? Write down the memory in as much detail as possible.

Step 6: Now that you have elicited the memory, let's become curious observers of it. Ask yourself the following questions:

- Where were you?
- Whom were you with?
- How old were you?
- How did you feel?
- What is your current interpretation of the memory?

Step 7: To close this mindfulness exercise, come back to the present moment. How do you feel? Take some more deep breaths and remember you are in a safe space.

Your Feelings about Money Today

Now that you've brought your early money memories to the surface, let's come back to the present moment and connect them to how money makes you feel today. Try the following exercise to help you draw out your feelings, and make sure to write everything down for your future reference.*

---

* The "Your Feelings about Money Today" exercise was developed in collaboration with Nadine Salz, MScOT, OT Reg. (Ont.), The Mindful Way.

EXERCISE

Step 1: Start breathing intentionally as described in the last exercise. Breathe in through your nose, feel the air come through your nose as your belly expands. Breathe out through your mouth, feel the air leave your mouth as your belly empties. As your mind drifts, remember to bring it back to your breath.

Step 2: Now practise visualizing while you breathe. Close your eyes and visualize yourself pouring a glass of water. Observe yourself opening the cupboard, selecting a glass, turning on the tap, filling the glass with water, and turning off the tap. Watch yourself take a sip of the water. Okay, now you know how to visualize.

Step 3: Now I am going to ask you to visualize a variety of scenarios. These all have to do with money, with the goal of eliciting your present feelings about money, which you might not be consciously aware of. Here are some examples of scenarios, but I encourage you to pick or create ones that are most relevant to you.

Visualize yourself:
- opening your wallet at the grocery store checkout
- on payday
- paying your mortgage or rent
- buying a lottery ticket
- buying yourself or a loved one an expensive present
- at the gas pump and watching the cost rise as you fill your car

Step 4: Without judgment, notice the feelings and thoughts coming up. How does your body feel? What are the physical sensations? What words or phrases are going through your mind?

Step 5: Name the feelings coming up without judgment. Refer back to the feelings previously discussed in this chapter, and check out Gloria Willcox's "The Feeling Wheel," referenced in the back of this book.[25]

Use the feeling wheel to explore the range of emotions humans experience. Remember, two things can be true at once. An experience can make you both scared and excited (e.g., quitting your job), and you can experience both relief and grief (e.g., inheriting money from a loved one who's passed).

Write down the feelings and emotions that correspond to each scenario.

Step 6: Now let's come back to the present and thank your feelings for presenting themselves to you.

Well done on getting through both mindfulness practices! Hopefully, you've identified your starting place with money and captured some feelings you may or may not have been aware of. It may take a couple of tries to get to the memories you need, so be patient and listen to any cues and feelings that come up. Now let's move on to the next chapter, where we're going to explore where these feelings come from.

Takeaways

- If money makes you feel shame, guilt, fear, anxiety, envy, or despair, you're not alone, and these are perfectly natural feelings to feel.

- It's important to differentiate between rational feelings about money, which are meant to help you or keep you from harm, and irrational feelings, which are holding you back from getting out of your own way.

- Identifying your earliest money memories will reveal part of where those feelings stem from.

- Acknowledging your current feelings about money will help you understand, let go, and heal from your negative feelings about money moving forward.

PART II

More Than a Buzzword: The Roles Trauma and Family Play in Our Money

3.

What's Your Money Story?

Owning our story and loving ourselves through that
process is the bravest thing that we'll ever do.
—Brené Brown

Now that you have a better idea of how money makes you feel, the next question to ask yourself is "Why is that?" The answer lies inside your personal money story. Your money story is the narrative you've developed throughout your life about your relationship with money and the main guide you've used for all of your financial decision-making up until this point. This story is based on the lessons you've learned and behavioural patterns you've either repeated or rebelled against from your parents or caregivers, as well as a few other factors I'll discuss in subsequent chapters on trauma, human behaviour, personal circumstance, and societal barriers. In short, your money story is the answer to why you keep self-sabotaging your finances or can't break out of patterns you'd like to leave in the past.

Once you've got your personal money story outlined and written down, you're in a much better position to identify the trauma responses, conflicting messages, and self-limiting beliefs you've held on to that have negatively impacted your finances all your life. Not only that, you'll be ready to start letting go of some of these things so you can start writing a brand-new money story that will open the door to a much healthier relationship with money and, ultimately, a path toward financial fulfillment (which we'll get to in the book's final chapter).

To give you some context, let me show you a snapshot of a money story from a 28-year-old woman named Nina.

Oh my gosh, I'm so bad with money. I've never been good with it. Whenever I have it, I spend it, which makes me feel so guilty. And then, what do I do to try to make myself feel better? I spend more of it, which makes me feel even worse! Ugh, I'm just like my mom, who I do not want to end up like. She's sixty-two and can't retire any time soon because she still has a mortgage and credit card debt but zero savings. But hey, what are you gonna do? Everyone I know is pretty much the same way, so at least I know I'm not the only one!

Let's break this money story down, shall we? The first thing I can identify is the presence of shame with the comment "*I'm so bad* with money." Right off the bat, we can tell that Nina feels like she is fundamentally flawed when it comes to managing money, a common yet powerful self-limiting belief. Next, she mentions that whenever she has money, she spends it and can't stop herself. This tendency to overspend is likely a trauma response to soothe her underlying pain temporarily, despite the fact that it will likely cause further damage to her financial well-being down the road. She also mentions the feeling of guilt whenever she overspends, which indicates she is aware that what she is doing goes against her intentions, but she isn't able to emotionally regulate to stop the behaviour. Next, she mentions her mom and recognizes that she is repeating a behavioural pattern that she observed growing up. She also mentions that she knows it's bad behaviour by acknowledging that she doesn't want the same fate as her mom, who is still in debt and unprepared for retirement in her sixties. Lastly, although she is clearly aware of the problem, she tries to rationalize it by saying everyone she knows has similar financial struggles. This is likely another defence mechanism to avoid her feelings of shame, guilt, and anxiety about the future so she can carry on with her day.

That's a lot of information from just a few short sentences. But when does anyone in real life ask you a question like "What does your relationship with money look like?" The answer is almost never. I interviewed dozens of people for this book who either listen to my podcast, watch me on YouTube, or saw me speak at an event, and when I posed a question like this, it was almost always the first time anyone had ever asked them about their relationship with money and the first time they'd ever verbalized it. Not only was it fascinating to hear money stories from people of all different ages and backgrounds from across Canada and the U.S., but it was also amazing to see the interviewees make connections to life events, family history, and money they never had before.

And that's what I want you to experience, too, which is why I'm going to share some real-life money stories with you to help you unlock some of the hard money lessons, mixed messages, and self-destructive habits you've brought with you from childhood into adulthood. We'll then get to work on figuring out what your money story is, so you can start rewriting it. Without doing this important self-exploration, you can go your whole life without realizing what has been driving your financial habits and beliefs up until this point. As we all know, the quality of our decision-making is only as good as the quality of the information we receive. If we grew up in a "Do as I say, not as I do" type of household or had very strong values pushed on us by our parents, it can cause a lot of confusion and harm when we become adults. That's why pinpointing the types of messages you received and lessons you learned is key to healing your overall relationship with money.

Money Lessons to Unlearn

Kids are absolute sponges when they're growing up, holding on to a simple comment, gesture, or tone of voice for the rest of their lives. For instance, when I was 12, I remember my seventh-grade teacher warning my class about the dangers of credit cards and to never buy something when we didn't have the cash to pay for it. I can't remember the exact context for this—it must have been during math class—but his words weren't the only thing that stuck with me all these years. He was unusually serious and even somewhat emotional when he was talking, which led me to believe that he wasn't just imparting some words of wisdom; he was going through something personally and needed to vent.

Thankfully, that was a helpful money lesson that I brought with me into adulthood, though it did make me perhaps overly cautious of credit cards for a long time. Unfortunately, a lot of the money lessons we learn aren't that helpful and can be incredibly harmful if we don't recognize and unlearn them when we enter adulthood. Moreover, most of these lessons aren't learned directly like my teacher's "Beware of credit cards!" remark in seventh grade. Most of the time, we learn them indirectly by observing our parents argue about the electricity bill or witnessing a traumatic financial event that affects the family's sense of stability, which was the case for Maria.

DISASTER IS ALWAYS JUST AROUND THE CORNER

Maria grew up in Brazil in the 1970s and experienced first-hand how money can put a stranglehold on your family. Her dad was the sole breadwinner, while her mom stayed at home to raise her and her three siblings. Back in those days, employees were paid monthly, so it became a ritual that at the start of each month, her dad would come home with his paycheque, pay off all their outstanding bills, and then give some money to her mom to buy groceries. However, around the two-week mark, the money was always all gone, so everyone would patiently wait until it was payday again and make do with whatever they had in the pantry for meals. Then one day, her dad, who was known to have a permanent smile on his face, came home and burst into tears at the kitchen table because he'd been laid off from his job.

"I know this definitely caused some childhood trauma in me, because it was so scary. Ever since that moment, I've always been planning for tragedy, always thinking, *What if? What if I lose my job? What if my husband loses his job? What if I die? How are my kids going to survive? What is my husband going to do without me?* And then always defaulting to 'No, we can't spend any money,' even when we actually can afford to do so."

The lesson Maria learned was that in a flash, the rug can be pulled out from under you, so hold on to your money if you want to survive.

That's why after she immigrated to Canada and started a family of her own, she maintained a frugal lifestyle and prioritized staying out of debt and living within her means, just in case something was to happen again. Although there are undeniable benefits to these habits, Maria now laments the fact that she was overly focused on living on less instead of truly living for most of her life.

For instance, she'd always assumed that there wasn't any wiggle room in the family budget to afford things like family vacations, since those were considered luxuries for the wealthy when she was growing up. It wasn't until she befriended a neighbour who travelled for months out of the year that she realized she could. "When I first met Carey, we started chatting about what we liked to do, and she asked me if I liked to travel. My automatic response was 'We can't afford to travel,' to which she responded, 'What do you mean?' Eventually, I shared that my husband and I both had well-paying jobs and no debt besides our mortgage, which was very small, but I still couldn't rationalize spending money on something that wasn't a necessity. But because she travelled all the time, she said she'd help me make a budget and find the money for a family trip to Italy. And she did! The money was there the whole time. I'd just been viewing my money as something to protect and use only for needs instead of wants my whole life. Honestly, if she hadn't stepped in and showed me a different perspective, I know I never would have taken that trip, which was such an amazing life experience and created so many memories for my family."

A rewritten lesson: Be prepared for potential financial loss, but don't let fear run all of your financial decision-making.

FRUGALITY STRIPS THE JOY OUT OF EVERYTHING

Anja had a similar upbringing but took a very different path once she left home. Her parents were immigrants from Serbia and were extremely frugal. Because they lived through the civil wars in the former socialist Yugoslavia during the 1990s, scarcity and instability were part of their everyday lives. When they moved to Canada for a better life, they instilled the same survival skills in their kids that had helped them for so many years, such as living a minimalistic lifestyle and not spending money on things they deemed wasteful. "One thing I learned from my parents was to never go to restaurants, because it was basically the same thing as throwing your money away. Still to this day, 30 years later, they never go to restaurants because they believe this!"

Maria from the previous story got the same advice from her parents, but how she reacted was to follow suit and make food at home to save money. Anja, on the other hand, went in the opposite direction. Feeling restricted under her parents' rules when she was growing up, when she finally went off to college and started earning an income of her own, for the first time in her life she made spending and enjoying all the things she had been denied her top priority. She went to restaurants, she bought nice clothes and expensive electronics. She did everything she could to chase that feeling of freedom that spending provided her.

The lesson Anja learned was that being frugal restricts your freedom, so it's better to spend your money and enjoy it while you can.

Unfortunately, she didn't track how much she was earning versus how much she was spending and started to accrue some hefty credit card debt. Breaking free from the confines of her parents' money attitudes led her down a path of limitless spending with some serious financial consequences. Eventually, she was able to realize that if she continued doing what she was doing, she'd be even more restricted in her life than she'd ever been in her childhood. She didn't want to be tied down by debt any more than she wanted to be tied down by strict spending rules. Slowly, she was able to find a balance between living within her means and also spending money in a way that made her feel free and happy.

A rewritten lesson: Overly strict financial rules can backfire when you feel deprived, so instead, try to find a balance between your income, your responsibilities and goals, and your desires.

BE READY FOR TAKEOFF

Similar to Anja's parents, Henry's parents were also forced to flee their homeland of China to seek refuge in Hong Kong during the Communist Revolution. Starting a new life with nothing had a big impact on both his parents, especially his father. As Henry tells it, "They lived in squalor in Hong Kong, because at the time, it was basically barren land except for the properties owned by the British elites. They lived in stone huts with no running water and experienced extreme poverty." When they got older, his parents moved to Canada for a chance at a better life. Henry's father found work and was able to provide the family with all their needs, though not much more. But one thing that Henry always noticed was his father's obsession with keeping cash around.

Because his father had had to uproot his life twice in a hurry, compounded by his lack of trust in the government and banking system due to escaping Communist China as a kid, having access to cash quickly was very important in their household. "My dad made it clear it was always important to save and keep cash. He would keep bundles and bundles of cash under the carpet. I think he always had this fear that he needed to be ready to run again."

The lesson Henry learned was that cash is a tool for survival, and it is vital to have access to it in a hurry.

So, when Henry entered his early 20s, he didn't think about things like investing for his future or building generational wealth, because that had never been a value in his family. Cash was king, after all. But when Henry's parents retired, despite them owning their home and having no debt, because they had kept only cash and at most invested in very conservative instruments like GICs, they had a very meagre nest egg to live on. Because of this, they were forced to live very humbly in their twilight years, depending on financial assistance from government programs for low-income retirees. As Henry got older and started reading personal finance books, he realized that although having cash for emergencies is important, it can also limit your financial freedom in later years.

> **A rewritten lesson: Cash is important for emergencies but won't be enough to afford a comfortable retirement. Save up cash for the short term and invest for the long term.**

OUR LUCK IS ABOUT TO CHANGE

Blake grew up with a dad who always believed his luck was about to change. "He grew up in Libya, and I think because he felt like he'd won the lottery by immigrating to Canada, making a new life here, and meeting my mom, he thought he could do it again and a big windfall was just around the corner. He'd say, 'Blake, what numbers do you want? Do you want to pick them this week? When we win the lottery, we're going to get a boat and buy anything you want.' It was that one thing that gave him hope that things would work out in the end."

Unfortunately, there's no amount of wishful thinking that can counteract something as catastrophic as the 2008 financial crisis. When the market crashed and the subsequent recession hit, Blake's parents could no longer make their mortgage payments and were forced to sell the family home. Luckily for Blake, they moved into a townhouse closer to his best friends from school, so he was pleased about the move. His parents actively hid the realities of the family's financial struggles from him and his siblings so they'd continue believing that everything was fine and there was no cause for worry.

> **The lesson Blake learned was that no matter what happens, luck will be on your side side and everything will work out in the end.**

When Blake started working in his early 20s, he maxed out his credit cards and spent everything he earned because he believed that everything would work out somehow, just like it had for his parents. That is, until he met his girlfriend, who came from a financially secure background and helped him realize that *he* was the one who had to work it out. You can't financially plan around divine intervention, and your odds of winning the Lotto Max are the same as everyone else's—1 in 33,294,800. If he wanted to experience even a semblance of the dream life he and his dad had fantasized about while he was growing up, it was up to him to start taking control over his money.

A rewritten lesson: Everything will work out when you take control of your finances and make it happen.

WEALTH IS A BURDEN

Stephen grew up in a wealthy family. His parents had an annual country club membership, a house in Seattle with the most breathtaking views, and a laundry list of expectations for Stephen. His father was a corporate lawyer and his mother was an interior designer, but both originally came from middle-class families. With their new wealth and status, they wanted to make sure their son continued to carry the torch by excelling in private school, making strategic friendships so they could network with the friends' rich parents, and, of course, becoming a lawyer, doctor, or successful entrepreneur, so they would be proud to answer the question "And what does your son do?" at cocktail parties when he was older.

But all Stephen dreamed about was becoming a musician. "They would have been thrilled if I told them I wanted to learn violin to one day become first chair in the Seattle Symphony Orchestra. But that was never my dream. I wanted to be a singer-songwriter like John Mayer, which they hated, because they thought that meant I would probably never make any money. So, they refused to buy me a guitar and pay for music lessons, telling me, 'We're not paying for you to throw your life away. If you want to do that, you can pay for it yourself.' So, I did. I got a job at a coffee shop, saved up, bought my own guitar and found a tutor, which they also weren't crazy about."

Even though from the outside looking in, Stephen seemed to have it all, he felt powerless in the face of his family's wealth. Instead of a blessing, the money and what it meant to his parents was just a big burden.

The lesson Stephen learned was that wealth means being restricted by other people's expectations of you.

So, when he finished high school, he told his parents he wasn't going to college and, instead, was going to take his guitar and drive across the U.S. to play bars and small clubs so he could be discovered. Unhappy with his decision, his parents cut him off and stopped speaking to him, gobsmacked that he could be so selfish as to destroy everything they'd set up for his future.

Cut to 12 years later: Stephen now lives in Nashville with his wife and son and works in music as a producer-songwriter. He makes a pretty good living and is doing what he loves, but he still has a strained relationship with his parents and most especially with money. "This sounds weird, I know, but I hate money. It's just never been a positive thing in my life, and I've seen what it can do to people. If it weren't for my wife taking control of our finances, I'd still be broke, because I would either spend it all or give it away to friends or musicians I wanted to support."

A rewritten lesson: Money itself isn't a bad thing, and it can actually be a tool for good in your life and those of others. It's up to you!

Mixed Messages to Untangle

It's one thing to learn clear-cut lessons about money, but what if we learn things that contradict themselves? Unfortunately, many of the lessons we learn are in direct conflict with each other, which can cause a lot of confusion and ultimately prove to be a recipe for financial disaster.

RICH PEOPLE ARE CROOKS / ALL OUR PROBLEMS WOULD BE GONE IF WE HAD MORE MONEY

Luke grew up in a fairly conservative Christian household in North Dakota where money was always tight but also seen as something sinful. "The biggest belief that I picked up from my parents was that if you have wealth, you probably did something wrong or bad to get it. I know a lot of that came from our Christian beliefs and that popular Bible verse 'Money is the root of all evil.' So, we always saw the accumulation of wealth through this negative lens, instead of considering all the good a person could do with it." At the same time, he also picked up the belief from his parents that if only there was more money, life would be a whole lot easier. They never owned their home or had much savings, and habitually lived paycheque to paycheque. But instead of taking any responsibility for their financial situation, Luke's parents were quick to blame the bank, the wealthy stealing from the poor, and the system keeping them down.

Since those were the conflicting messages Luke adopted growing up, when he was an adult, he continued down a similar path, spending freely, not prioritizing saving, and making late payments on his truck. It wasn't until the bank repossessed it while he was at work one day that he got a big wake-up call. "Up until then, I never really thought about the negative consequences of my financial actions. So, it was a big learning lesson to have my truck taken away, especially in front of all my co-workers, which was really embarrassing. Because my parents only ever talked about money in a negative way, when I was struggling financially, it never even occurred to me to contact my bank to see if we could work something out. In my mind, the bank was part of this financial system you couldn't trust or was meant to keep you down."

After that, he realized how little he really understood about personal finance, which motivated him to start reading books and listening to podcasts to educate himself. Since then, not only has he learned that the full Bible verse is "the love of money is the root of all evil" (1 Tim. 6:10), referencing how one shouldn't be money-obsessed or overly attached to material possessions, but that having money isn't a bad thing on its own. Accumulating wealth can make it a lot easier not just to experience more security and stability in life but also to help you pay it forward and aid others in need as well.

> **A rewritten lesson: Money isn't evil and accumulating wealth can provide security, stability, and a means of helping others.**

WE CAN'T AFFORD THAT / TREAT YOURSELF

Jennifer grew up with a single mom who was always on a quest for a better-paying job and a better life. "When I was younger, we moved around a lot. Like every couple of years, we'd literally pack up everything in the car and drive to a new town, as if we were hitting the reset button to try again. It was very unsettling as a child. I think my mom thought that if we started again somewhere new, things would be better, but it would always turn out that we were worse off than before." Then one day, they stopped moving. Jennifer's mom met someone, got married, and the best part was her new husband was a doctor with a high and stable income. Having experienced only scarcity and instability up until that point, Jennifer reasoned that, finally, they'd been struck with some good luck for a change. "We'd come from this place of not having any money for anything, then all of a sudden, we had so much. My stepfather bought a ton of expensive things, and at the time, I thought things were good and I could enjoy it."

Unfortunately, a few years into the marriage, it became apparent that the new husband had a drinking problem, which started to affect his job and his spending. It got so bad that he eventually stopped working and had to start selling their belongings to pay for groceries and the bills while also depending heavily on credit. At the lowest point, they sold the family car, their one source of transportation. "When I asked them why they were selling it, they just told me, 'Having a car is a luxury. We don't need a luxury like that.'"

Because of the mixed messages and financial ups and downs that Jennifer experienced growing up, she's had a hard time feeling settled most of her life. When she turned 18, she started doing the same thing her mom did, moving to a new city every few years, thinking that the next place would be better. At the same time, she racked up mountains of credit card debt, feeling extremely guilty in the process for spending money on things that her mom and stepdad used to call luxuries but were actually necessities. "Them selling the family car and making me feel ashamed for wanting to keep it because it was a 'luxury' has always stuck with me. It's why it took me until my 40s to finally get my first car, which, looking back, is wild."

Thankfully, the stay-at-home order during the pandemic forced Jennifer to take a good look at her finances and realize she didn't want to continue the same cycle her mother was stuck in. She began educating herself about budgeting, started her own upcycling business, which has tripled her income, and paid off all of her consumer debt.

A rewritten lesson: Necessities aren't luxuries. Only treat yourself when you feel good about doing so and don't have to rely on credit.

MONEY WILL KEEP YOU TRAPPED / MONEY BREEDS GREED

Taylor grew up in a small town in Ontario, in a household where her mom stayed at home to raise her and her two siblings while her dad worked for the government and controlled all the finances. Because of this, growing up, she learned that when it came to money, the man had all the power. "Whenever we'd go ask my mom for money to go to the corner store, she'd always say, 'Go ask your father,' and so we picked up pretty quickly that she had zero economic power. It got complicated as we got older, when their relationship went through some bumps. She tried leaving my father a few times, but always came back because she didn't have the resources to commit to leaving him, plus she didn't know anything about money, like how to pay bills or earn a living."

When Taylor left home, she promised herself she'd never put herself in the same position and be dependent on a man. That's why she and her partner keep all of their money separate and she's focused on reaching financial independence on her own. Although she's on a personal journey to financial freedom, during our chat together, it became clear that she also had mixed feelings about money in general. Her entire career has been in the non-profit sector, and she describes herself as an eco-socialist. She sees the oppression and damage that our current capitalist system causes people every day and wishes we could live in a world where money was distributed more equally and the mere mention of universal basic income didn't trigger a response like "Then what's the incentive to work? That will just create a society of lazy people."

Because of her conflicting feelings about money being a source of freedom but also a means of propping some people up while keeping some people down, she's struggled with guilt when negotiating her salary and asking for a raise. She has also struggled to feel deserving of more money working for a non-profit, because when administration costs go up, it could mean fewer resources for the main cause. It wasn't until she started dating her partner, who earned twice as much as she did, that she realized that asking for more money wasn't greedy, but was an important way for her contributions to be validated and valued. "My partner works hard, but he doesn't work twice as hard as me, so why is he earning twice as much if his contributions aren't double mine? It just made me think that what you earn isn't automatically a reflection of your work ethic or contributions, so if you feel like you're not being paid fairly, you need to speak up, and it's not being selfish or greedy if you do it."

A rewritten lesson: You can strive for financial independence and get paid your worth while still making a positive change in others' lives.

Toxic Money Behaviours

After hearing the real money stories from Maria, Anja, Henry, Blake, Stephen, Luke, Jennifer, and Taylor, I hope you've been able to recognize the huge impact the lessons you picked up throughout childhood can have on your relationship with money. These are only eight of dozens more I could share that would confirm the same thing. So, what now?

As financial psychologists Brad and Ted Klontz explain in *Mind over Money*, people with a damaged relationship with money typically fall into three camps when it comes to money: they either avoid it, worship it, or use it to fulfill a need in a relationship.[1] When you know which camp you fall into, it can be a lot easier to understand why you do some of the things you do with money that you could never explain before. Let's find out which camps you fall into (and it might be more than one).

I DON'T WANT IT ANYWHERE NEAR ME

Denial

Avoiding money can take a number of different forms. It can look like denial, in which you literally avoid money at all costs. This could look like throwing unopened bills into the trash, never logging into your bank or credit card accounts, not tracking your income, spending, or net worth, and avoiding calls from collection agencies. If you saw your parents do this, for example, you may have brought this behaviour with you into adulthood. If, instead, money was a big negative presence in your household, with your parents constantly arguing, complaining, and stressing out about money, your coping mechanism as an adult may be to deny money a place in your life, so it doesn't continue to cause you the same stress and pain.

Rejection

Money avoidance can also look like rejection, as we saw with Stephen. Because money had caused such turmoil in his life when he was growing up, he didn't want anything to do with it. So, whenever money came into his life, he would try to get rid of it by spending it or giving it away as a way to reject its power over him.

Underspending

Similarly, if money was a source of pain when you were growing up, instead of spending it or giving it away, you may choose to avoid it by stashing it in a savings account and refusing to let it out by underspending, as we saw with Maria. This is your method of seizing control over money instead of letting it control you, even though denying yourself things that could bring you comfort or joy will inevitably cause *you* more pain in the long run.

Excessive Risk Aversion

Lastly, there's excessive risk aversion, which is "an irrational unwillingness to take any risks with one's money [because] a person in the grip of risk avoidance reacts to any risk, however slight, with enormous anxiety."[2] Therefore, to avoid this feeling of intense anxiety, a person assumes that inaction is better than action, because at least if you do nothing with your money, there's a greater chance you won't lose all of it. People with this type of behaviour tend to be like Henry's father, who took no risks with his money by keeping only cash and conservative investments, but in so doing, gained no real returns to make that money stretch further in retirement.

BOW DOWN TO THE ALMIGHTY DOLLAR

As you can guess, worshipping money is on the complete opposite side of the spectrum and involves clinging to the belief that having more money will solve all of your problems, and thus you should do anything to get it and keep it. If you need a good representation of what money-worshipping looks like in today's world, I highly recommend watching Lauren Greenfield's documentary *Generation Wealth*. It's not only eye-opening but heartbreaking to see how we've evolved into a society that idolizes money above everything else, usually to our own detriment.

Extreme Risk-Taking

Along the same lines, unreasonable risk-taking by gambling or trading speculative investments like cryptocurrency, non-fungible tokens (NFTs), or "hot" stocks you've done zero research on is also a form of money worship. By taking on so much risk that there is likely to be a greater downside than upside, you're effectively buying into the get-rich-quick fairy tale that has been peddled by sleazy salespeople and now social media con artists for years. Despite the fact that most of us know a friend of a friend's second-cousin who got rich by playing the stock market or buying and selling the latest crypto coin, it's important to remember that most real people never disclose their losses, and there are a lot more losers than winners when it comes to taking on big risks like this.

Workaholism

If you're thinking, *I would never fall into any of those traps. I believe that the only way to get rich is by hard work*, let me ask you: What would you define as *hard work*? Are you part of the get-up-at-four-in-the-morning rise-and-grind hustle culture? Have you bought into the idea that everyone has the same number of hours in a day, and if you haven't created six different passive income streams and don't have a side hustle on top of your day job, you're lazy and thus deserve to be broke? If the answer is yes, guess what? Workaholism is a form of money worship, too.

Workaholism is the belief that hard work will lead you to wealth, and wealth will lead you to a life of prestige, attention, respect, higher self-worth, and overwhelming happiness. So, if you don't have wealth, you must not be working hard enough. The solution? Work even harder! The thing is, and this is something that I personally went through a few years ago, there is a limit to how much you can actually work, and burnout will be waiting for you when you reach your breaking point. Not only is burnout not fun to go through (believe me), it can also lead to some pretty serious physical and mental health issues like heart disease, prolonged fatigue, migraines, depression, insomnia, and a higher mortality rate.[3] I really want to stress how dangerous workaholism is because I see it as one of the most widespread problems among Generations Y and Z right now, largely due to pro-workaholism messaging being promoted online. It's important not to work all the time, and there are many better ways to build wealth other than just working harder (hint: it's working smarter).

Hoarding

If you've ever seen the reality TV show *Hoarders*, you may already be familiar with how damaging hoarding can be to a person. But hoarding isn't just a form of money worship. It's also a disorder that is usually caused by another underlying disorder such as obsessive-compulsive personality disorder (OCPD), obsessive-compulsive disorder (OCD), attention-deficit/hyperactivity disorder (ADHD), and depression.[4] It can also be triggered by experiencing extreme scarcity in your life or inheriting the trauma of scarcity from your family, and it's something you will likely need professional help to overcome.

Nevertheless, hoarding occurs when a person places a strong emotional attachment to either material objects they perceive as valuable (even if they aren't, like old newspapers or damaged teacups) or money itself. Henry's father could fit into this category, since he was known to hoard cash around the house due to his childhood trauma of growing up in extreme poverty. Even though I wouldn't classify myself as a hoarder, I've had hoarding tendencies throughout my life that I still have to combat when my insecurities flare up.

For example, I was recently talking with my bookkeeper, and she said to me, "You know, you really shouldn't keep that much cash in your business chequing account. Why not put some of it into your savings account, where you can earn some interest on it?" She was right and I knew it, but because of the scarcity I felt before I could earn my own money as a teenager and my inherited trauma from both sets of my grandparents (which I'll discuss in Chapter 5), seeing a pile of money in one account often makes me feel safer than seeing two smaller numbers in separate accounts. It's completely illogical, because it's still the same amount of money. That's why it's always great to have someone in your corner to call you out on some of your limiting money behaviours when you can't see them for yourself.

Overspending

One of the most common forms of money worship is overspending. The routine of spending excessively on yourself or others provides you with feelings of safety, comfort, love, and wholeness that saving money or spending reasonably just doesn't allow. What's interesting is this form of money worship is also caused by experiences with scarcity. Just as Anja displayed, when you grow up in a household where money feels restrictive, you want to break free by doing the one thing you were always denied: spending. It's like when you go on an extreme diet, denying yourself all kinds of foods, only to end up eating way more at the end of the day because you're so hungry, or bingeing on treats on the weekend or "cheat days" because you feel deprived.

Compulsive Buying Disorder

Lastly, we have compulsive buying disorder (CBD), which is a disorder just like hoarding. Compulsive buying disorder is when you spend excessively and can't seem to find the slow-down or stop button, just as Nina described herself at the start of this chapter. CBD is essentially an addiction to shopping, and just like any addiction, it's a way to soothe or suppress your pain by doing something to get a big dopamine hit. This is why people with this disorder buy stuff over and over again even though they can see how it's ruining their financial lives. The drive to get that dopamine hit is way stronger than the drive to stop. Like hoarding, CBD is typically caused by another underlying disorder, such as a mood or anxiety disorder, eating disorder, substance abuse disorder, or other disorder linked to issues with impulse control. CBD should be taken very seriously, and unfortunately, it plagues 5% of the Canadian population[5] and 5.8% of the U.S. population, 80% of which are women.[6]

A LITTLE BIT NEEDY

In the final camp are those who use money to fulfill a specific need in their relationships, such as to feel needed, to express love, or in the following case, to not need anyone at all.

Financial Infidelity

As you can guess, financial infidelity, which is lying about or hiding money matters from your partner,[7] stems from having severe trust issues with people close to you. These issues are typically rooted in childhood trauma in which some sort of abandonment or betrayal occurred. With that said, it can also stem from wanting to protect your independence because you witnessed the hardships that can come from depending on someone else. For example, it would have been completely understandable if Taylor had exercised financial infidelity with her partner to maintain her autonomy. Considering her mom had zero economic power and thus felt trapped in her marriage, Taylor's fear of not having full authority over her finances stands to reason. Thankfully, she didn't and was able to recognize the importance of transparency and honesty to maintain a healthy relationship.

Enabling

Enabling is less about maintaining power and more about giving it up. We likely all know of kids who got all the latest gadgets and toys, only to find out later that it was because their parents felt guilty for overworking and not spending enough time with them. In effect, these parents were giving material things to their child as a surrogate for their time and attention, likely to squash any feelings of guilt they had for not being present.

I've also seen this behaviour in parents who grew up in low-income households and want to provide their kids with everything they didn't get. That's why there are so many media stories of baby boomers sacrificing their own retirement to fund their kid's college education or provide them with the down payment on their first home. They are trying to provide the financial support to their kid that they never got at the same age, despite the fact that doing so might be to their own financial detriment.

Dependency

Finally, there's dependency. I see this often with adults who still depend on their parents to pay their bills or financially support their lifestyle when they are more than capable of earning a sufficient income themselves. I also see this in some conservative circles with women espousing older "traditional" values and expecting their male partners to be their financial providers, correlating their income level to their level of love and loyalty. Then again, I've also heard the same narrative in more liberal circles, such as in some of my favourite female-sung rap songs, in which they say if a man can't buy them everything their heart desires, he'll be kicked to the curb and replaced with a man who can. But dependency can also look like depending on the government, family members, or the universe to provide all your financial needs, instead of stepping up to the plate yourself when you are perfectly able to.

Repeat or Rebel

Before moving on to writing out your own money story, there's one more important question we need to address. You may have even already asked yourself this while reading the previous money stories: Why do some people repeat the same behaviours as their parents and why do others rebel? We saw it with Maria and Anja. They both came from similar financial backgrounds but reacted in opposite ways. Why is that?

When you grow up in an environment where the prominent views and behaviours around money are extreme, you're going to be

conditioned to believe that *money = extreme*. Without any outside intervention, you're either going to stay on one end of the spectrum or sprint
to the other. It's hard for you to find that perfect middle ground, which
is where you need to be to experience financial fulfillment.

THE FOLLOWER

I've got to say, the majority of people I interviewed modelled their financial behaviour after their parents' instead of rebelling against it. A
simple explanation for being a follower is that there's comfort in sticking
to what you're familiar with, even if it's harmful or self-destructive. As
the saying goes, better the devil you know than the devil you don't.
That's why I see a lot of people invest exclusively in real estate, for example, because that's what their parents invested in and that's the only
way they learned how to build wealth. The stock market, on the other
hand, no thank you, that's too risky.

On top of that, we are conditioned as children to believe that what
we learn from our parents is gospel. We assume our parents know everything, and we're taught to follow their example exactly. This is fine
when you're a child, but once you enter adulthood, you shouldn't be
blindly following everything your parents tell you anymore, especially
when it comes to money. Remember, we're living in a time when information about almost anything is accessible in nanoseconds. If you want
to learn how to trade a stock, Google, Alexa, or ChatGPT will provide
you with a full tutorial before you've even had time to sit down at your
desk. Several decades ago, this wasn't the case. If your parents wanted
to learn about money, their only options were to go to a "free" seminar
where they'd inevitably be pitched some sort of financial product, talk
to a financial advisor at the bank who would provide heavily biased advice and also push some sort of financial product, or check out the few
personal finance books available by the same five white guys in suits
who promised to make you a millionaire if you just stopped thinking
like a poor person. In other words, it's astounding how well most of

our parents did despite the lack of unbiased and actionable information available back then.

Another more complex explanation for staying on the same course as your parents is that you're simply trying to finish what they started. Think of it like a relay race. They hand you the baton and you feel like if you just put your head down and work a bit harder, you'll finally reach the finish line. Another way to think about it is that by repeating the same patterns, you're trying to recreate the same scenarios your parents experienced so you can change the outcome. You're essentially trying to complete your parents' unfinished business.

Remember Jennifer who moved around a lot as a kid? It's no coincidence that she started to do the same thing as an adult. Her mom was always on the lookout for a better life in a new city. It never worked out for her, but maybe, Jennifer thought, it would be different if she gave it a try. Maybe she would finally move somewhere and strike gold.

This is the type of behaviour displayed by many trauma victims. Why do many children who lived with an alcoholic father go on to marry an alcoholic husband, for instance? They are simply repeating a pattern with the intention of breaking it. In their minds, if they can just put themselves in similar circumstances and try again, maybe this time the man in their life will show them love and attention and they'll finally be able to heal. But as we all know, doing the same thing and expecting a different result is what Albert Einstein famously defined as insanity. Nevertheless, many of us do this exact thing with our money and are still confused as to why we aren't in a different financial position than our parents. If you want a different outcome, you've got to throw out their blueprint and make a new one.

One last explanation could be that you simply don't believe you are worthy of a different outcome. If your self-esteem has been eroded throughout your childhood or you surround yourself with people who are negative and want to keep you down on their level, you'll eventually believe that the financial situation you find yourself in is what you deserve, so why bother trying to improve it?[8]

THE REBEL

It's a very different story when you choose to go in the opposite direction as your parents after leaving the nest. And it makes a lot of sense that you would do this, especially if you grew up seeing the mistakes they made and the hardships they went through. But why do people run to the other end of the spectrum instead of settling in the middle? Why do people who grew up in extremely frugal households become spendthrifts when they're older? Why do people who grew up with extreme wealth adopt a more frugal, minimalist lifestyle instead? Again, because they were conditioned to believe that *money = extreme*, the only answer to "How do I *not* become like my parents?" is to do the exact opposite of them.

Unlike the follower who may be trying to complete their parents' unfinished business, the rebel is trying to make up for lost time. They look back on their childhood and think, *Look at all the things I never got. Now I can finally get them on my own.* But instead of using moderation, they go from a place of too many restrictions to none at all. Instead of getting one thing they never got on their childhood Christmas wish list, they try to get their hands on everything they were ever denied and then some. Picture them as the White Rabbit from *Alice in Wonderland*, who is always stressing about how he is late. Rebels feel like they are years late to the life they deserve, so they have a lot of catching up to do, never mind the financial consequences.

This can also manifest in people who want nothing to do with money. Maybe they feel like their family had too much, and in adulthood, their guilt drives them to make up for lost time by giving everything away to balance things out. I also see something similar in people who grew up with parents who overspent and undersaved, resulting in them not having enough money for retirement and forcing them to work well into their senior years. Not wanting the same fate, these kids rebel as adults and join a movement like FIRE (Financial Independence, Retire Early), which encourages people to live incredibly frugally while saving an extreme percentage of their income (e.g., 70%), with the ultimate goal of having enough money saved up so they can retire in their 30s or 40s and never have to work again. Although I know many people who've achieved FIRE and are happier for it, almost all of them have admitted that, in retrospect, they wish they had taken their time instead of living in such an extreme way to get to their goal.

Finally, this rebellion could also be chalked up to psychologist Jack W. Brehm's reactance theory,[9] in which a person rebels if they believe their freedom is being threatened, and they'll do whatever they can, even if it means putting themselves in harm's way, to defy that threat. For example, we saw a lot of this when people refused to wear masks or stay at home at the height of the pandemic because they believed their freedom was being stripped from them. So, if you grew up in a household in which there were too many restrictions around money and you felt like your freedom was being threatened, guess what you're going to do? Rebel.

Deconstructing Your Money Story

Now that you have a better understanding of both extremes, the question is how do you find that sweet, sweet midpoint to achieve the perfect equilibrium? You need to deconstruct the financial blueprint you've been using up until now, which was based on the lessons you learned and behaviours you observed while growing up. Only when you truly understand that blueprint you've been using up until this point can you keep the good stuff, toss out the bad, and craft a fresh, new blueprint to lead you to the financial life you've always wanted but didn't know how to achieve.

We'll go through how to write that brand-new money story in the final chapter of this book, but until then, grab that piece of paper or journal and answer the following questions. Take your time, be as detailed as possible, and don't hold back (remember, only you are going to read it).

EXERCISE

1. What was the socioeconomic status of your family when you were growing up (low, middle, high income)?

2. Did your parents speak openly about money, or did they only do so behind closed doors?

3. As a kid, were you privy to any of your parents' financial struggles or conflicts?

4. How did your parents respond when you asked them questions about money (e.g., "How much is our house worth?" or "How much do you earn?")?

5. What were your parents' views on poverty and wealth?

6. When you were growing up, how was money viewed, valued, and spoken about in your family?

7. What were some of the good and bad lessons you learned about money when you were growing up (e.g., never depend on a man for money; if you struggle with money, you've likely done something to deserve it; more money will solve all of your problems)?

8. What were your first financial experiences like, such as getting an allowance, getting your first bank account, getting your first job, getting your first credit card, and making your first big purchase (e.g., your first car)? Were they positive or negative experiences?

9. What are some financial characterizations you've placed on yourself (e.g., I'm bad with money; I'll never be wealthy; I'll always struggle with money; I'm only as valuable as my net worth; no one will respect me if I don't earn a high income)?

10. What are some harmful money behaviours you've observed yourself doing regularly?

11. What are some of your deepest fears and insecurities with money, and where do you think they came from (e.g., parent's trauma or your own trauma)?

12. What does money mean to you (e.g., safety, power, influence, success, achievement, access)?

13. What made you pick up this book?

Takeaways

- The lessons we learn about money in childhood, even indirectly, can stay with us for the rest of our lives whether they are helpful or not.

- Often, some of the lessons we learn are in direct conflict with each other, which is why some of our values and beliefs about money are confused. We need to untangle those lessons and rewrite them.

- Depending on the lessons we learned and behaviours we adopted while growing up, our toxic money behaviours can fall into three camps: avoiding money, worshipping money, or using money to fulfill a specific need in relationships. These may explain why you keep repeating habits that are financially unhealthy.

- Once you enter adulthood, you're likely to either follow or rebel in regards to the lessons you learned and behaviours you observed.

- The only way to craft a brand-new money story is to deconstruct your current one.

4.

It's Not You, It's Your Trauma

*Until you make the unconscious conscious, it
will direct your life and you will call it fate.*
—Carl Jung

In our society, we can be quick to blame an individual alone for the financial situation they find themselves in. Likewise, we can be quick to blame ourselves and believe that with so many people out there thriving, maybe there's something wrong with us if we're still struggling. And to be fair, it's easy to see where this line of thinking comes from.

"You don't want to be poor anymore? Then get a job and get to work."

"It's not that hard to stay out of debt. Just change your habits. It's not rocket science."

"If you want to change your financial life, then YOU need to change."

"Stop buying stuff you can't afford to impress people who don't matter to you."

"Want to become a millionaire? It requires hard work, discipline, and taking a good look in the mirror."

Do any of these statements sound familiar? They should, because they are all based on real things said by some very prominent and privileged money experts who've built successful brands off of blaming the individual for their financial shortcomings. If the loudest voices in the room are telling you that *you* are the sole problem, you're going to start believing them at a certain point, along with the millions of people who already do.

But what if we started asking ourselves a different question? What if instead of asking ourselves, "What's wrong with me?" we asked, "What happened to me?"[1] Because what these popular money gurus seem to consistently ignore when doling out their cookie-cutter (and judgmental!) financial advice are the roles that trauma and circumstance play in people's finances. If being good with money came down to only hard work, changing habits, and motivation, the wealth gap wouldn't be nearly as wide as it is today.

Just in case you're thinking, *But what about personal responsibility? Sometimes people are poor because they made bad choices,* I want to remind you that there's a big difference between an explanation and an excuse. I fully agree that we all need to take ownership of the financial decisions we make, but if those decisions keep driving us into a bigger debt hole each month and we have no idea why or how to stop it, we need to consider that there's something deeper going on. Only when we discover what that thing is can we truly start making change.

Get Grounded

In the previous chapters, we cracked the surface of uncovering your relationship with money, but now it's time to grab your shovel, because we're about to dig much deeper to explore the impact that trauma has had on your finances, whether you're aware of it or not. Some of what I discuss in this and the next chapter may stir up some feelings in you that you really don't want to stir up or aren't ready to. That's perfectly okay. That's also likely an indication that there is something going on underneath the surface that needs to be uncovered, identified, and worked through, which can be done with the help of a mental health professional (which we'll discuss in Chapter 8). You are the expert on you, so take this section at your own pace and seek support where you need it.

With all that said, I want to introduce you to some grounding techniques to help if anything heavy does come up for you. These simple exercises will remind you that you are in a safe space, so you can regulate your emotions. If you ever feel anxiety, panic, or experience a traumatic flashback throughout this chapter, you can use these exercises to calm down and come back to your safe reality.

First, there's the 5-4-3-2-1 technique that involves naming five things you see, four things you feel, three things you hear, two things you smell, and one thing you taste. Another technique I love using is called the calm place imagery exercise, in which you close your eyes and envision a space that evokes feelings of calmness and safety, such as the hiking trail near your house or a cottage in winter with a lit fireplace and pillows and blankets all around. Some other great and quick ways to get grounded include drinking a glass of water, chewing some ice or a piece of gum, savouring a mint, smelling a calming scent like tea or an herb, breathing in and out slowly, or crossing your arms over your chest and tapping each shoulder with the opposite hand's fingers back and forth.

You've Got Trauma? Same.

Before COVID, I never would have labelled myself as someone who suffered from trauma. That's because, to me, the term *trauma* was exclusive to victims of horrific events, such as sexual or physical violence, child abuse, natural disasters, or war. I hadn't experienced any of those things myself, though I was aware that some members down my family line had. Not only that, but over the years, it started to feel like the word *trauma* was everywhere. I remember thinking to myself, *There's no way everyone has trauma. What is going on with the world?* only to realize later on that it wasn't that everyone suddenly had trauma. Instead, people were finally speaking up about it instead of hiding it as so many past generations did.

When everything shut down in March 2020 and my work dried up, for the first time in years, I had all the time in the world to reflect, as so many of us did. Although my immediate thoughts turned to how to get more toilet paper and where to buy face masks like everyone else's, I also started to ruminate over feelings, attitudes, and hurt from my past that I kept buried. This is what got me to seek help from a therapist again after not seeing one since Twittergate 2017 and what helped propel me on my current healing journey.

What I started to learn in session after session with my therapist was that although I may not have experienced one big, horrific event, that didn't mean that I wasn't suffering from the effects of trauma. Not all trauma is created equally, but no matter how big or small the traumatic event you experienced, its impact on you can be significant. Moreover, the more I learned about trauma, the more my own feelings and behaviours with money started to make a lot more sense. I started to connect the dots and see that although improving my financial literacy had helped me develop a relatively good relationship with money over the years, there were still toxic parts of the relationship that no amount of financial education could fix. I needed an entirely different tool box for that.

As I was discovering this about myself, I was also able to view my financial counselling work through a new lens. When all my speaking engagements and brand partnerships got cancelled at the start of COVID, I quickly pivoted and started promoting my financial counselling services more than I'd ever done before. Previously, the work I did with clients was about 80% basic financial planning and 20% counselling. During COVID and beyond, it became a more balanced 50/50 split, because more clients were looking for someone they could trust to talk to about their worries, fears, and shame about money, not just budgeting and debt repayment strategies.

Listening to my clients share their feelings, then digging deeper into their upbringing and significant life events to try to make sense of those feelings, made it glaringly clear to me that all of us have experienced trauma on some level and that trauma can have a profound impact on our finances.

What Is Trauma?

Derived from the Greek word for "wound,"[2] trauma is described as the lasting emotional response from a distressing event or series of events. Experiencing a traumatic event can make you lose your sense of safety, sense of self, as well as your ability to regulate your emotions and navigate your relationships. A key characteristic of trauma is that long after the event has taken place, you may feel continued shame, helplessness, powerlessness, anxiety, and fear.[3]

Put differently, trauma is not an event that has occurred; it's the effect that an event had on your brain and body afterwards. Moreover, if left untreated, it can cause you to become stuck in the past and obstruct your growth. As psychiatrist Bessel van der Kolk explains in *The Body Keeps the Score*, often what happens long after experiencing a traumatic event is "the brain may keep sending signals to the body to escape a threat that no longer exists."[4] In other words, until you identify and treat your trauma, you'll continue to encounter smells, sounds, words, objects, people, or even thoughts that will remind you of the traumatic event and trigger your brain and body to react as if there is a threat to defend yourself against when in reality you are perfectly safe. You can remember the different components of trauma by reciting "the three E's—the event, the experience, and the effects."[5]

An important thing to note is that you don't personally have to experience the event to suffer from trauma. You can also have trauma if you witness a traumatic event (e.g., you see a violent mugging outside your office window), hear a first-hand account or story of a traumatic event experienced by someone else (e.g., you learn that your friend was injured in a car accident), which is known as secondary trauma,[6] or are repeatedly exposed to other people's trauma (e.g., you work as a health care worker, police officer, or mental health professional), which is known as vicarious trauma.[7]

I can't ride a bike or drive a car, which I never considered to be trauma-related until recently. Well, I *can*. One never forgets how to ride a bike, and I do have my driver's licence. So, perhaps a better way to say it is I *won't*. When I was young, I had one too many close calls with cars while riding my bike around my neighbourhood, which instilled this deep fear inside me every time I grabbed the handlebars. Although I continued to ride my bike throughout childhood and early adolescence, every time I rode, my palms would get sweaty, my heart would race, and I'd start imagining a car side-swiping me or a truck popping out of a back lane unexpectedly. Once I became too big for my bike, instead of getting a bigger one, I chose to never ride a bike again. Now the only bike I feel safe on is one that's indoors and stationary.

As for driving, my fear started the week after I got my driver's licence, when I was 19. I was driving up Burnaby Mountain to attend a class at Simon Fraser University and unexpectedly hit the car next to me when switching lanes. I remember it so clearly. I looked at my mirrors, shoulder-checked, and signalled before merging, since those steps were still fresh in my mind after passing my test, then BAM! To this day, I have no idea how it happened. But it did. Luckily, no one was hurt and there was minimal damage to both cars, but it startled me to my core and made me lose trust in my driving abilities. After that, I limited how often I drove to school, and once I graduated and moved out of my car-dependent suburb to live in the city, I stopped driving entirely. I've driven only a handful of times in the 20 years since. Without being conscious of it, I then built my life around never having to drive again. Every place I've lived has been close to transit and within walking distance of all my necessities, and the family car my husband and I share is a stick shift, which I never learned to drive (a convenient excuse), so my husband is in the driver's seat whenever we want to do a big grocery shop or get out of town. Thankfully, he loves to drive.

These events happened when I was a child or just finishing adolescence, yet they still have a profound impact on my day-to-day life. I still feel extreme fear and anxiety when I think about going for a bike ride or having to drive somewhere, because my trauma causes my brain to tell my body, "Hey, threat ahead! Activate your defences!" even though the actual threat is long gone.

Big-T and Little-t

Because trauma comes in all shapes and sizes, there are two major categories to know. The first is big-T trauma. These types of trauma occur when you've experienced or witnessed an event or recurring events that are big, distressing, and potentially life-threatening, and if left untreated, they could lead to post-traumatic stress disorder (PTSD). Examples of big-T traumas can include the following:

- war
- genocide
- natural disasters
- vehicular accidents
- physical abuse

- sexual abuse
- incest
- kidnapping
- mass shootings
- murder
- burglary
- death of a parent or child
- racism
- sexism and gender discrimination
- sexual orientation discrimination
- ableism

When we think of trauma, we usually think of big-T trauma, and we believe that anything outside the examples I shared is an overreaction to an event. Have you ever reacted to something that made you fearful or anxious only to hear someone say, "Stop being so dramatic!" or "You're so sensitive"? Just as I discussed in Chapter 2, there are no wrong answers when it comes to how you feel, and there's actually a helpful term for trauma outside of big-T trauma: little-t trauma. Little-t traumas are typically caused by recurring events, usually smaller in nature but still distressing, and generally non-life-threatening, though they may threaten your ego or identity.

A compounding problem with little-t traumas is that they can occur again and again, leaving little if any mental space for you to process them and heal. And if you don't process your trauma, no matter whether it's big or small, it gets frozen in time inside your senses, which helps explain why being triggered can feel so debilitating. As Toronto-based psychotherapist Suzanne Wiseman explained to me, "When we get triggered, we are responding at the age of the event. If we couldn't understand or process what happened then, how could we possibly process or understand what is presented to us as adults? So, if the event happened when you were five, when you're triggered, it's your five-year-old self reacting, which could explain why your reaction to something insignificant can come off as sensitive or dramatic." Examples of little-t traumas can include the following:

- bullying or harassment
- relationship breakups
- divorce
- infidelity
- unhealthy friendships
- job losses
- legal troubles
- financial struggles
- death of a pet

Although I've already included racism, sexism and gender discrimination, sexual orientation discrimination, and ableism as big-T traumas, they can also be categorized as little-t traumas, especially if they are caused by smaller and/or recurring events.

These are just examples, and depending on your situation and experience, the category a trauma falls into may vary. But the point is not to be able to say whether your trauma is big-T or little-t—it's to identify that you have it and figure out how it's affecting you, so that you can heal.

Not only that, it's important to recognize that trauma is something that happens *to you*. You can't help it. It's not a choice you make, it's not always avoidable, and the size of the event has nothing to do with your mental strength or weakness. A singular event can affect different people in different ways for a multitude of reasons, and even if you've never experienced a big traumatic event before, that doesn't mean you haven't been heavily impacted by a series of little traumatic events. Remember, a wound is still a wound no matter the size, and a thousand tiny cuts can be just as lethal as one big gash. When it comes to trauma, we're trying to deal with its impact.

Personal Trauma vs. Financial Trauma

Besides big-T and little-t trauma, we must also differentiate between personal trauma that *indirectly* affects your relationship with money and financial trauma that *directly* affects it.

Personal trauma is trauma that negatively affects areas of your personal life, including your finances, but isn't linked to a financial event. For example, if I felt safe driving, I wouldn't have avoided applying for jobs that required a commute, or turned down paid speaking opportunities that were too far for me to use transit or to hire an Uber, which would have been too expensive. Not only that, but since my husband and I are both self-employed and work from home, we likely could have saved thousands of dollars by choosing to buy a home in the country or suburbs. But because I'd need a car to freely get around there, that was a big reason why we chose to remain in the city with public transit and assume a higher mortgage and cost of living.

Another example could be someone who was neglected and verbally and emotionally abused as a child. Growing up, they may have been made to feel stupid, worthless, and incapable of becoming successful by their parents, their teacher, or students in class. This trauma likely would have eroded their self-esteem as an adult and could hold them back from pursuing higher education, negotiating higher pay throughout their career, learning how to take control of their finances, or taking risks with their investments to grow their wealth. Because of that early trauma, they might have internalized the idea that they didn't have the skills or didn't deserve to rise above their station in life.

Financial trauma, on the other hand, is connected to a specific financial event and directly impacts how you think, feel, and behave with money. Just like personal trauma, financial trauma can also be categorized as big-T trauma (e.g., experiencing a market crash and losing your life savings) or little-t trauma (e.g., living paycheque to paycheque for an extended period of time). You may have financial trauma if you've ever experienced any of these situations:

- growing up in poverty or financial insecurity
- being unable to pay your bills on time
- homelessness
- being in debt for a long period of time
- filing for bankruptcy
- losing money through a scam or identity theft

- lending money to a friend or family member and never being paid back
- being forced to sell your home or having your home foreclosed on
- losing money through a bad investment or market downturn
- living through an economic recession or market crash
- being fired or laid off from a job
- long bouts of unemployment or underemployment
- financial abuse in which someone you financially depend on controls your access to money or you are unable to leave an abusive relationship because you can't afford to

A lot of my financial hang-ups have to do with growing up with less, witnessing my dad go on strike at work for several months when I was a kid, which affected the family finances, being laid off from two jobs in university, which I depended on to pay for school, being unemployed for a year after graduating university, and experiencing the Great Recession in my early 20s. When these financial traumas are triggered, they can make me feel like I'm on the brink of financial ruin, I have no financial security, and my whole financial life could turn upside down in an instant.

ADHD or Trauma?

I knew I needed to include a section in this chapter about attention-deficit/hyperactivity disorder (ADHD), because over the years, not only has there been an influx of financial social media influencers ("finfluencers") publicly sharing their ADHD diagnoses, but they've also been vocal about how undiagnosed ADHD may be the reason why so many people struggle with repeated overspending, falling back into debt, and making rash investment decisions. Although this can be true for some people, it's important to point out the connection between ADHD and trauma.

As a reference, symptoms for ADHD can include inattention and difficulty keeping focus, hyperactivity and trouble keeping still, and impulsivity, like acting hastily without thinking of future consequences.[8] Since ADHD diagnoses have been on the steady rise for the past two decades,[9] it's no wonder so many people with these symptoms can have difficulty sticking to a budget or following through with their financial goals. Nevertheless, it does raise the question "Are more people afflicted with ADHD now compared to 20 years ago, or is there something else at play?" For example, are people with trauma actually being misdiagnosed with ADHD? A growing body of research suggests that may be the case.

Looking at this Venn diagram comparing the symptoms of ADHD and trauma, what do you see?

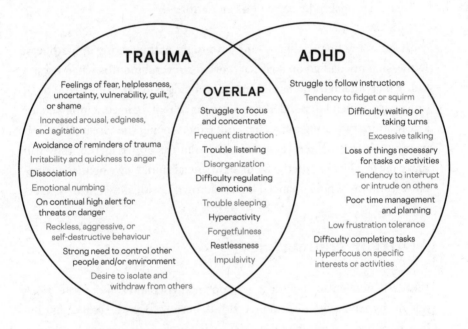

What you should notice is how much symptom overlap there is between trauma and ADHD, and thus how challenging it is to accurately diagnose one over the other from a clinician's perspective. Moreover, since there is no brain scan or genetic testing available for ADHD (there is no gene for ADHD as there is for muscular dystrophy, for example),[10] just a list of behaviours to observe, compounded by the pressure clinicians are under to make appointments brief (instead of thorough) and prescribe medication to inhibit symptoms (instead of referring out to a therapist), there may also be a bias to diagnose for ADHD instead of trauma.[11]

In a study conducted by Todd Elder, an economics professor at Michigan State University, he estimated that 20% of the 2.5 million children in the U.S. who use ADHD medication like Ritalin have, in fact, been misdiagnosed because of some of these pressures.[12] Besides trauma being sometimes confused for ADHD, some research also suggests that childhood trauma may even stimulate ADHD symptoms in both children and adults,[13] while other research has found that if you have ADHD, you're more prone to experience a traumatic event.[14]

I'm sharing these studies to highlight the close link between ADHD and trauma, which is often ignored, and to encourage you not to rule out trauma as either the real cause of your ADHD-type symptoms or a compounding factor to your ADHD. Regardless, ADHD and trauma affect a lot of people, and symptoms of both can have a negative impact on how people manage their money. This book is not a diagnostic tool, but I will try to help you improve your relationship with money, no matter what you're working with.

What Are Your Traumas?

EXERCISE

Right now I want you to pause and let everything you've learned sink in. When reading some of the examples of big-T, little-t, personal, and financial trauma, how did it make you feel? What examples could you identify with? Did any events you've experienced come to mind that may be considered traumatic that you haven't thought about in years?

If so, I'd encourage you to write down how you feel and any possible memories that have come to the surface. This will become helpful as we move on, in the next section, to explore how traumas present themselves in your body and behaviour and what role these traumas play in your personal money story, too.

Another tool you can use to identify trauma buried inside you is to take the ACE quiz.[15] The CDC-Kaiser Permanente Adverse Childhood Experiences (ACE) study is one of the biggest studies on childhood trauma's effects in adulthood. The study found that there is a direct link between childhood trauma and the development of chronic disease, incarceration, and employment and financial challenges later in life.[16] Nevertheless, whatever your experience is, there are things you can do to heal from your trauma. A high score does not mean it's too late or you're beyond help.

When Your Emotions Take Over

When you recognize the trauma in you, it's important to understand how that trauma interferes with your emotional regulation, which is your ability to manage your emotional state. If you don't have awareness and governance over your emotional state, you behave, albeit subconsciously, in ways to protect or soothe yourself that may actually cause you and your finances harm in the short or long term. Succumbing to emotional dysregulation could look like abusing alcohol or drugs, avoiding people and isolating yourself, presenting violent or angry behaviour, being hypervigilant, or taking unnecessary risks to your safety. It could also look like underspending, overspending, overworking, avoiding your finances, gambling, or hoarding. Let's look at a few examples to see what I mean.

JARRED

Jarred gets pulled into his boss's office and receives some disappointing news. His colleague, Hakeem, is being promoted. This infuriates Jarred, because he was promised a promotion months ago, he has several more years of work experience than Hakeem, and he even helped train Hakeem when he first started at the company. This event brings some past personal trauma to the surface, such as when Jarred was neglected as a child while his two younger half-brothers were given preferential treatment by his mother and stepfather.

Having this trauma triggered, Jarred may feel emotionally destabilized, and he may experience the urge to go into fight mode to protect himself and soothe his pain. This could take the form of arguing with his boss unprofessionally, giving passive-aggressive jabs to Hakeem, and splurging on new clothing after work to make himself feel confident and worthy. In this scenario, not only would he damage his relationships with his boss and colleague, which could negatively affect his career, but he would also spend money earmarked for emergencies on clothes he doesn't need, putting himself in a more vulnerable financial position. If Jarred's emotions were regulated, instead, he may have listened to his boss respectfully and remained cordial with his co-worker. But after work, he would have started a job search from a place of hope and optimism (instead of desperation and anger) for a new employer who would better respect his experience and skills, and he also would have stuck to his budget and savings goals.

AALIYAH

Aaliyah attends her friend Simone's birthday dinner, and it's decided beforehand that everyone at the dinner will split the bill equally plus pay for Simone's meal and drinks. When the server comes around, one of the guests decides to order a few bottles of expensive wine for the table without asking permission from any of the other guests. No one speaks up, but Aaliyah really wants to say, "I don't want expensive wine! I'm on a fixed budget because I'm still paying off my credit card!" Instead, she stays silent, and when the bill comes, she adds even more debt to her pile. This event triggers a response in her that is connected to years of financial abuse wherein she was taught that she didn't have a voice and couldn't safely communicate her wishes or needs.

Aaliyah's ex-boyfriend controlled all the finances and racked up thousands of dollars in credit card debt in her name, damaging her credit score and leaving her with a sizable debt burden to pay off when they broke up. Whenever she'd confront him about his spending, he'd get loud and angry, prompting her to go quiet to avoid further aggravating him and escalating the situation. Seeing the guest take charge and make a financial decision for the table without consulting anyone else brought her right back to her old relationship and made her respond with silence as she was conditioned to. With a better handle on her emotions, she'd have been more prepared to advocate for herself and say something like "The price tags on those bottles of wine are a bit high. How about we get some bottles that are more affordable for everyone?" or "That sounds great, but I'm actually not drinking tonight, so I'm going to opt out of that part of the group's bill."

In both of these scenarios, Jarred's and Aaliyah's personal and financial traumas were triggered, causing their emotions to take over to the extent that they couldn't calmly and clearly express their true feelings and wishes. As you can guess, we do not want to live in emotional dysregulation, because it can undo a lot of hard work we've done in our lives and with our finances. We want to live in a space of safety and connectedness, so we can make the best decisions for ourselves without having our emotions cloud our judgment. But in order to do this, we need to understand how the autonomic nervous system (ANS) works.

Polyvagal Theory & You

The first time I learned about Stephen Porges's polyvagal theory,[17] so many of my emotional responses to situations finally started to make sense. What this theory explains is how the ANS governs your three basic emotional states through biological pathways called the sympathetic and parasympathetic. The ANS is a network of nerves throughout your body that automatically and unconsciously controls your body's internal processes, like your heart rate, breathing, digestion, and body temperature. It also controls how you react, automatically and unconsciously, to certain situations based on human instinct as well as past trauma.

The sympathetic pathway leads to the emotional state of fight or flight, also known as mobilization. This system first appeared in prehistoric fish around 400 million years ago and was a necessary part of evolution for humans' survival, especially back when the roar of a predator or a rustle in a bush could mean imminent danger.[18] Although we no longer have to worry about regularly fighting or fleeing a wild animal that wants to eat us, the fight or flight response still comes in handy with modern-age threats.

If you've ever hit the brakes because a pedestrian has suddenly run into the street, or jumped out of the way when you pass a loudly barking dog, that's your sympathetic system mobilizing you to protect yourself. What's so interesting, and why most of us don't even realize we're experiencing a fight or flight response when we're in it, is that these responses precede our conscious mind because by the time the danger is fully registered, it's too late. This is what Porges describes as "neuroception," when the ANS scans our environment for signs of safety and danger before our conscious minds do, kind of like our own internal home security system. For example, the other day, I went into my basement's bathroom, turned on the light, jumped and screamed, and then moments later registered that it was because there was a small black spider in the sink (and I'm deathly afraid of spiders). I reacted before I even knew what I was reacting to because my ANS knew about my fear of spiders and activated a flight response so I could get away from the threat.

The parasympathetic pathway, in contrast, breaks off into two different systems: the dorsal vagal and the ventral vagal. The dorsal vagal also first appeared in prehistoric fish but well before the sympathetic was developed, around 500 million years ago. This is the original survival mode that involves freezing and disappearing. In her book *Anchored*, Deb Dana describes a turtle's response to being scared: it "immobilizes, disappears into its shell, and waits until it feels safe enough to peek out at the world again."[19] For a real-life example, pretend you're hiking a forest trail, and you suddenly see a bear half a mile ahead. Your nervous system will quickly concede that you can neither fight the bear nor outrun it. Instead, it will tell your body to freeze and wait for the bear to move on or see you and lose interest, so you can avoid being attacked.

Pete Walker later expanded on immobilization responses to include the fawn response in his book *Complex PTSD: From Surviving to Thriving.*[20] When it doesn't make sense to freeze, you may instead resort to appeasing or pleasing a threat to avoid conflict. For example, when an angry driver who believes you cut them off pulls up next to you and rolls down their window to give you a piece of their mind, you might respond by appeasing, apologizing, flattering, and killing with kindness to avoid further conflict or escalating the driver's road rage.

In either scenario, both freezing and fawning are states of immobilization and are activated when mobilization won't help your chances of survival.

Lastly, there's the ventral vagal, which is the emotional state of safety, connection, and well-being. The ventral vagal was the last system to develop around 200 million years ago and is activated when we feel safe and engaged with ourselves, others, and our environment.[21] In this state, you feel calm, secure, connected, joyful, open, and curious. This is where we want to live most of the time.

All three of these states work together and form what Dana dubbed the polyvagal ladder. We all start at the top of the ladder in the ventral vagal in a place of safety and connection, but when a threat arises, our ANS pushes us down the ladder into the sympathetic pathway. If that system won't protect us from harm, we'll be pushed even further down

VENTRAL VAGAL

State of safety, connection, and well-being

SYMPATHETIC

State of fight or flight (mobilization)

DORSAL VAGAL

State of freeze, fawn, or shutdown (immobilization)

the ladder into the dorsal vagal pathway. We are going up and down this ladder throughout each day, but in the end, the ventral vagal is what we always come home to once the threat is gone. But for people with personal or financial trauma, it can be a challenge to not get stuck on some of the ladder's lower rungs and thus live in an almost constant state of emotional dysregulation.

Stuck in Survival Mode

The response examples I gave make a lot of sense when you think of danger in the conventional sense, but thankfully, it's rare that we ever stumble upon a bear in real life. Instead, in a normal setting, these responses may be set off by a word or phrase, a tone of voice, a facial expression, body language, a sound, a smell, or an image.

Our responses may also manifest themselves differently in modern life. When you're in the fight response, it doesn't necessarily mean you're ready to rumble, nor does a freeze response mean you'll freeze like a deer in headlights. Instead, when you're pushed into the sympathetic pathway, you go into hyperarousal, where your fight response looks like anger, aggression, and confrontation, and your flight response looks like anxiety, panic, and avoidance. When you're pushed into the dorsal vagal pathway, you go into hypoarousal, where your freeze response looks like dissociation, numbness, and emotional shutdown, and your fawn response looks like codependency, people-pleasing, and a lack of personal boundaries.[22]

In terms of how these responses could affect your dealings with money, if you get triggered and are pushed into fight mode, a casual conversation about the monthly budget with your partner could turn into a heated argument about how you think they overspend every month. In flight mode, you may avoid looking at your credit card statement for fear of seeing how much interest you've accrued. Freezing could look like emotionally shutting down whenever your partner wants to talk about your retirement plans, preventing you from making any progress. And fawning could be lending money to your cousin to avoid conflict even though you know they will never pay you back.

Although these emotional states are important and play a vital role in your survival, they cause a problem when you react or make decisions from a place of fight, flight, freeze, or fawn. It's like that common saying: don't make permanent decisions based on temporary emotions. But this reaction can often happen if you have past trauma that thrusts your neuroception into overdrive. Because your ANS perceives that there is danger at every corner when there isn't, you're effectively stuck living in survival mode and forced to make decisions from an extreme and emotional headspace.

To mitigate this problem, you need to learn how to identify your triggers, recognize when your neuroception is making a false alarm, take the moment you need to regulate, and get yourself back up to a place of calmness and safety in your ventral vagal. If you can do this, you'll be more capable of staying composed and non-judgmental while talking to your partner about their spending. You could look at your credit card statement rationally and critically so you could strategize a realistic debt repayment plan. You could listen to your partner about their ideas for your future retirement and participate in a productive conversation about how to reach that goal together. You could tell your cousin you aren't able to lend them money, or if you can and wish to help them out, say it's a one-time gift that they don't need to repay, but set a clear boundary that you won't help them out financially again.

Going back to some of the feelings we discussed in Chapter 2, with what you just learned, you may now better understand why you feel shame, guilt, fear, anxiety, envy, and despair (among other feelings) when it comes to money. Your past trauma keeps pushing you into your sympathetic or dorsal vagal pathways, which then causes you to react defensively when confronted with aspects of your financial life. Or money itself could be a trigger from past financial trauma, making you hold on to the belief that money is a threat you need to protect yourself against.

Nevertheless, the best place to view money is from that place of security and connection in the ventral vagal, because, despite your past experiences, money *isn't* a threat. It's not here to hurt you, even if you feel like it has burned you in the past. Money is just a tool. It's neither good nor bad. It's neutral and should be viewed that way. If used correctly, it can actually support the security and connection that the ventral vagal provides, instead of causing you harm and disconnection the way you may have gotten used to.

It Starts at Birth

When we're talking about the factors that affect your emotional reactions and regulation, there's more at play than just trauma and your nervous system. Your attachment style plays a huge role in your relationship with money. You may not know this, or you may have heard the term on TikTok and didn't know what it fully meant, but everyone has a particular attachment style. It's formed around the emotional connection you had with your main caregiver (like your mother) as an infant and reinforced by other bonds you forged throughout childhood and early adulthood. The quality and style of these connections inform how you deal with intimacy and react in different types of relationships, such as familial relationships, friendships, romantic relationships, and even your relationship with money.

Attachment theory came from the minds of psychoanalyst John Bowlby and psychologist Mary Ainsworth in the 1960s. Ainsworth's most notable contribution to this theory was the now classic Strange Situation study, which was first conducted in 1962 with her team observing a sample of one-year-old Caucasian middle-class children from the Baltimore area. The study involved a small room with toys, a one-way glass window for observation, and a mother and her child as participants. In the experiment, at different intervals, the mother would be present with her child in the room, leave the child with a stranger (another woman) in the room, or leave the child alone with no adult present.[23]

This study observed how the children reacted when their mothers left and returned, as well as how they behaved alone. What the researchers discovered was that there were three main classifications of behaviour displayed by the children participants that would persist as they grew up and foreshadowed how they would act in relationships throughout adulthood. A fourth classification was later added by one of Ainsworth's Ph.D. students, Mary Main.[24]

Secure	If the child showed signs of distress like crying when the mother left, but regained composure and resumed happily playing with their toys when the mother returned and comforted them, they'd be classified as being secure.
Anxious	If the child showed signs of distress when the mother left, but upon the mother's return continued to show distress or rejected contact when the mother tried to soothe them, they'd be classified as being anxious.
Avoidant	If the child showed no signs of distress when the mother left, and upon the mother's return displayed little or no interest in the mother's presence, they'd be classified as being avoidant.
Disorganized	If the child showed a combination of anxious and avoidant behaviours, they'd be classified as disorganized (or anxious/avoidant).

Attachment Styles in Adulthood

It's one thing to behave like this when you're barely crawling, but some of these behaviours can cause a lot of pain, confusion, and destruction when they manifest in adulthood. Let's take a look at how attachment styles play out.

SECURE ATTACHMENT

To no one's surprise, the children who ended up developing into the most well-adjusted adults fell into the secure attachment style. This is because, when faced with being abandoned, they showed a natural distress for their mother's absence. However, when their mother re-appeared, they recognized that the threat was gone and they could feel safe again to continue playing with their toys.

In other words, these children were able to display healthy emotional regulation, starting in the ventral vagal, going down into the sympathetic when confronted with the threat of abandonment, then rising back into the ventral vagal when their mothers re-emerged and the threat disappeared. Children develop this secure attachment style when they experience a secure upbringing where they can generally rely on their needs being met. This means feeling safe, seen, heard, supported, and valued, as well as having their feelings validated and being comforted and soothed when their feelings get hurt. Adults with secure attachment are empathetic, self-assured, not afraid to ask for support, calm and rational in the face of conflict, and resilient when dealing with disappointment, hardship, or failure. It's estimated that 50% of the population has a secure attachment style.[25] Grabbing some familiar examples from TV, I've found that these characters do a great job of displaying secure attachment styles: Miranda's husband, Steve Brady, and Charlotte's husband, Harry Goldenblatt, from *Sex and the City*; Beth Pearson from *This Is Us*; and Jim Halpert and Darryl Philbin from *The Office*.

If your upbringing wasn't secure, but instead involved rejection, neglect, fear, or a lot of inconsistency, you likely would have developed one of the insecure attachment styles.

ANXIOUS ATTACHMENT

The children who continued to act out in distress when their mother returned were seen to have an anxious attachment style. Their behaviour showed that they weren't able to easily regulate their emotions or jump back into the ventral vagal after the threat of abandonment was gone compared to the securely attached children. Being abandoned is one of the worst fears of someone with an anxious attachment style, and intimacy is a very important need. They will go to great lengths to keep someone close to them, but even still can feel that abandonment is looming regardless of reassurance.

Anxiously attached adults are often described as clingy, needy, and anxious, as well as overly sensitive to someone's moods and actions, preoccupied with their relationships, and needing frequent reassurance of closeness. Anxious people also usually fall into self-blame when faced with conflict and use fight or fawn as their go-to defence responses, which they enact through protest behaviour. Protest behaviour is any action someone takes to try to regain closeness or garner attention to make them feel safe again. Unfortunately, in reality, most protest behaviour risks causing the opposite effect, depending on the other person's attachment style. This behaviour can look like making frequent phone calls or sending text messages until they get a response, playing mind games to keep the other person engaged, using blame or guilt to draw them back in, threatening to leave or end the relationship, trying to make the other person jealous, keeping score, sulking, expressing hostility, and manipulating.

People develop an anxious attachment style when they grow up with caregivers or experience a long history of relationships with people who are inconsistent and unpredictable with their presence, attention, and care. About 20% of the population has an anxious attachment style.[26] Rachel Berry from *Glee*, Ross Geller from *Friends*, Kelly Kapoor from *The Office*, and Leslie Knope from *Parks and Recreation* are all classic examples of characters with an anxious attachment style.

AVOIDANT ATTACHMENT

Avoidantly attached children not only showed little or no distress when they were abandoned by their mothers in the study, but also ignored or gave no attention to their mothers when they came back. On the face of it, you might assume that an avoidant child was simply independent and didn't react either way because they were confident their mother would return. But at the heart of this behaviour, that's not the case. What looks like being unbothered is actually a defence mechanism, while internally they are dismissing their feelings and suppressing their need for closeness. Because the threat of being abandoned is so overwhelming, they fall into either a flight response by using avoidance or a freeze response by using dissociation and emotional shutdown, as a way to protect themselves from hurt.

Contrary to anxiously attached people, avoidants' biggest fear is intimacy and vulnerability, though not because they don't want or need both of these things. Everyone, no matter their attachment style, desires intimacy and bonding with others. It's in our biology. But avoidants likely experienced a lot of rejection growing up and had emotionally unavailable caregivers, so it was instilled in them from an early age that the only person they could trust and rely on was themselves. That's why avoidants often engage in deactivating strategies to keep others at a distance as a means of self-preservation.

As explained by Amir Levine and Rachel S. F. Heller in *Attached*, "A deactivating strategy is any behavior or thought that is used to squelch intimacy. . . . If you're avoidant, these small everyday deactivating strategies are tools you unconsciously use to make sure the person that you love (or will love) won't get in the way of your autonomy."[27] In other words, deactivating strategies are behaviours to ensure that attachment to a person won't get in the way of a carefully crafted shield of independence.

Deactivating strategies can look like being noncommittal, blaming others when things don't go your way, pulling away at any sign of intimacy, forming relationships with no chance of a future, hiding things or keeping secrets, and avoiding contact with others. That's why avoidants can often be described as cold, emotionally unavailable, detached, and generally uncomfortable or negatively responsive to anything resembling intimacy or vulnerability. About 25% of the population is avoidant.[28] Jess Mariano from *Gilmore Girls*, Miranda Hobbes and Samantha Jones from *Sex and the City*, Nick Miller from *New Girl*, and Eleanor Shellstrop from *The Good Place* are all great examples of avoidants.

DISORGANIZED ATTACHMENT

Lastly, there are those people who have both anxious and avoidant qualities, a category I discovered through therapy that I fall into—which is a pretty unique spot to be in considering that only 5% of the population has a disorganized attachment style. If you're disorganized, you fear intimacy because, historically, it's involved rejection, disappointment, and hurt, but at the same time, intimacy is your greatest desire. This confusion of feelings is largely due to being raised by a caregiver who was inconsistent with their attention, care, and love, used fear tactics or humiliation in parenting, and may have even been abusive.

Because of this, someone with a disorganized attachment may have a hard time opening up and letting people in due to a lack of trust in others, can be hot and cold in terms of pulling people in and then pushing them away, and can have a deep-down low opinion of themselves and feel unworthy of love. It could also be why they constantly flip-flop from anxious to avoidant responses, because of their inner conflict between not trusting others and desperately wanting closeness at the same time. Liz Lemon from *30 Rock*, Serena van der Woodsen from *Gossip Girl*, and Chandler Bing from *Friends* are all characters with a disorganized attachment style.

What's Your Attachment Style?

EXERCISE

After reading through these descriptions and examples of different attachment styles, which one resonates the most with you? I found it super helpful when I was able to discover what my own attachment style is. You can work with a therapist to better understand what your attachment style is, or you can complete one of the many attachment style quizzes available for free online.

Labels Can Change

There are a few things I want to point out before moving on and discussing how these attachment styles relate to money. First and foremost, attachment styles should be viewed as more of a spectrum than set-in-stone personal characterizations. Knowing what you know now, what you'll likely start to witness in your own life is how you may act more secure in some relationships and more anxious, avoidant, or both in others. This is because we play off other people's attachment styles. For example, I'll start to feel more secure if I'm hanging out with someone who has a secure attachment. But if I'm with someone who is more avoidant, I'll start acting more anxious (and vice versa). That's one of the tricky things about the insecure types—the very behaviours someone uses to protect themselves, to gain closeness or distance, tend to elicit the opposite style in the other person, essentially making up the difference. Unfortunately for anxious and avoidant folks, this result is usually the exact opposite of their desired outcome. These behaviours can lead to self-fulfilling patterns, especially if they go on unchecked. It's also good to note that secure types aren't immune to having anxious or avoidant tendencies depending on whom they are with and the environment they're in.

The ultimate goal is to adopt more secure characteristics in your own life for all the same reasons that being in the ventral vagal state is better for you. Even if you had a difficult upbringing or experienced severe trauma that propelled you into an anxious, avoidant, or disorganized attachment style, labels can change. Through therapy and treatment, you can become more secure over time.

Moreover, like me, you may have discovered that you fall into one of the insecure attachment styles but can't relate to their origins. I fall into the disorganized attachment style, but growing up, I never experienced abuse or fear-inducing behaviour from my parents or any other caregiver. So, how did it happen? It could have developed from other close bonds in your life, like other familial relationships or childhood friendships, or it may have even developed from your own parents' attachment styles. When exploring these ideas with my parents, I discovered that one parent was anxiously attached and the other was avoidant. Since anxious + avoidant = disorganized, a logical explanation could be that I simply adopted both attachment styles from my parents. Nevertheless, if you're still scratching your head and aren't sure where your attachment style came from, don't worry. This is something you can unearth over time, and it's more important to address how it plays out in your life.

Money in Your Relationships

As you read about the attachment styles, you may have started to recognize patterns you've repeated in your past relationships that you
weren't fully aware of before. If you add money into the mix, you
may also notice how money can trigger fight/fawn (anxious) or flight/
freeze (avoidant) responses that can lead to some unfortunate financial consequences.

According to a 2020 study conducted by researchers at the University of Arizona, they discovered after examining 635 young couples
that the more securely attached you are, the more financially responsible and satisfied you'll be.[29] Conversely, if you fall into one of the insecure attachments, you'll have a higher chance of behaving irresponsibly
with your money and will consequently have an overall lower level of
satisfaction with your financial life. Why is this? Well, when you're
secure and are better equipped to regulate your emotions, it's much
easier to make calm and rational financial decisions in times of crisis,
and be more resilient in the face of financial hardship, like job loss or
investment failure. It's also easier to be more open to asking for help,
communicating with your partner, and improving your financial literacy without fear of judgment or embarrassment for asking a "stupid"
question. But only 50% of the population is secure, remember. What
about the other 50%? When you're insecure, it's a very different story.
As the data shows, you're more likely to act against your best financial
interests by succumbing to your attachment style's go-to behaviours.

MICAELA

Micaela and her boyfriend, Amir, have been together for just over a year
and have decided to move in together. Amir really wants Micaela to
move into his two-bedroom condo, since it's located right downtown,
but he presumes they'll split the rent 50-50, and Micaela can't afford
the higher rent. She currently lives in a bachelor basement suite on the
edge of town. Micaela has always known how much her boyfriend earns

($180,000 a year) because he's very open about it, but throughout their relationship, she's never shared what she earns ($76,000 a year) for fear that he will judge her, or worse, think twice about being with her because of her lower income.

That's why she's always tried to keep up with his spending on vacations, nights out, and shopping sprees, to maintain this illusion of financial equality. However, this has started to get her into some serious credit card debt. Amir really wants to stay in his apartment because it's close to his work, but Micaela is financially overextended as it is. Because of her anxious attachment, she's likely to default to her fawn response and agree to move into her boyfriend's condo to make him happy and avoid conflict, even though it will cause her to get into an even bigger debt hole.

This is just one example of letting your anxious attachment be the driving force in your financial decision-making, but other behaviours could arise, including these:

- holding back important financial information, such as income, debt-level, or net worth, to avoid your partner perceiving you as being inadequate and unlovable
- obsessively hoarding cash for fear of being abandoned and needing to start over
- constantly offering to pay for things or buying gifts to prove your value in the relationship
- deferring to your partner to make all financial decisions for you
- never expressing your true desires about money to your partner to appease them and avoid conflict
- depending on your partner for all your financial needs to fulfill a deep desire to be taken care of

Although these behaviours on their own can cause a big negative impact on your financial well-being, when your anxious insecurities get activated, you may also resort to some money-related protest behaviour in order to regain closeness with your partner, such as:

- making a large purchase on your shared credit card to get your partner's attention
- keeping score of what assets you brought into the relationship or what financial sacrifices you've made (e.g., "If it wasn't for me, you wouldn't be able to afford your fancy new car!")
- threatening to leave your partner and explaining that it's going to be a very expensive divorce
- booking an expensive weekend getaway with your friends to punish your partner
- selling some of your partner's prized possessions to elicit a reaction

If Micaela were more securely attached, she'd have an honest conversation with her boyfriend about her financial situation so they could find a solution together, such as sharing the rent proportional to their incomes or finding a cheaper place to live.

ELI

Eli has just gotten married to his husband, Marcus, after four years together, but now Marcus wants to combine their finances to feel like they are a family unit. Eli has always avoided conversations about money or shut them down by turning them into fights, and any time Marcus suggests getting a joint bank account or shared credit card, he walks away. Eli also has a number of savings and investment accounts that he's never told Marcus about, because in his mind, "It's my money, so it's my business," but they also serve as his secret safety net in case the relationship turns sour. His excuse for all of this is that he likes his independence and it's just simpler keeping their finances separate. However, his real issue is that pooling their money and talking about future financial plans together is way too much intimacy for him to handle.

Even though he agreed to get married and is very happy in his relationship, he can't help but continue to use money as a way to maintain some distance and protect himself in case he has to leave the relationship or his husband leaves him. Although, in my opinion, there is no one right way to manage money as a couple, because Eli is avoiding important money conversations with his spouse, he is clearly using money as a defence mechanism. Not only will his unwillingness to talk about money and his willingness to keep secrets from Marcus hurt his relationship in the long run; there are also a lot of monetary benefits to working as a team that he'll miss out on. But more than that, because of Eli's behaviour, he may actually invoke a self-fulfilling prophecy. When Marcus discovers Eli's financial infidelity, he may choose to end the relationship, leading Eli to believe that he was right to be so secretive and distant all along.

When you're avoidantly attached like Eli and feel as if things are getting too intimate and you need to break away, you might engage in one of the following examples of deactivating strategies:

- refusing to get financially naked by revealing your income, assets, and debts, because it's "your money, not theirs"
- keeping finances separate and refusing to have a discussion about a more cohesive financial management style
- focusing on your own financial goals alone and shutting your partner out of any future financial plans
- hiding purchases or making purchases that impact you both without consulting your partner
- having secret bank accounts or credit cards that you don't tell your partner about
- avoiding money conversations by either walking away, disconnecting and ignoring your partner, or escalating the situation into a fight and using shame and blame to derail it
- taking your money away as a threat to undermine the stability of the relationship

If Eli were more securely attached, he'd be able to express some of his fears surrounding joining finances and eventually find a compromise with his husband so they could work as a team while also preserving some financial autonomy.

Although the examples I've just shared are based on romantic relationships, the same goes for familial relationships and friendships, too, wherever there is financial dependence or integration. Not only that, but these behaviours can come up even in your direct relationship with money, which is where we'll finish this chapter.

Your Attachment to Money

While conducting research for this book, I took an online course called the *Trauma of Money*, which teaches individuals about their relationship with money and also helps train coaches, therapists, and educators to be more trauma-informed with money. One exercise the course had students do was write a letter to money as if it were a person we had a one-on-one relationship with.* My initial thought was *This is corny. Money isn't a person, it doesn't have feelings, and it can't talk back.* But what I soon discovered was that money can often have such a big presence in our lives, its pull on us can be just as powerful as a real-life relationship.

After giving students 10 minutes to complete their letters, the floor opened up to allow for sharing. A number of students read their letters aloud and let their raw emotions pour out. One student shared how she felt like money was in and out of her life so unpredictably that she had a hard time trusting that money would be there when she really needed it, as if she was on a constant emotional roller coaster with money and couldn't get off. Another student said he felt abandoned by money and felt like it was never something he could rely on long-term. As more and more students shared, all I could think of was how they were describing money in a similar way to how an insecurely attached person would describe their inconsistent and neglectful caregiver when growing up.

Of course, one reason for this could be that they were simply pro-

---

* The course references that inspiration for this exercise was taken from Jen Sincero's book *You Are a Badass at Making Money.*

jecting their feelings about real-life relationships onto money. But I'd like to think that money deserves its own seat at the table. Besides the people in your life, it's something that you think about, engage with, and depend on for your comfort, security, and survival every single day. Day in and day out, no matter what's going on in your life, it's there, even if it's just hanging out in the background.

If you grew up in a financially secure household in which money was always there for you, you likely have a secure relationship with money in adulthood as well. You feel confident with your financial abilities, unafraid to ask questions about money or ask for support when you're in financial need, calm and rational in the face of financial conflict, resilient when disappointed by a financial outcome, and able to overcome financial hardship and failure. But if you grew up in a financially insecure household, you may also have an insecure relationship with money.

If you have an anxious attachment style, you may react to certain financial situations with the same protest behaviours that show up elsewhere, such as communicating with your financial planner too often or checking your bank accounts multiple times a day, overspending or buying something flashy to get attention from others, refusing to move financial institutions for fear of being disloyal, blaming yourself and feeling guilty for minor financial mistakes or negative financial outcomes, keeping score and comparing your financial life to others' financial lives, and having no boundaries with your money, such as spending money outside of your values or giving away money to appease others.

If you have an avoidant attachment style, you may engage in deactivating strategies to distance yourself from money, such as hoarding cash at home or investing in cryptocurrency since it's unregulated, blaming others for your financial problems, being secretive about your financial life with loved ones, avoiding looking at your bank statements or bills, and having a general mistrust in the stock market and the financial industry at large.

If you have a disorganized attachment style, your financial situation may be just that—incredibly disorganized.

Takeaways

- Instead of asking, "What's wrong with me?" start asking, "What happened to me?"

- All of us have experienced trauma on some level, which has had a big impact on our relationships with money.

- Big or little, trauma is trauma, and it's not your fault it happened to you.

- Unhealed personal or financial trauma can cause you to be more emotionally dysregulated, which could lead to emotionally charged and regrettable financial decision-making.

- We can all be classified into one of four attachment styles based on our upbringing (secure, anxious, avoidant, or disorganized), and these styles can inform how we approach money in our personal relationships as well as money itself.

- Our attachment styles can vary depending on how others' attachment styles influence us, which can affect our money. But ultimately, to be more secure with our money, we need to invite more securely attached influences into our lives.

5.

Blame Your Ancestors

Our ancestors speak to us through our genes,
but we can choose to listen and heal.
—Dan Siegel

If you read the previous chapter and thought to yourself, *Yeah, I can't relate to any of this*, I bet you're thinking that you're just one of the lucky ones who haven't been touched by trauma. You might have even done a full inventory of your childhood and life up until now and concluded that you had a fairly secure upbringing and can't recall any painful events that have negatively impacted you or your relationship with money. I'm happy for you, but not so fast.

Remember when I said that all of us have experienced trauma on some level? The truth is, your trauma doesn't necessarily come from you. Even if you've never personally experienced or been exposed to a traumatic event, that doesn't mean you haven't been carrying around trauma for most of your life. You may be carrying someone else's trauma—trauma from someone in your bloodline whom you may have never even met or known much about before. This is what's known as intergenerational trauma.

Intergenerational trauma is a phenomenon in which you adopt the same emotional and behavioural responses to a traumatic event that was experienced by one of your ancestors.[1] This could look like your fear of frozen lakes stemming from your grandma's traumatic fall through the ice while skating as a child à la Amy from *Little Women*. Or it could look like your wariness to invest and compulsion to live extremely frugally because your grandparents barely survived the Great Depression. It could also look like your uneasiness to increase your income and elevate your economic status coming from generations of your ancestors being enslaved in Canada or the United States.[2]

As its name suggests, this type of trauma can be passed down from generation to generation until the cycle is broken and the trauma is finally metabolized. Without such a disruption, this trauma can continue down your family line and become even harder to link to its original source, since family history can be lost and forgotten over time. This is often why we see repeated fates when examining our family trees. If a trauma keeps getting passed down to new generations without any intervention, how realistic is it to expect a different outcome? There could be something powerful yet invisible holding you back. To move forward in a new direction, it helps to discover where the trauma came from and whom it belonged to in the first place.

How You Can Inherit Trauma

Before discussing the impact of intergenerational trauma on your financial life, if you're thinking this all sounds a bit mystical or even made up, I get it. It's completely natural to feel skeptical about a very new field of study. But as psychiatrist and professor Rachel Yehuda explained, "Where we are with epigenetics today feels like how it was when we first started doing research into PTSD."[3]

PTSD is now a well-known diagnosis for severe trauma symptoms, but that wasn't always the case. PTSD was excluded from the first two editions of the *Diagnostic and Statistical Manual of Mental Disorders* (DSM) released in 1952 and 1968 by the American Psychiatric Association, despite mounting evidence, especially from returning soldiers from the First and Second World Wars and the Vietnam War. The DSM is *the* handbook used by mental health professionals in North America and around the world to diagnose patients. If a diagnosis isn't in there, it's as if the disorder doesn't exist. Because PTSD wasn't included until the manual's third edition in 1980,[4] for years, patients with PTSD were either misdiagnosed or denied coverage by their insurance provider, since most mental health professionals must abide by the DSM's codes to bill for treatment.[5]

Similar to the skeptics who once doubted PTSD, there are plenty of cynics of epigenetics, the study of how your environment and behaviours can affect your genes' expression without permanently changing or mutating your DNA.[6] Although it's true that more research is needed with larger sample sizes, what has been uncovered so far is still pretty incredible, and I don't doubt that epigenetics will become a bigger part of future discussions on trauma.

The prefix *epi* comes from the Greek word for "on top of," and *genno* means "give birth." Thereby, epigenetics is the science of how you can *inherit* modifications that are *on top of* your DNA that can control whether certain genes inside you are turned on or off. The good news is that because these modifications don't actually alter your DNA sequence, they are also reversible if identified and treated. If not, they can continue to be passed down to future generations on some level.[7]

One notable example of this happening was after the Dutch Hunger Winter, which took place in the Netherlands from 1944 to 1945, during the Second World War. In 1940, German forces occupied the Netherlands and established a new government controlled by the Reich. When Allied forces landed in Normandy in 1944 to liberate the Netherlands and surrounding countries from German occupation, Dutch railway workers across the country went on strike to aid the Allies by blocking German reinforcements from coming through. In retaliation and to squelch resistance from Dutch citizens, German forces halted food shipping via rail throughout the country for six weeks. Compounded by freezing temperatures that made food transportation through the canal system almost impossible, this spurred an extreme food shortage that caused mass starvation and killed 20,000 people.[8]

And it didn't just affect those who experienced the famine first-hand. It also affected babies in utero at the time. Sixty years later, researchers discovered that mothers who were pregnant during the famine bore children who were 30% more likely to become overweight.[9] Because these mothers were starving for a period of time while pregnant, a gene in their unborn children involved with metabolism was turned off so they could survive with fewer calories.[10] But once they were born and the famine subsided, this gene stayed off, causing them to have a slower metabolism and thus burn calories at a slower rate than children born before the famine. Not only did this increase their chances of obesity in adulthood, but it also made them more susceptible to heart disease, diabetes, and a higher mortality rate.[11]

If you can inherit a predisposition for obesity because of the environment your pregnant mother was in, could you also inherit trauma from your parents in the form of fear, anxiety, and shame? Brian Dias of Emory University and Kerry Ressler of McLean Hospital, Harvard Medical School, aimed to find this out in their 2013 experiment. To see whether future generations of mice could inherit the fear of a particular smell, they conditioned a group of male mice to fear the smell of acetophenone (a scent similar to cherry blossoms), giving them a shock every time the scent was released. Over time, the mice came to associate the smell with pain and would consequently show signs of fear whenever the scent was present.

The researchers then tested out their theory by releasing the scent with no shock to the next generation of mice and the next generation after that, and even substituted their biological parents with foster parents in some groups to control for any behaviours they'd learn from their caregivers. What researchers discovered was that the same fear was passed down to the second and third generations, no matter if they were raised by their biological parents or by foster parents. However, the fear became somewhat diluted in further generations, manifesting as simply a heightened sensitivity to the smell.[12] Dias also tested what would happen if he desensitized the male mice to the scent so they would no longer associate it with the pain of being shocked. Once these mice were desensitized, their sperm shed their characteristic fearful epigenetic signature, and when they had new offspring, the young mice no longer showed a fear or heightened sensitivity to the smell either. In effect, although trauma can be passed down, it can also be unlearned and stopped, too.[13]

Humans are not mice, but there are many other studies that provide evidence for how trauma can be passed down. One such study was conducted in 2016 by Rachel Yehuda (whom I quoted earlier) that looked at the epigenetic effects of the Holocaust on survivors and their offspring. From a young age, she had been curious about this connection as she grew up with many families who had survived the concentration camps.[14] What she found was that Holocaust survivors with PTSD were more likely to produce offspring who were more susceptible to increased stress levels, anxiety, depression, and PTSD.[15]

This is all to say that although the science is new, it is there and we will be seeing more of it in the coming decades. But even if your skepticism hasn't shifted, I'd still encourage you to keep an open mind and continue to explore this with me. You never know what you may discover about your family's past and its effect on how you view money, just as I was surprised to learn about mine.

A History of Poverty

If you have a family history of poverty, those traumas can run deep. Even if you grew up in a middle-income household and haven't had any first-hand experience with this type of scarcity, that doesn't mean it doesn't live inside you, inherited from your relatives. It may also explain some of your feelings toward and behaviours with money that you've never been able to quantify before. Let me walk you through my family history as an example.

ON MY MOTHER'S SIDE

Back in 2015, I interviewed my maternal grandpa, Jacques Hardy, for a special episode of my podcast. My grandma, Columbe Hardy (née Brouillard), had passed away not too long before then, and it was a big regret of mine that I had never interviewed her about her life, to gather that information and have a recording of her voice. I didn't want to miss my chance with my grandpa. I ended up learning a lot about where my shame and anxiety with money came from.

Jacques was born in a rural area of Saint-Sylvère, Quebec, in 1930. He was one of nine children and, like so many families back then, grew up in extreme poverty. He didn't get above a ninth-grade education and, from adolescence, worked various jobs for little pay with frequent bouts of unemployment in between, until he finally found a steady paycheque, room and board, and an education through the Canadian Armed Forces when he was 19. As he told me, when doing his medical exam before going to base camp for training, he weighed only 108 pounds—markedly underweight for a man of his age and a sign of what kind of scarcity he had experienced most of his life.

Going back even further, his father (my great-grandfather), Julien Hardy, also had a tough childhood with much financial instability. He was orphaned at the age of five and raised by his uncle Cyril until he was 11, when he started working odd jobs to earn a living for himself. When he got married in his early 20s, he started his own butcher business with only $25 in his pocket and a horse and a buggy to his name. He would continue to butcher and sell meat door-to-door for the next 14 years. Unfortunately, Julien's career ended tragically when he sold a large order of meat to a new customer who ended up skipping town and never paying his bill. This forced Julien to declare bankruptcy to appease his creditors and resulted in him struggling to make ends meet until his premature death in his 50s.

Consequently, after his death, the majority of his nine children struggled to stay afloat, but eventually, they found their way out of poverty and into some version of a low-to-middle-income life—except for his child, and my great-uncle, Roger. Struggling with an alcohol and gambling addiction, he ended up losing the family home in a bet gone wrong, causing the eviction of his mother and siblings from the only home they knew together. Due to his addiction, Roger never found his financial footing, though he did end up married with children. My mom vividly remembers visiting this uncle when she was young. She said, "I'd never seen poverty like it before. You could smell it. You could feel it. There was a reason we never stayed long when we visited his home, whereas with other relatives, we'd have lengthy visits and even stay the night. I remember leaving there and thinking I would never let that happen to me."

Curious if my grandma Columbe had a similar upbringing, I got my cousin Virginie Paré to interview her grandma Marie Brouillard (my grandma's older sister and my great-aunt) for me, since my French-speaking skills are not up to par. What I found out was that my grandma was born on a small farm in 1930 in Saint-David, Quebec, just 83 kilometres from where my grandpa grew up. She was number 10 of 11 children and, similar to my grandpa, grew up with next to nothing. Not only that, she experienced two traumatic events that had a big impact on her childhood and the family's finances: their barn burned down and her father died early.

When my grandma was only three years old, a big storm descended upon the family farm, causing a lightning bolt to strike their barn, burning it to the ground along with the winter's supply of hay for their cattle. To keep the cows alive, my grandma's parents, Joseph Brouillard and Marie-Rose Verrier, were forced to borrow money from family and friends to buy more hay. Unfortunately, they weren't able to pay off their debts before Joseph died a year later. As recounted by my great-aunt Marie, their father came home one day after working the fields complaining of a sinus infection. That night, he went to sleep but never woke up. He was only 40 years old. No barn, mounting debts, and the loss of the main financial provider pushed the family further into poverty.

The eldest son, Gaston, assumed the position of head of the household at only 16. As he and his brothers became old enough to work, they took jobs at the local lumber mill with the intention of supporting the women back home, who were maintaining the farm. Unfortunately, likely to suppress their own traumas, the men drank most of what they earned, leaving hardly anything left over for everyone to live on. The women in the family ultimately had to support themselves by selling the eggs and milk they produced on the farm, collecting strawberries from the fields and selling them in the village, and receiving charity from the local church.

It's no wonder my grandma was driven to become a teacher at only 16, so she could start earning her own money. And she did just that, teaching for the next 11 years, until she eventually married my grandpa and became a homemaker, raising four children of her own.

ON MY FATHER'S SIDE

Moving over to the paternal side of my family tree, I only ever knew my grandma, Audrey, because my grandfather was no longer in the picture after they got divorced. Nevertheless, I was able to interview my grandma and learn more about both of their childhoods. Audrey Wilson was born in Insch, Aberdeenshire, Scotland, in 1935 to an unmarried mother who gave her up and a father who never acknowledged her. At first, she was given to her maternal grandmother to be raised alongside her half-sister (another child born out of wedlock and given up). However, her grandmother soon realized she couldn't afford to raise both children, resulting in Audrey being put in an orphanage until age four.

At that time, she was given to her foster mother, Jessie McIntosh, a widow with two children. Audrey explained to me that the only reason she was taken in was that Jessie was penniless after her husband's death and unable to work because her daughter was chronically ill. Orphans came with government support. In other words, my grandma was treated more like a paycheque than a part of the family throughout her formative years. Despite having her basic needs met, she was constantly criticized by her foster mother for being an orphan born to an unwed mother, and made to feel like an outsider. This treatment is likely what led her to start working at a bakery at 16 to get out of the house and start earning money for herself, which led her to meet her future husband. She later trained to be a teacher, and her tuition was paid by the government—the one silver lining, she said, of being overseen by the state. As soon as she came of age, she got married, gave birth to my dad, and moved to British Columbia, where she continues to live today.

Although I have less information about my paternal grandfather, what I do know is he was one of nine children and also grew up in extreme poverty. All nine children lived in a small council house for low-income families, with an alcoholic father and a mother who died in her early 50s. To escape his chaotic household, he cut his education short and started working as a baker's apprentice at age 11, a profession he'd continue for the rest of his life. He owned his own bakery for the majority of his career.

MY ANCESTORS

Going further up my family tree and checking the records that family members have saved over the years, I could see that poverty was a recurring theme for centuries. On my maternal grandparents' side of the family, their ancestors can be traced back to the *filles du roi* (daughters of the king). These were groups of women in the thousands recruited and compensated by King Louis XIV of France to emigrate and ultimately help populate New France (now Quebec) between 1663 and 1673.[16]

Why would any woman in the 1600s choose to leave France for the harsh winters, sickness, and dangers of New France to marry a man she'd never met and start a family with him? Money. You don't leave your home country like that unless you feel like you have no other choice. As one archive describes it: "They were poor, abandoned, with no future in France." So, for these women, this was their ticket to a better life.[17] Although their prospects may have seemed better in Quebec compared to France, as family documents show, my ancestors nevertheless lived hand-to-mouth for generations.

On my paternal grandparents' side, it's a similar story. My ancestors were either poor Scottish farmers or in service working for wealthy landowners for hundreds of years. If you've ever watched *Downton Abbey*, my ancestors were the ones barely earning enough to afford the rent on their farmland or cleaning chamber pots and working 14-hour days for the Crawleys.

The Impact of Generational Poverty

Looking at my family history, I can make sense of some of my deepest fears and anxieties about money. I've always had an irrational fear that I would either go bankrupt or be evicted from my home, for instance, even though neither my parents nor my grandparents ever struggled with paying their bills on time. I have a vivid memory from when I was

13 and heard my parents deliberate about whether they should pay off the mortgage on our family home (a one-level, three-bedroom ranch-style house) or sell it to buy a bigger, more expensive home so my two sisters and I could finally have our own bedrooms. You'd think that as a teenager, I'd be jumping at the chance to no longer share bunk beds with my kid sister, but I remember pleading with my parents to just pay off the mortgage instead. I obviously didn't understand the concepts of leverage and real estate appreciation at the time, so to me, it was reckless for my parents to get into even more debt and risk possible foreclosure if something happened. It was only when doing research for this book that I was reminded about my maternal great-grandfather's bankruptcy and learned about my great-uncle losing the family home, and my fears finally started to make more sense.

Similarly, ever since I could remember, I've had this unrelenting drive to start earning money as young as possible and to never depend on a man financially. Again, I couldn't directly connect those feelings to my parents, but then I learned about both my grandmothers starting work at 16 and the financial difficulties my great-grandmothers experienced after their husbands died young, and it certainly made me think.

Finally, I've always had this feeling deep down that I'd never become wealthy. Sure, I'm working hard at becoming financially independent in the sense that I know I'll be mortgage-free one day and have plenty saved up for a comfortable retirement. But despite being immersed in the world of personal finance, being accredited, and knowing all the tools I need to build wealth, deep down I just never thought it was likely, or even possible, for me. Considering that no one in my family has ever had wealth as far back as records go, I think it makes a lot of sense why I'd feel this way. How could I feel confident that I could achieve something that none of my ancestors were able to make a reality?

I used to think that there was something wrong with me for not believing I could reach those financial heights—especially being part of the personal finance space, where so many content creators, financial experts, and entrepreneurs have proven that it is possible to go from broke to millionaire in your lifetime. It's not that I don't believe that anyone can build significant wealth by practising smart financial advice like investing in appreciating assets, increasing your income over time, and taking calculated risks; I just always thought that when it came to me, there was a ceiling. Wealth beyond a middle-class life just wasn't in the cards for me. I'd live comfortably, more comfortably than any of my ancestors by far, but not at that next tier of wealth.

A lot of this thinking comes from the self-limiting belief I've developed from my intergenerational trauma. And as odd as it sounds, it's a huge relief to learn this about myself. I feel like I finally have permission to let go of all these traumas, for my sake and for the sake of their original owners. They weren't mine to begin with, so I can stop carrying them around with me and avoid passing them down, too.

As Mark Wolynn shares in his book *It Didn't Start with You*, "Once we recognize that we have been carrying thoughts, emotions, feelings, behaviours, or symptoms that do not originate with us . . . [we can release ourselves] . . . from unconscious family ties and loyalties, and end the cycle of inherited trauma."[18] Once we recognize that not all of our feelings about money come from us but instead were inherited, we can finally start to do the work to break free.

A History of Wealth

If you also have a family history of poverty, you can likely relate to some of what I've shared, and I'll walk you through an exercise shortly so you can discover more about your lineage and its financial imprints on your own life. But what if you have a family history that doesn't look like this? What if there were times when your ancestors had money and times when they didn't? Or what if you come from a long line of wealthy landowners, business owners, politicians, or even royalty? Does that make you exempt from intergenerational trauma? Well, if you take a good look at some of the most famously wealthy families, such as the Trumps,

Rockefellers, Vanderbilts, Gettys, and Windsors, the answer becomes pretty obvious—NOPE!

REBECCA*

To get a better understanding of what I mean, let's take a look at Rebecca's story, a fourth-generation descendant of one of the wealthiest men in Virginia. Rebecca's great-grandfather, Walter Greenmount, founded a grocery store chain in Virginia in the early 1920s. Although Walter grew up in poverty on a humble family farm, he was always ambitious for more, and after serving in the First World War, he started his own business, which grew into a multi-million dollar enterprise by the 1950s. By then, Walter started preparing his first son, John, to take over. When he did, John was able to expand the business into one that earned nine figures in annual sales by 1980.

At that point, John decided to sell the company for over $200 million to a big food conglomerate. Walter retired and lived for another decade, while John started an investment firm (known as a family office) to manage the proceeds from the company's sale and preserve the family's wealth for future generations. Just like his dad, John started preparing his only son, David, to take over the family business when he finished college, which he continues to do today. Rebecca, David's daughter, however, chose a different path for herself and became a therapist.

Reading this story, you may think that there doesn't seem to be much trauma going on. Besides the poor upbringing Walter experienced as a young boy on a small farm, he was able to fulfill the American dream and go from pennies to his name to multi-millionaire in his lifetime, while also setting up his children and grandchildren to never have to worry about money ever again. What's the problem? The problem is that having money doesn't solve all of life's problems. It solves a lot of them, to be sure, but it also causes a slew of new ones.

---

* Rebecca's name and the details of her family history have been altered for her privacy.

The Impact of Generational Wealth

Two years after Rebecca's grandfather sold the family business and right after her father, David, graduated college, her parents conceived her unplanned. Because of this, they got married a month later, and at a very young age, Rebecca's mother, Sophie, was ushered into a very different lifestyle than what she was used to. Rebecca said, "All of a sudden, my mother is in her first year of marriage. There's this giant liquidity event happening with the business. It's a huge transition period for the family, with my dad suddenly being thrown into all of these positions of leadership and he doesn't even know if he wants it."

Remember what I shared about epigenetics? Sophie experienced a lot of feelings like anxiety, stress, and likely shame for getting pregnant unexpectedly and having family pressure to get married before she started showing. Those feelings could have been passed down to her unborn child to some extent. As a therapist who, ironically, specializes in trauma, Rebecca believes that her body was already keeping score in her mother's womb. She said, "My body told a story before I could even talk. I was always the heir of a fortune, and everyone knew it before me. Knowing what my mother was feeling, the incredible weight she was carrying, and the expectations that were already put on me as the heir . . . as I look back, I can see how all the pieces fit together."

David would eventually take the position of leader in his family's investment firm, and from the outside looking in, it would seem as if he was happily carrying the torch for his family's legacy. But that's why it's important to remember that you never really know what's going on in someone else's life.

Rebecca noted that because her father didn't get a choice about assuming the family business or taking a different path, he never got to properly self-actualize: "He never did the work most people get to do, which is discover who you are outside of your family. He's 59 years old and still doesn't know who he is." Not only that, once Rebecca was born, her mother began to feel the full force of upholding the family name. She was told how to raise her children, how to dress, how to support the family from the sidelines, and ultimately, how her life was now all about the success of the family. With her identity effectively taken from her, and her husband never figuring out what his identity was in the first place, it was a recipe for disaster from the start. A few years into their marriage, David had an affair, and because Sophie was expected to put duty before anything else, she buried it deep down and never fully recovered from the betrayal. Eventually, she resorted to taking Prozac and Xanax to soothe her pain, which led to a serious pill and alcohol addiction.

When Rebecca was 13, her parents divorced and lines were drawn in the sand. Because there was a pre-nup in place, her mother got a modest house and continued to have her basic bills covered after the divorce, but nothing more. After the split, Rebecca felt trapped between two worlds—her father's excessive wealth and her mother living on a low income for the rest of her life. Rebecca now manages her mother's finances and provides her with an additional sum of money every month from her own personal savings for her to live on.

Rebecca also remarked that although money has been such a big part of her family, no one ever talks about it. Because of how their family office is set up with all the family's assets being pooled together, there's a lot of tension and distrust among family members, as well as fear that someone is going to pull their money out and affect everyone's bottom line. But more significantly, the older members of the family never discuss money with the children, including basics, like how to budget, use credit responsibly, and pay bills, because there is a concern that discussions about money may disincentivize them from working hard and achieving success on their own. But as Rebecca said, "What are the markers of success? Because I feel like I'm so much more successful than some people in my family for all of the things I've accomplished on my own, like finishing my master's degree, starting my own therapy practice, and helping hundreds of trauma victims over the years. But because I don't have an income that shows that, to my family, it's as if it doesn't count for anything."

Because of her upbringing, when Rebecca got married to her now ex-husband, who came from a middle-income family, she felt unequipped to handle their finances and let him take full responsibility. Unfortunately, her ex was brought up to believe that carrying consumer debt is normal, and he maxed out their credit cards and even took out equity on their home to pay for things like dining out and entertainment. When they divorced and she had to manage money on her own for the first time as a single mom, she got into the habit of giving away more money than she could afford, because though she had never learned how to budget from her family, she did learn about the importance of charitable giving. When she didn't have enough money left over to cover her own needs, she felt immense shame. She came from wealth but had zero financial literacy, and she was afraid that her family would find out and judge her for her financial failings.

You may be wondering at this point, *If she came from money, why was she ever struggling financially? Isn't she rich?* There's a difference between being rich and coming from a rich family. Her father controls her inheritance and trust, not her. This means that although she is privileged to have enough set aside in her trust for her eventual retirement, everything else is her financial responsibility. Not only that, but if she ever needs access to more money or just a financial leg up from her father, there are always strings attached.

For example, one thing Rebecca is really proud of is that she bought her own car with cash. But one day, she got into an accident and totalled it. Without being asked for any help, her father stepped in and bought her a brand-new vehicle—and not one that would fit into her middle-class lifestyle, like a Toyota sedan. No, instead he bought her a luxury Volkswagen SUV, which caused her some embarrassment for looking like she was showing off to the neighbours. On the surface, this gift doesn't seem all that bad, but as Rebecca explained, "If I take the car from him, that means that I can't ask for any of his time for months or even years. Because it's not just a car; it's something he can hold over my head for as long as he wants." Nevertheless, Rebecca took the car, but because of the way her dad handles family relationships and money, what it cost her was being unable to call him or ask for anything, like his attention or time, for six months. "But he would say he showed up for me. The thing is, I never asked for the car, and that's not what I really wanted from him anyway."

The last thing Rebecca shared with me is how burdensome money has become for her family and how a scarcity mindset can exist even when there is monetary abundance. Everyone in her family is suspicious of each other's motives and potential moves for power, and they are all terrified of touching the principal, losing it all, and not being capable of earning it back. That's why family members withhold information from each other about their lives and careers, for fear that it will be used against them or come off as a threat. It's also why money is often used as a means of controlling others, as Rebecca's aunt does when she continually tells her kids that she'll cut them out of her will if they don't abide by her wishes. As Rebecca says, "Although there's not poverty of financial resources in my family, there's certainly poverty of spirit." Luckily, she's been able to do a lot of self-work over the years, but unfortunately, she describes many members of her family as scared, lonely, and without a true connection to their identity or self-worth outside of the wealth that holds them captive.

Trauma Doesn't Care If You're Rich or Poor

Do you remember learning in school about Maslow's hierarchy of needs?

As a refresher, at the base there are your physiological needs, such as having enough water, food, shelter, and clothing. Above that, there are your safety needs, such as having security and stability, employment, health, and access to resources. Next, there are your love and belonging needs, like having friendships, family, intimacy, and a sense of connection with others. A level above that is your esteem needs, such as feeling respected and recognized, and having high self-esteem, a sense of personal agency, and freedom of choice. And right at the top are your self-actualization needs, which are knowing who you are and being able to reach your full potential as a person. The idea is that as you have your needs met at the lower levels, you're able to progress up the hierarchy to fulfill the next level of needs.

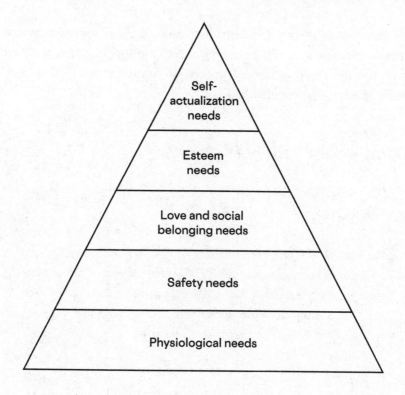

If you come from a history of poverty, you're carrying the trauma of your ancestors not being able to fulfill those bottom two tiers of needs. If you come from a history of wealth, you could be holding on to the trauma of not fulfilling those top three tiers of needs. I know most of us would still prefer to have rich people problems versus poor people problems, but in order to be truly happy and satisfied with your life, every need in this hierarchy is important.

Something Rebecca said that's stuck with me ever since was a comment her ex-mother-in-law made after Rebecca's divorce was finalized: "She spent years resenting me and my family's wealth because she grew up in poverty and hated how unfair it was. But after seeing how disconnected my family was over the years, all the in-fighting, suspicion, and greed, she looked at me and said, 'Maybe being middle-class isn't so bad, after all.'" At the end of the day, trauma doesn't care how much money you or your ancestors had or didn't have. Both the lack of and abundance of money can be a huge burden and cause a number of different forms of trauma that can flow through generations until it is finally identified, deconstructed, and extinguished.

What's Your Family History?

EXERCISE

Now that you've seen two examples of how family histories with money can impact future generations, let's take a look at yours. Taking inspiration from an exercise in Mark Wolynn's book, *It Didn't Start with You*,[19] I encourage you to take out a piece of paper and make your own genogram, which looks something like this:

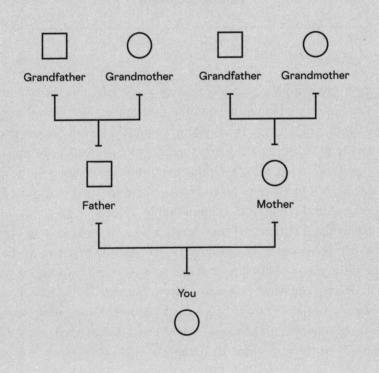

Start with you, your parents, and your grandparents, but feel free to expand this genogram to include older generations if that information is available. If you have no idea about your family history, this exercise could serve as a great opportunity to contact your parents or other relatives to find out (use this book as an excuse—I sure did).

Begin by writing out the histories of each of your grandparents from childhood through adulthood, paying special attention to any big or traumatic life events they may have experienced that could have affected their outlook and behaviour with money. Remember, these can be financial traumas (i.e., poverty, bankruptcy, investment loss), but also personal traumas, too. If one of your ancestors experienced sexual abuse, violence, or a natural disaster, for example, these traumas could have manifested through money as a way to soothe that pain or prevent the pursuit of financial success because of a distorted belief that they weren't worthy of it. Someone who experienced sexual abuse as a child may try to suppress that hurt by shopping in excess to get a temporary boost of joy and adrenalin. Someone who was often neglected as a child may use money in adulthood to garner attention from others to fill that void. This is just to say that while you are outlining your family history, there are no wrong answers, just as when you followed the exercises to help you identify your feelings about money. In fact, the more information and detail you include, the easier it will be to make some important connections between your family's past and you today.

Step 1: Start by choosing one of your grandparents and write out their history, including important moments and traumatic events that you believe may have stuck with them and could have eventually been passed down to you. Note down any of their feelings, behaviours, and actions that can easily be linked to some of their traumas. For my maternal grandfather, the history would look like this:

Gen-1 Trauma	Gen-1 Response
Grew up in poverty.	Was extremely frugal all his life.
Had to start supporting himself and earning an income at age nine.	Never turned down work and prioritized working hard no matter what.
Had no financial stability until age 19 after enlisting in the army.	Was loyal to the armed forces and worked there for most of his career up until retirement, but also never took any big risks with his career to potentially earn a better living.
Father went bankrupt.	Avoided consumer debt and stuck to very conservative investments.
Father died in his 50s.	Became hyperfocused on death and the afterlife from his 50s onward, and became very involved in his own estate planning.
Brother lost the family home.	Paid off his house early and put a lot of importance on paying off or staying out of debt.

Step 2: Next, let's move on to their offspring (your parent) and do the same exercise. Compared to my grandfather, my mom had a fairly trauma-free life. Nevertheless, she learned and inherited a lot of the same characteristics as my grandfather when it came to money, even sometimes at the exact same age. Here's how I'd describe my mom:

Gen-2 Trauma	Gen-2 Response
Grew up in an extremely frugal household.	Was frugal throughout adulthood, though less extreme than her father.
Was told she'd be kicked out of the house once she turned 18 and was expected to pay her own way from then on.	Started working at 13 and always feared not earning an income and having gaps in employment.
Had financial stability with needs met, but not much extra.	Was loyal to the school district where she worked her entire career. Felt safety in being a long-term employee and didn't often take career risks.
Grandfather went bankrupt and father was averse to debt or higher-risk investments.	Never got into consumer debt and stuck to moderately conservative investments.
Grandfather died in his 50s and father had a heart attack at 60.	Became more spiritual in her 50s and very focused on having enough money for retirement.
Uncle lost the family home and father put a lot of importance on staying out of debt.	Aggressively paid down her mortgage until it was paid off in her 50s, uses debit instead of credit for most purchases, and avoided non-mortgage debt most of her life.

Step 3: Finally, it's time to look inward. Refer back to the notes you took when doing the exercises in Chapters 2 and 4 on your feelings about money and any personal or financial traumas you've experienced.

Then do the same exercise you just did for your grandparent and parent. For me, it would look like this:

Gen-3 Trauma	Gen-3 Response
Grew up in a fairly frugal household.	Have been frugal throughout adulthood and have always been cautious about spending beyond my means.
Was told I needed to pay my own way through university.	Started working at age 13 babysitting, then got my first part-time job at 15. Always worked overtime or took extra shifts if available, and panicked when there were gaps between jobs.
Witnessed my dad's side business fail and the dot-com bubble burst right before he was about to take a job at a start-up.	Was afraid of self-employment or taking major career risks until my 30s.
Great-grandfather went bankrupt, and grandfather and mom were averse to debt or higher-risk investments.	Never got into consumer debt and stuck to moderately conservative investments until my 30s when I learned more about investing and the risks of playing it too safe.
Great-grandfather died in his 50s, grandfather had a heart attack at 60, and mother became more concerned about saving enough for retirement in her 50s.	Have always worried about dying or being widowed young. Became hyper-focused on saving enough for retirement in my early 20s.

Great-uncle lost the family home, and grandfather and mom put a lot of importance on staying out of debt.	Have always been aggressive in paying down my mortgage, have never used a line of credit or taken out a personal loan and paid off my student loan less than a year after graduating from university.

Do you see any patterns when comparing your life to your family's past? Do you share any of the same feelings or behaviours as your grandparent or parent? If so, how does that make you feel? Relieved? Unsettled? Confused? Not all the habits that come from these experiences will be bad, but it still helps to understand why we do what we do, especially if we want to make changes. Hold on to those feelings for a bit, because we're not quite done delving into family histories.

The Impact of Historical Trauma

If you come from a line of people who experienced violence, hate, and oppression for a long stretch of history, in addition to any personal or financial trauma you've inherited from your direct ancestors, you may have also inherited historical trauma. For thousands of years, humans have been tortured, oppressed, abused, conquered, enslaved, and colonized, creating populations of traumatized people who then pass down their trauma to their bloodline uninterrupted.[20] This is what historical trauma looks like, and carrying it around with you can have some severe financial consequences. We can start to see how these generational wounds have affected people today by going back to the Middle Ages.

As Resmaa Menakem shares in his book *My Grandmother's Hands*, during the medieval period in Europe "torture wasn't just wildly popular, it was a spectator sport" with public executions and civil justice taking the form of cutting off limbs, burning bodies, and decapitation. As he points out, "It is not hard to understand why so many people . . . fled to the American colonies," especially considering that flight is a survival response.[21] But what happens when large groups of traumatized people flee their countries for a new land? Especially when they haven't worked on healing any of their trauma? They push that trauma through to even more people, and not just their descendants.

You've heard the phrase "hurt people hurt people," right? Well, that's exactly what happened when the New World started to form. European colonizers passed on their trauma to entire civilizations of Indigenous people by murdering their families and stripping them of their land, resources, and culture. They did the same thing when they chose to abduct millions of Africans from their homeland and forced them into slavery for centuries. Menakem explains these atrocities as white people trying to soothe their trauma by blowing it through other human beings, whether it was done consciously or unconsciously, even though it provided no true healing, only temporary relief of their dirty pain.[22]

Over time, the descendants of those colonizers continued the cycle and perpetuated the trauma within the social system itself by creating institutions and passing laws to keep Indigenous groups and Afro-descendants oppressed not only culturally but financially, too.

INDIGENOUS TRAUMA

In 1887, U.S. Congress passed the *General Allotment Act*, which forced the division of Native American land into parcels to weaken the tribes and press Native Americans into traditional farming as a means of assimilation. One big caveat was that if they wanted to become U.S. citizens, accepting this land division was their only option. If they didn't comply, their land would be taken away and sold off to white settlers. But even when they did comply, often the land that they were given was desert land or unsuitable for farming.[23] Although the act was repealed in 1934, the damage had already been done. Native Americans were stripped of 90 million acres, or 65% of Native land, that they could never get back.[24]

Similarly, the *Indian Appropriations Act* of 1851, which created the reserve system, kick-started the slow displacement and segregation of Native Americans, and the *Homestead Act* of 1862 continued this marginalization to allow for the expansion of white settlers in the West.[25] And don't forget the several hundred years prior to this legislation in which European settlers murdered Native Americans and stole their land in order to build their own homesteads. It's estimated that prior to European settlement in North America, there were between 5 and 15 million Indigenous people living on the land. After the American Indian Wars, which took place from 1622 to the late 19th century, only 238,000 Indigenous people remained.[26]

This brings us to Canada. Modelled after the U.S. *Homestead Act*, the *Dominion Lands Act* was passed by Parliament in 1872 to strip First Nations people of their land and move them onto reserves to promote colonization in the western parts of Canada by white settlers.[27] A few years later, in 1876, the *Indian Act* came into effect, and it is still in effect today (though it has been amended through the years). Just like the acts in the U.S., this legislation was meant to suppress, isolate, and assimilate First Nations people to fit Euro-Canadian culture while taking away their land and resources for colonizer use. Until amendments were made to the act in 1951, it was illegal for First Nations people to gather in groups of more than three, leave their reserve without a pass, hire a lawyer, own property, or practise their culture. The act also specifically repressed First Nations women. If they chose to marry a non-status man, such as a white man, their Indian status would be revoked, which took away important rights and benefits that status provided, like tax exemptions, health services, and education.[28]

There were also the horrors of the residential school system, which operated from the 1880s to 1996 and was protected by the *Indian Act*. First Nations, Métis, and Inuit children were removed from their families, given white names, forbidden to speak their native language, and forced to adopt Christian ideology.[29] Although these schools were conveniently left out of many Canadian history textbooks, a bigger spotlight has been put on them in the last decade. Still, that does little to address the trauma experienced within Indigenous communities as a result of the system's existence for over a century.

This is just a glimpse of how European colonizers have blown their trauma through Indigenous people in North America for centuries. Similar events have traumatized Indigenous groups in regions such as Australia, New Zealand, the Pacific Islands, Africa, and elsewhere in the world.

So, what are the financial implications of these traumatic events on Indigenous people in North America? Native American households have eight cents of wealth for every dollar a white household has in the U.S.[30] Indigenous peoples (First Nations, Métis, and Inuit) in Canada experience the highest levels of poverty compared to any other group, with 25% of Indigenous adults and 40% of Indigenous children living in poverty.[31] Given the snapshot of history we just looked at, is it any wonder? Not only were their only forms of wealth—their land and resources—stolen from them, but the heavy restrictions that were later placed on them made it nearly impossible to ever get this wealth back. It's like playing a game of *Monopoly* but having your initial $1,500 taken away from you and given to your opponent, and then being told that you aren't allowed to buy any property or collect $200 when you pass Go. You can, however, still go to jail.

Knowing about all this historical trauma, we can understand why so many Indigenous people struggle with depression, anxiety, low self-esteem, anger, suicidal ideation, and substance abuse,[32] not to mention how their attachment styles have been affected by being taken away from their parents at young ages. It also makes sense that Indigenous people may feel resistant to keeping their money at a bank, investing in the stock market, trusting anything the government promises, or following the new rules of how to succeed in today's capitalist society.

How can we expect Indigenous people to spontaneously heal from their historical trauma when they have been lied to and gaslit from the beginning, have been provided no real support outside of their communities to heal, and are only now, hundreds of years later, getting any semblance of acknowledgement for the atrocities they've suffered?

And they're not the only group of people who've been traumatized and impoverished by colonizers.

BLACK TRAUMA

From 1526 to 1867, the same time period in which European colonizers were settling in North America and displacing Indigenous inhabitants, the transatlantic slave trade took place. It's estimated that over 15 million[33] African men, women, and children were captured and forced onto ships headed to the Americas to work as slaves (or subsequently born into slavery) with about 300,000 going to the United States and the majority going to Brazil and the Caribbean.[34] Because conditions on these ships were inhumane (slaves were considered cargo, not human) and the voyage through the middle passage was especially treacherous, approximately 15 to 25% of enslaved people on board died from disease, malnutrition, abuse, and suicide.[35]

But the journey from Africa to the Americas was just the start of centuries of unbelievable brutality. Although most historical books and films focus solely on slavery in the U.S., slavery did, in fact, exist in Canada, although that fact has also been largely kept out of the history textbooks, too. From 1629 to 1834, there were more than 4,000 enslaved people held captive and forced to work in the worst conditions imaginable in Quebec, Ontario, and the Maritimes.[36, 37]

When enslaved people arrived in the New World, they switched from being cargo to chattel (movable property) and were sold to the highest bidder. After that, and for the next almost 400 years, they were subjected to back-breaking labour from sunrise to sunset without pay, forcible breeding, barely habitable living conditions with insufficient food and no medical attention, not to mention regular torture, physical and sexual abuse, mutilation, and death at the hands of their captors.

If those were the experiences of your family, imagine how it would feel to be told, "But that's all in the past. Slavery was abolished in 1865. Move on." Move on how, though? There have been no apologies. No reconciliation. No reparations. No healing. Slavery may have ended, but it left behind another group of traumatized people with nothing in their pockets and laws set up to keep it that way. Similar to the statistics that showed the wealth gap between Indigenous and white people, in the U.S. "the median white household has a net worth of $171,000, 10 times the net worth of the median Black household, $17,100" and "the 400 richest American billionaires have more total wealth than all 10 million Black American households combined."[38]

The effects of the trauma Afrodescendants experienced and continue to pass on to new generations are what Joy DeGruy defines as "Post Traumatic Slave Syndrome" in her book of the same name. As she puts it: "The enslavement experience was one of continual violent attacks on body, mind, and spirit. . . . In the face of these injuries, those traumatized adapted their attitudes and behaviors in order to simply survive, and these adaptations continue to manifest today."[39]

These adaptations helped Black enslaved people survive for centuries, but as they continue to be passed down to new generations post-slavery, they now work to hold many Afrodescendants back from rising out of poverty, building generational wealth, and reaching financial fulfillment.

In subsequent generations, adaptations within a financial context might look like not pursuing higher education because reading and writing used to be forbidden and a punishable offence, thereby limiting lifetime income;[40] not obtaining sufficient financial literacy to make better choices because for centuries enslaved people were unpaid for their labour, never had access to financial education, and were made to feel as if money and prosperity were exclusive to white people; not taking opportunities to elevate their financial status because even after emancipation, Black people continued to be terrorized and lynched by white people for simply starting a business or finding paid employment; spending every dollar they earn because historically anything they saved could easily be taken away with zero retribution; buying things that promote the illusion of wealth instead of actually building wealth to try to transcend 400 years of enforced poverty in a single lifetime.

When your ancestors lived in survival mode and were conditioned to believe that they were subhuman for hundreds of years, it's unrealistic to think that these traumas that have been passed down can be undone in one or two generations. Especially when many white people still refuse to believe the real extent of the brutality that occurred. Healing takes time, and it's not just an inside job in this situation. Governments and white people need to acknowledge the hurt that was caused, take responsibility for their ancestors' part in it, and most importantly, stop pushing their own historical traumas through Black and Indigenous people by upholding racist systems and ideologies that still exist today.

OTHER HISTORICAL TRAUMA

Although I've spent some time describing historical trauma experienced by Indigenous and Black people in North America, there are many other events that have caused historical trauma in other groups of people with severe financial consequences, too. I'll touch on just a few of those traumatic events in Canada and the U.S. that you may have a connection to, though a more thorough list could take up entire books.

As I mentioned earlier when discussing epigenetics, if you're a descendant of a Holocaust survivor, this could mean you are more susceptible to higher stress levels, anxiety, depression, and PTSD. Not only that, this trauma may manifest in other ways, such as a compulsion to collect valuables and keep cash, since your ancestors had all of their wealth and belongings taken away from them, or workaholism to try to earn back all of the money your family lost.

If you have relatives who were imprisoned in Japanese internment camps during the Second World War, you likely also inherited historical trauma. In 1942, after the bombing of Pearl Harbor, orders were signed in both the U.S. and Canada to forcibly remove citizens of Japanese descent from their homes and place them in internment camps in the name of preventing espionage from Japanese enemies.[41] Although all internment camps were closed by 1946 and some reparations were provided to surviving families 40 years later, in the end, 120,000 Japanese Americans and 21,000 Japanese Canadians were displaced and had no homes or businesses to go back to, because they'd already been seized and sold by the government.[42]

Similar but lesser known was the internment of Ukrainians in Canada during the First World War. It's been documented that through the *War Measures Act*, the Canadian government was able to strip 8,579 "enemy aliens,"[43] who were mostly Ukrainian civilians, of their freedom, property, and wealth and either force them into internment camps or labour in the frontier wilderness between 1914 and 1920.[44] Although individual reparations were never made, after an arduous campaign by the Ukrainian-Canadian community, the government did finally acknowledge this internment in 2005, and the Canadian First World War Internment Recognition Fund was created in 2008 with a $10 million endowment by the government to support projects that commemorate these events and educate others about this largely forgotten or denied part of Canadian history.[45]

Since families had to rebuild from nothing upon release, they were set back decades, if not longer, to try to recoup any wealth they had previously accumulated, which impacted their children's and grandchildren's prospects of getting a higher education and earning a higher income. Nevertheless, no amount of money can undo the trauma and resulting psychological issues of being taken away from your home and imprisoned for the crime of simply being Japanese or Ukrainian in North America.[46]

PATRIARCHAL TRAUMA

To end this chapter, I want to discuss a form of historical trauma that affects roughly half the population: patriarchy. Since the beginning of time, women have been oppressed, beaten, raped, refused an education, treated like chattel, and often forced into a lifetime of unpaid servitude to their fathers, brothers, or husbands. They also continue to be marginalized by the lack of equal pay for equal work while being gaslit into believing that the glass ceiling was broken long ago and any difference in pay is based purely on aptitude and experience.

The effects of being born and raised in this oppressive system is what psychologist Valerie Rein describes as "Patriarchy Stress Disorder."[47] To survive and protect themselves from male threats and control throughout the ages, women have used many tactics, including being submissive, soft-spoken, or silent, having no opinions, expressing a sexy or sweet demeanour, and remaining uneducated. And even today, when you watch dating shows like *The Bachelor* or *Love Island*, scroll social media, or pay close attention to how women are described in the press, those characteristics are still upheld as the "ideal" for women. However, these same characteristics hold women back from realizing their full potential and becoming financial equals with men. If you're submissive, people will doubt your abilities to lead a team or company or manage your own finances. If you're soft-spoken or silent, people may not hear your ideas or solutions in the workplace. If you're unopinionated, people will question whether you have ideas of your own or provide real value. If you're uneducated, people will distrust your skills and capabilities. If you act sexy or sweet, people may not believe that you can be anything outside of that.

Although I'm a feminist and believe that women should be allowed to express their true selves in whatever way they want, women continue to be judged based on the way they speak, dress, and look. The complicated part about all of this is that although these adaptations are holding women back, they can still serve as a form of protection in the face of a real threat. For example, I choose silence whenever I get hollered at by a group of men on the street for fear that anything I say back will provoke a violent response. I also find myself withholding my opinion at times in discussions with a group of men when I fear they will attack not just my opinions but also my character, education, and experience.

Even though a lot of progress has been made since the start of women's suffrage, over 100 years later, women still earn only 83.7% of what men earn[48] and own 32 cents of wealth for every dollar a man owns.[49] Just like the income and net worth statistics I shared about Indigenous and Black people, these numbers tell us that if you've been told you're worthless for generations, it's hard not to believe it yourself. But the truth is, you're not worthless, and it doesn't have to continue like this. There are tools I'll share later on that we can wield to improve our financial futures and the next generations'.

Takeaways

- Even if you've never personally experienced or witnessed a traumatic event, you may still be carrying around the trauma of your ancestors via epigenetics. This can have a big impact on how you think, feel, and approach money to this day.

- You have the power to unpack and process trauma that came before you to be able to let it go and overcome patterns that have been repeated for generations.

- No matter if you have a history of poverty or wealth, the trauma from previous generations can run deep and keep a tight hold on your financial future.

- If you have a family history of cultural or gender-based oppression, you may also be burdened with historical trauma, which may also be impeding your financial prospects.

PART III

Stacked Against You: The Invisible Barriers Holding You Back

6.
You're Only Human

The investor's chief problem—and even his
worst enemy—is likely to be himself.
—Benjamin Graham

You're only human. But as it turns out, being human means that you're hard-wired to make a ton of costly money mistakes—which you can learn to overcome. Although trauma and the lessons you've learned growing up are considerable factors in why you've held on to so many unhealthy money behaviours all these years, the study of behavioural finance also shows that much of our faulty decision-making with money comes down to being a *Homo sapiens* who did not evolve with money management in mind.

Remember when we explored polyvagal theory (in Chapter 4) to better understand how trauma can trigger you into a state of fight or flight (sympathetic) or freeze or fawn (dorsal vagal)? Well, trauma isn't the only thing that will trigger these survival responses. If you believe your financial security or livelihood is threatened in any way, your primitive instincts will kick in, rational thought will be tossed out the window, and your emotions will take over. In the face of financial crisis, you'll be pushed out of your happy place of safety and connection (ventral vagal) and back into survival mode. Although these instincts can be helpful in other areas of your life, when it comes to your finances, they can be downright disastrous.

For example, let's say you hear on the news that the stock market took a tailspin recently. You log into your investment account and see that your portfolio has dropped in value by 20%. What's your reaction likely to be? Chances are, your brain will register the loss in your portfolio as a threat to your survival, just as if a predator was headed straight for you. This will trigger you to "Run for your life!" but since running away from your computer screen won't do much good, instead you'll do the next best thing: hit the sell button and cash out your investments to keep them safe from further loss. The unfortunate thing is that you would be much better off either ignoring those instincts and doing nothing, or doing the exact opposite of what your instincts are telling you and hitting the buy button to snag more shares at a discount. After all, historically, after every crash, the market rebounds to an even higher high than its previous peak.

We only need to look back a few years to see how this exact scenario happened on a massive scale at the start of the pandemic. As news of COVID-19 spread globally, investors started to panic. Fearing that this market crash would be different from those before it, because most of the world had never lived through a global pandemic before, investors started to sell their stocks at a rapid pace, in favour of hoarding cash until the world was safe again. That's why between February 12 and March 23, 2020, the Dow Jones dropped by 37%[1] and the S&P 500 went down 34%[2] in the U.S., and the S&P/TSX Composite Index plummeted by 37% in Canada.[3] What those numbers mean is that way too many people watched *Contagion* on Netflix and started preparing for the end of days by selling off their retirement nest eggs so they could hoard cash the same way they were hoarding toilet paper and cans of soup. Not that I'm judging—I was one of those people who stupidly watched *Contagion* days after the news broke and subsequently did a full inventory of every toilet paper roll and non-perishable food item I had in my house (I couldn't help myself).

Remember when I said, "Don't make permanent decisions based on temporary emotions" in Chapter 4? There's never a better time to heed this advice than when you see your investments sink and the financial news prints panic-inducing headlines like these:

- "Coronavirus crash wipes $5 trillion off world stocks"
- "This was the fastest 30% sell-off ever, exceeding the pace of declines during the Great Depression"
- "Coronavirus triggers the worst market crash since 1987"

With that said, if 2020 wasn't your first ride on the roller coaster that is the stock market, there's a good chance you might have thought to yourself back then, *Wait, haven't I seen these headlines before?* The answer is an emphatic yes, you have! Surrounding every market crash, you'll find almost identical "The sky is falling!" messaging in the financial news to drum up fear and draw in readers with the ultimate goal of getting clicks and selling advertising. Just take a look at some of the news archives from the Wall Street crash of 1929, Black Monday in 1987, the dot-com-bubble burst in 2000, and the 2008 market crash. Here's a quick snapshot of some of the headlines from the 2008 financial crisis:

- "The worst market crisis in 60 years"
- "Worst crisis since '30s, with no end yet in sight"
- "Are we headed for another Great Depression?"

And here are some headlines from 1987's Black Monday:

- "Panic sweeps financial markets smashing records of 1929 crash"
- "The crash of '87: Nowhere to go . . . but down"
- "Stocks plunge 22.6%—Does 1987 equal 1929 and who gets hurt?"

See some glaring similarities? Every headline is shouting from the rooftops that your world is crumbling right before your eyes and you'd better get ready to revert back to the penny-pinching ways of your Depression-era grandparents. That doesn't exactly make it easy for you to regulate your emotions and stay cool, calm, and collected, especially when the media tells you that you're on the brink of financial ruin when the market dips or crashes. Again, it's important to remember that the market has returned from every crash so far and will do so again.

Unfortunately, cool, calm, and collected is exactly what you need to be if you want to come out ahead. The only way to ensure you'll make smart financial decisions is by taking emotion out of the equation. Now, in practice, that's impossible since we're not robots (though I fear we're getting scarily close, if *Black Mirror* is any indication of where we're headed), but you can at least get emotions out of the driver's seat. As behavioural finance researcher and author of *The Confidence Map* Peter Atwater shared with me, "accompanying those feelings, there are predictable behaviours. We go from overconfidence to panic to underconfidence to recovery, and this happens over and over. If we can recognize those feelings, we can better recognize the behaviours that usually follow and thus learn to become more objective when it's time to make important financial decisions."

In other words, we shouldn't strive to suppress our emotions, because they carry a lot of important information with them. Just as we discussed at the beginning of this book, uncovering your feelings about money will provide you with a powerful tool to help you better control them and ultimately become better at financial decision-making. Being able to clearly identify and express how you're feeling when something happens, like when the market crashes, will help you build the resilience necessary to not just withstand but confidently navigate the often anxiety-inducing financial world. But to get there, you need to understand the different biases that have been stirring up those feelings and impacting your financial life up until now, accept them as part of being human, and then craft a plan on how to circumvent them when they arise.

To Be Human Is to Be Biased

Every human alive has biases, and that's not always a bad thing, since they've kept our ancestors alive for millennia. The biases we carry today are adaptations that previous humans generated, and then passed on, in order to survive in their different environments. Evolving over the course of thousands of years, these biases get pretty firmly ingrained in our minds.

With that said, it's important to point out that most of our biases are unconscious, which is why so many people struggle with making financial decisions that will help them instead of hurt them when a lack of financial literacy isn't the issue. It's not that people struggling with money issues are stupid, materialistic, or weak. They're simply being human and following their natural-born instincts. Even when you are conscious of your biases, it's still easy to fall prey to them. The problem is, in the context of money, these instincts are long outdated and need to be reined in. Fortunately, once you become aware of these biases, you'll be more capable of managing them in the future.

I'VE GOT A SHORTCUT FOR THAT

In order for us humans to make decisions quickly, especially in high-stakes situations, we need a way to streamline our thinking. As explained by Cleotilde Gonzalez, research professor at Carnegie Mellon University, "Heuristics are the 'shortcuts' that humans use to reduce task complexity in judgment and choice, and biases are the resulting gaps between normative behavior and the heuristically determined behavior."[4] In other words, our survival depends on mental shortcuts (heuristics), and biases are their by-product.

In prehistoric times, these shortcuts helped our ancestors make swift judgments about a situation being dangerous or safe or solve problems when it came to food, shelter, mates, or predators.[5] In these situations, and in more modern ones we experience today, we're using what's called reflexive reasoning. When you're faced with a decision and need to make a choice right away, you'll react automatically and unconsciously the same way your knee will jerk when the doctor taps it with that little rubber hammer. This is super helpful when you're faced with a decision such as when to safely cross the street, but when it comes to pretty much anything involving finance, we need to enact more reflective reasoning, wherein we go slow, consider a number of factors and scenarios, and put logic ahead of gut-feeling or emotion.

Reflexive and reflective reasoning are what psychologist and Nobel Prize winner Daniel Kahneman calls the two systems in his book *Thinking, Fast and Slow*. He says, "System 1 operates automatically and quickly, with little to no effort and no sense of voluntary control," whereas "System 2 allocates attention to the effortful mental activities that demand it . . . often associated with the subjective experience of agency, choice, and concentration."[6] Because System 1 requires so much less effort, there's an evolutionary and real-life pressure to default to System 1 to conserve mental energy. But relying too much on System 1 for decision-making has its consequences.

As Kahneman goes on to share, although System 1 runs the show most of the time, when it stumbles into trouble, it will lean on System 2 to jump in for help. For example, System 1 can easily come up with an answer for 2 x 2 (4), but it'll get stuck when asked to answer 39 x 267 (10,413). Alternatively, if System 1 is presented with a difficult problem, it will try to provide an answer anyway, even if the answer is wrong. This is why we can't always rely on our reflexive reasoning to steer us in the right direction.

One famous example of this principle is the Müller-Lyer illusion. Look at this illustration of two lines and tell me which line is longer— A or B?

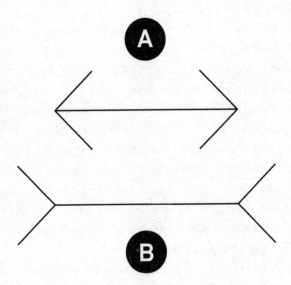

If you answered line B, you'd be with the majority of people who used their reflexive reasoning to deduce that it was longer than line A. But it's a bit of a trick question, because they are the exact same length. If you had gotten your reflective reasoning to jump in for some extra help, you would have noticed that the wings on either side of each line are creating an optical illusion to make your brain think that one line is longer than the other.

Another example of this is demonstrated through psychologist Shane Frederick's cognitive reflection test (CRT),[7] which is a series of three questions that most people get wrong on their first try (including me). The questions are these:

1. A bat and a ball cost $1.10 in total. The bat costs $1.00 more than the ball. How much does the ball cost?
2. If it takes 5 machines 5 minutes to make 5 widgets, how long would it take 100 machines to make 100 widgets?
3. In a lake, there is a patch of lily pads. Every day, the patch doubles in size. If it takes 48 days for the patch to cover the entire lake, how long would it take for the patch to cover half of the lake?

Were these your answers?

1. 10 cents
2. 100 minutes
3. 24 days

If so, I'm sorry, those darn reflexes got the best of you again. Here are the correct answers:

1. 5 cents (A dollar more than 5 cents is $1.05, and $1.05 + $0.05 = $1.10.)
2. 5 minutes (No matter how many machines are working, it still takes 5 minutes to produce a widget.)
3. 47 days (If it doubles in size every day, and on the 48th day, the lake is fully covered, then you can deduce that the day before, the patch is only half the size.)

Notice how fast your brain provides the first (wrong) answer, but to get the second (and correct) answer, you need to slow down and think it through more intentionally. Thankfully, getting these questions wrong has zero real-life consequences, but if you were to use your reflexive reasoning when determining which stock to pick or whether you should get a fixed or variable rate mortgage for the next five years, there could be some very real and costly repercussions. For that reason, it's important to be able to identify the different biases that will make you want to respond reflexively when what you should really do is reflect and *then* respond.

Biases That Are Holding You Back

All the way back in 1776, philosopher Adam Smith first introduced rational choice theory to explain why humans behave as they do. In his essay *An Inquiry into the Nature and Causes of the Wealth of Nations*, he proposed that people have a tendency toward self-interest, are rational beings unswayed by emotions, and always weigh the costs and rewards of each decision they make. These principles were later woven into modern finance, a movement that started in the 1950s largely due to economist Harry Markowitz's modern portfolio theory, which posited that people make rational financial decisions and act on available information rather than any sort of emotional motivation or cognitive bias.

Although many academics and professionals still follow these schools of thought, with the introduction of behavioural economics in the 1970s and its subsequent subset of behavioural finance, I find it difficult to understand how anyone can ignore the very real fact that we humans are anything but consistently rational. There are so many things that cause us to lose self-control and make choices that go against our own best interests. In fact, there are literally hundreds of biases that we exhibit on a regular basis. But for the purposes of this book, I want to focus on the following eight biases that I believe have the biggest impact on our financial lives.

LOSS AVERSION

Let's go back to 2020, when everyone was seemingly preparing for the apocalypse. When you saw the stock market take a nosedive, the dooms-day news headlines splashed everywhere, and people on social media freak out like you've never seen before, what did you do? Did you check your investments and think, *I'm just gonna ride this out*, or *Looks like a good time to buy more shares*, or did the hysteria get to you and cause you to make a decision you later regretted? It's okay if you did. Again, you're only human. Despite how much I know about behavioural finance, even I couldn't entirely block out the noise and decided to hit pause on my investment contributions for a few months to maintain my sanity. You may not think that's a big deal, but as someone who has been teaching people to stay calm in the face of economic uncertainty for years, at the time, I took it as a personal failure.

Then I remembered that I, too, am human and just as susceptible to loss aversion as anyone else. Loss aversion is a cognitive bias driven by the desire to avoid loss, because we feel the psychological pain of losing twice as much as the pleasure of gaining.[8, 9] Because we are predisposed to put surviving ahead of thriving, our motivation to avoid loss far out-weighs our desire to pursue gain. On paper, it may not make sense, but it's a big reason why so many people are fearful of taking calculated risks, even if it means forfeiting a higher income or future wealth.

As a personal example, at the start of my career, I used to never nego-tiate my salary when interviewing for a new job. This was largely due to my fear of not getting the job because I asked for more than the posted base salary. I wanted to avoid the loss of a potential new job more than I wanted to earn a higher income. Did I get those jobs? Yes. Did I leave thousands of dollars on the table in order to snag those jobs? Also yes.

Another example of loss aversion I see all the time is with brand-new investors. They make an appointment with a financial advisor to start investing, and one of the first questions they are asked is "How much risk are you comfortable taking with your portfolio?" Since most inexperienced investors associate the word *risk* with the potential for loss rather than the potential for gain, most of them will choose to play it safe. Even though they have decades to ride out any ups and downs in the market, the idea of losing any amount of money is just too much to stomach. So, they'll say something like "I want to keep my money safe. I can't afford to lose any of it," to which the advisor will note down that their client has a low risk tolerance and proceed to invest their money in something conservative.

Unfortunately, what these advisors usually fail to make their clients understand is that there is no such thing as a completely risk-free investment. If you invest in conservative investments like money market funds, GICs or CDs, or bonds, although you won't be as affected by big swings in the stock market, you are still opening yourself up to inflation and interest rate risk. So, not only will you be earning lower returns than if you were to invest in higher-risk investments like stocks (the price you pay for "safety"), but those returns will be further corroded by rising inflation and the fluctuations that occur with interest rates. What breaks my heart is having conversations with these investors years later and them coming to the realization that they've missed out on years of growth by playing it too safe.

The interesting thing about loss aversion is that not everyone exhibits this bias equally. If you come from a financially secure or wealthy family and observed close relatives take risks and be rewarded for it, you'll have a drastically lower aversion to loss compared to someone who grew up in a low-to-middle-income household and only saw evidence that taking risks rarely paid off.[10, 11, 12] Unsurprisingly, this is because if you have a high level of resources, status, and influence at your disposal, you're in a much better position to weather any losses that come your way. So, even if your relatives made a bet that didn't pay off, the lesson you may have come away with is that you can always bounce back after a setback. Conversely, if you're living paycheque to paycheque or you're constrained by a strict budget where every dollar counts, any loss, no matter how small, can be catastrophic and difficult to recover from, which is a lesson that can be hard to unlearn later on.

It's also been found that if your social circle is made up of financially secure people who have low levels of loss aversion, this will rub off on you, too, and you'll invariably feel more comfortable with loss and more confident with taking risks yourself. Alternatively, if your circle is predominantly made up of financially insecure people who have high levels of loss aversion, then you're more likely to adopt the same fear of loss as everyone around you.[13] This is why looking at your family history and comparing it to other families' will help you to better understand how your family has always just gotten by whereas others have continued to build empires. It's a lot easier to build wealth by taking risks when the fear of losing everything isn't constantly clouding your judgment.

STATUS QUO BIAS

Another reason we may be resistant to taking risks is because we humans are creatures of habit, and our status quo bias makes us resistant to newness or change. We like things just as they are and feel threatened when the status quo gets disrupted.

This type of bias is perfectly depicted in Spencer Johnson's classic book *Who Moved My Cheese?* wherein two mice, Sniff and Scurry, and two Littlepeople, Hem and Haw, are stuck in a maze with the sole goal of finding cheese to survive on. Both duos explore the maze every day to find said cheese, and on one particularly lucky day, they both find an ample supply in a section of the maze called Station C. They then get into a routine of visiting Station C every morning to eat more cheese, but as the days go by, Sniff and Scurry soon realize their supply is running low. At that point, they decide to switch up their routine and continue exploring the maze for new cheese.

Conversely, Hem and Haw get lax and overly comfortable in their routine and continue visiting Station C until one day, the cheese is all gone. Instead of following Sniff and Scurry's lead, they continue to visit Station C every morning with the hope that, at some point, new cheese will magically appear. It never does, and as hunger sets in, Haw urges Hem to leave Station C with him and venture out to find new cheese elsewhere. Hem refuses, believing more cheese will appear if they simply stick to their routine. As you might guess, eventually Haw abandons Hem and explores the maze on his own, realizing that the only way to survive is to do something different when circumstances change. In the end, his efforts are rewarded when he stumbles upon Station N in the maze, where Sniff and Scurry are already happily indulging in a mountain of new cheese.

In short, the message of Sniff, Scurry, Hem, and Haw is to adapt or be left behind. This advice may sound simple and obvious, but in reality, it can be hard to do. I remember that while working at an office several years ago, I confided in one of my co-workers about my plans to hand in my notice. After a few years at the company, I realized there was no room for me to grow or increase my income, so my only option was to leave. My co-worker's response was very reminiscent of Hem's: "Oh, I could never do that. I can't imagine having to start somewhere new, get familiar with how things are done there, and meet new people. No, I'm happy to stay here." Although I'll never know for certain what would have happened to me if I'd stayed, I do know that I was eventually able to quadruple my income within six years because I left.

Now, part of the reason I saw my income increase so quickly was because I became self-employed in a different industry that lent itself to higher earning potential. But data still shows that even if you remain an employee or stay in the same industry, you can increase your income at a much faster rate by switching companies every few years rather than staying loyal to your current employer. Statistics show that the average salary increase when switching employers is 14.8%, whereas the average wage increase is only 5.8% (if you're lucky and actually get a raise each year, which I never did).[14]

Another example of status quo bias I see a lot is people's resistance to any new financial services or products that could make processes more efficient, save them money, or make them more of it. Raise your hand if you know someone who refuses to do online banking, still uses a chequebook, keeps all of their paper receipts in a box to track their spending, has financial statements mailed to them, or defers all investment management and financial decision-making to their financial advisor instead of learning how to do it themselves. I can't even tell you how many people I know who do one or all of these things, and some of them are even millennials who grew up during the big tech boom. With that said, I completely understand how it can be scary to change something you've been doing all your life, but wouldn't you rather be a Haw than a Hem? Wouldn't you rather make the change now instead of getting left behind later on? There are many benefits you could gain from making that change.

A glaring example of resistance to new financial products is Canadians' refusal to ditch high-fee mutual funds in favour of cheaper equivalent exchange-traded funds (ETFs) for their investment portfolios. According to Morningstar, Canada has some of the highest mutual fund fees in the world, with the average management expense ratio (MER) equalling 2% of assets under management.[15] That means that if your portfolio earns an 8% annual return, after fees your return is actually only 6%. It also means that the fund will take its 2% fee even if your portfolio earns a low or negative return (no matter how the fund performs, the management team is still going to take its cut).

Let me show you how much making this one simple change can cost (or save) you over time. Pretend you invested $10,000 and made an annual contribution of $12,500 for 25 years. With an 8% annualized return, over the course of 25 years, you'd end up with $1,055,414.94 minus $285,541.45 in fees for a grand total of $769,873.49. A 2% fee may not seem like much at first, but over time, it can turn into six figures and could cost you reaching millionaire status. Knowing this, you'd think that most Canadians would refuse to pay 2% and look for a cheaper alternative, like ETFs, which have an average MER of 0.31%[16] (though you can find ETFs with an MER as low as 0.05%). Using the same numbers as the previous example, if you were to switch to an equivalent ETF with a 0.31% fee, you'd end up with $1,004,377.01 *after* fees over the course of 25 years—a savings of $234,503.52 just because of the lower fees![17] That extra $200K sure could go a long way in retirement. Plus, as all savvy investors know, there's a lot you can't control when it comes to investing, but the one thing you can control is the fees you pay. Nevertheless, as reported by the Investment Funds Institute of Canada (IFIC) in 2023, Canadians still had a total of $1.94 trillion invested in mutual funds compared to only $382 billion in ETFs.[18]

The situation is the same for people who refuse to leave the big bank they've been with since childhood in favour of an online bank or credit union that charges no or minimal monthly bank fees. A typical monthly bank fee in Canada is about $15 a month. If you were to pay that $15-a-month fee for 25 years, you would spend $4,500 on fees. Whereas if you used an online bank or credit union, that money could be put to better use. For example, it could be added to your annual investment contribution.

Still, as of 2022, Canada's big six banks held around 93%[19] of all banking assets in the country, showing how Canadians still prefer to stick with banks that they're more familiar with, despite paying more for that familiarity. The math may be right there, but sometimes it's just not enough to convince someone to change their routine.

PARADOX OF CHOICE

When I share some of these examples with people, what often follows their shock at how fees can really eat into their future wealth are intense feelings of distress and eventually analysis paralysis. When you realize you're leaving thousands of dollars on the table by investing in high-fee mutual funds or paying monthly bank fees, and your status quo bias hasn't deterred you, you want to take action right away to make up for lost time. But which ETFs should you switch to, because there are thousands to choose from? What no- or low-fee financial institution should you use instead, since there are over 20 online banks and 1,600[20] credit unions in Canada, not to mention the thousands in the U.S.?

With so many options available, how do you know which one is the best to choose? Enter the paradox of choice, popularized by psychologist Barry Schwartz in his book of the same name. When we are presented with too many options, we humans just can't take it. Our brains become overloaded with information, making it difficult to come to a decision. As explained in the 2000 research paper "When Choice Is Demotivating:

Can One Desire Too Much of a Good Thing?" when there are too many choices, "individuals experience conflict and as a result tend to defer decision, search for new alternatives, choose the default option, or simply opt not to choose." Remember System 1 (reflexive) and System 2 (reflective) from Chapter 6? When this type of situation arises, both systems become completely overwhelmed, causing you to either go blank or make a decision in haste that you may question later on.

The authors of the paper, Sheena S. Iyengar and Mark R. Lepper, go on to share that based on their experiments, in which consumers were presented with an array of gourmet jams, shoppers were more likely to purchase one when offered only six choices as opposed to a more extensive selection of 24 or 30.[21] In other words, when we're presented with too many choices, our cognitive bias causes us to freeze, get someone to make the choice for us, make a choice we may regret or be less than satisfied with later on, or not make a choice at all.

This may be why most Canadians choose to stick with one of the big six banks despite learning about the fees they're paying. Just like with gourmet jams, it's a lot easier to choose between six well-established banks than hundreds of smaller and lesser-known online banks and credit unions, which would require further due diligence before a thoughtful decision could be made. Similarly, it's easier to stick with the mutual funds you already have, even though they have high fees, than try to sift through the thousands of ETFs available on the stock exchange.

CONFIRMATION BIAS

This may actually be a bias you've heard of, because we saw a ton of it on display during the pandemic. Confirmation bias is the propensity to look for and interpret information in a way that confirms our personal beliefs or values. When we lean into this bias, not only will we view information through a lens that always proves we are right, but we'll either refute or discount information that proves we are wrong. As behavioural science researcher Eugene Malthouse put it, "it is hard to change a mind that is already made up—particularly if the subject in question is ideologically-charged."[22]

In his 2022 paper "Confirmation Bias and Vaccine-Related Beliefs in the Time of COVID-19," he explored how confirmation bias played a huge role in the pro- versus anti-vaccine divide during the pandemic. With a sample size of almost 4,000 participants, he conducted an experiment to see if the subjects' existing beliefs impacted their judgment when evaluating the effectiveness of a fictional COVID-19 vaccine. Despite all participants receiving the exact same data and information, Malthouse discovered that participants who had pro-vaccine views coming into the study were more likely to find that the data proved the vaccine was effective, whereas participants with anti-vaccine views were more likely to find evidence to prove that it wasn't. Even without this study, I'm sure we can all recall seeing heated debates on platforms like Reddit or Facebook between people who argued that vaccines were our only hope and those who believed they were the devil's poison, with each side being able to find just as much evidence as the other to prove its point.

When we have a strong opinion about something, our confirmation bias makes us see what we want to see and ignore what we don't. No matter if we're debating vaccines, politics, or the latest pop culture scandal, when we've got a stance on something, it's very difficult for us to move our feet instead of instinctually digging our heels in even deeper.

Just take a look at the comments section of any money expert's or finfluencer's social media channel. Even if they are talking about something that on its face is non-controversial, like the benefits of investing in index funds, you'll likely find heated exchanges between people who are proud indexers versus those who believe stock-picking is the best way to build wealth. I know this to be true, because I'm one of those indexers. If you were to look on my bookshelf right now, you'd find that 80% of the books I have on investing are about index investing. Why do I keep buying books on the same topic? Because I'm human and it makes me feel good to read something that supports what I already agree with. I have a harder time reading books about the benefits of active investing, because they challenge my pre-existing views and beliefs. But the only way to learn and grow is to let yourself be challenged.

OVERCONFIDENCE BIAS

Another bias I see often in the comments section when people are debating the best investing strategies is overconfidence bias. This is our tendency to overestimate our financial prowess, and it can lead us to take on more risk than we really should. This overconfidence stems from our belief that on an individual level, we're better than the average person. I'd like to say that social media started it, but overconfidence bias has been around for a very long time.

For example, in 1980, Swedish psychologist Ola Svenson conducted a study to see how groups of college students would rate their driving competency compared to the average driver. What he discovered was that 70 to 80% of participants rated themselves as being in the top half of drivers.[23] Statistically, it's impossible for that many drivers to be above average, and unfortunately, this overconfidence hasn't waned over time. Since 2008, the American Automobile Association (AAA) has conducted an annual survey called the "Traffic Safety Culture Index" to study driver behaviour, overconfidence, and the level of risk that drivers take.[24] What the survey finds, year after year, is that most drivers believe they are better than the average driver, and because of this, they take unnecessary risks, believing that their elevated driving skills will prevent them from getting into an accident. In the 2016 study, the AAA even noted that the general attitude of overconfident drivers was "do as I say, not as I do," wherein they engaged in "the same dangerous behaviors that they deem as 'unacceptable'" in other drivers.[25]

Overconfidence doesn't just exist on the road; it's also heavily present among investors when evaluating their investing skills, especially young people. In a 2022 report by the Financial Industry Regulatory Authority (FINRA)[26] in the U.S., the organization found that investors under the age of 35 were more likely to engage in riskier investment behaviours, like trading options or cryptocurrency, than older investors. They also found that 60% of young investors use social media as a source of investment information and are more likely to invest for reasons other than a long-term goal like retirement, such as to make money in the short term, or simply for entertainment or social activity purposes. Here's where it gets a bit dicey: FINRA also found that not only do investors (young and old) not realize they are paying investment fees (be it MERs or currency exchange fees), but over all, they have very low investment knowledge, with participants scoring on average 4.7 on a 10-question investing quiz.

This is all to say that there are a ton of investors out there who have very little investment knowledge and experience, but their overconfidence bias is pushing them to walk over to the proverbial blackjack table and go all in with their chips because they've got a good feeling that they're about to win big. Unfortunately, this usually isn't the case. Award-winning financial journalist Spencer Jakab revealed just how many of these overconfident investors lost their bets by riding the meme stock wave in 2021 in his book *The Revolution That Wasn't: GameStop, Reddit, and the Fleecing of Small Investors*. But you can also just check out the SPIVA Scorecard to see how even the most skilled portfolio managers can't get it right. As reported at the end of 2022, in the past 15 years, only 6.60% of actively managed funds outperformed the S&P 500 in the U.S., and only 15.10% outperformed the S&P/TSX Composite Index in Canada.[27]

Although I think it's important to be confident in your financial decision-making, there's a big difference between confidence and *over*confidence. Confidence is a "trust in one's abilities, capacities, and judgment,"[28] whereas overconfidence is believing that you are better and more skilled than others when chances are you're really just, well, average. The biggest pitfall with being overconfident is that you allow zero room for learning new things or self-improvement, which are vital when it comes to being good at financial planning. If you want to learn how to do things right, at some point, you're going to have to admit you've been doing things wrong.

PRESENT BIAS

Since I mentioned how young investors typically invest with more of a short-term mentality, let's explore present bias.[29] This is our tendency to put short-term needs above long-term needs and can explain why so many of us have a hard time thinking into the future with our money. It's also why most of us give in to instant gratification and are reluctant to pump the brakes and be patient, even if doing so means sacrificing a bigger reward.

For instance, in a 2015 research paper called "The Role of Time Preferences and Exponential-Growth Bias in Retirement Savings," the authors asked survey respondents whether they would prefer $100 today or $120 in 12 months.[30] Without taking into account factors like inflation or compound interest, it's pretty clear that if you were to wait a longer period of time, you would earn a higher payout, and thus the logical choice would be to wait. Nevertheless, over half of respondents said they'd sacrifice getting more money in the future if they could get it right away.

Why do we do this? Within an evolutionary context, it makes a lot of sense, actually. As we discussed with loss aversion, we are programmed to put surviving ahead of thriving, because eons ago, our ancestors' prospects of living a long life weren't very good. Because of this, it made sense to focus on the present, which was a guarantee, instead of making plans for a future that was unknown. But a lot has changed since then, and thinking long-term is the best way to ensure you won't end up destitute in your twilight years. Don't forget, the average life expectancy is 79 for men and 84 for women in Canada,[31] and 73 for men and 79 for women in the U.S.[32] Thanks to health care and technology, we are living on average 25 years longer today compared to a century ago.

Knowing these numbers, you'd think we'd have a stronger sense of urgency to save for the future. Instead, time and time again, we lean into our present bias and exclaim, "YOLO! I've got plenty of time to get serious with my money later!" and then procrastinate over doing exactly that. Let me tell you, as someone who talks to people about their finances every single day, one regret I hear over and over is "I wish I'd started sooner." I can also tell you that time goes by way faster than you want it to. When I was younger, I remember my mom telling me that time flies so much quicker as an adult than as a kid. You'll blink and decades will have gone by. But like any other kid, I rolled my eyes and thought, *Yeah, whatever.* Then I blinked and here I am, rapidly approaching 40. She was right.

SUNK-COST FALLACY

Have you ever thought to yourself, *Well, I've come this far*, when considering whether you should continue to pursue something, such as a new business, romantic relationship, or attempting to trim your own hair, instead of cutting your losses and moving on when it just isn't working out? Sometimes success doesn't happen right away, after all, and abandoning ship before you get there could feel like a real personal failure. Maybe you just need to invest more money into your business to see it finally turn a profit. Maybe your partner will prove that they are, in fact, committed to your relationship if you just stick around for a few more months. Maybe you've got a hidden talent for cutting hair, and you can start saving hundreds of dollars a year by doing it yourself from now on. Or maybe you should put the scissors down, because what were meant to be California-girl curtain bangs are looking a lot more like girl-in-a-punk-band micro bangs that will take at least four months to grow out.

Hair, luckily, grows back, but you can't get back the time you wasted on a going-nowhere relationship, and you certainly can't get back all the money you spent trying to make a business work that was never going to. So why didn't you just quit early on, especially at the first clear sign that things were not going to end well?

We humans are susceptible to the sunk-cost fallacy, which is "our tendency to follow through on an endeavor if we have already invested time, effort, or money into it, whether or not the current costs outweigh the benefits."[33] It can be hard to tell sometimes what's worth persevering for and what's not, but we do have a bias to keep going when we've already invested, even if signs point to it being a bad investment. This is largely due to our loss aversion bias, because giving up will make whatever we invested into it feel like a total waste. At least if we keep going, we can trick ourselves into believing that we haven't lost anything yet.

One famous example of this happening on a grand scale was the supersonic Concorde airplane. Initial development for the hyper-speed plane started in 1962, but took until 1976 to get up in the air. Not only did it take over a decade for the 16-plane[34] fleet to get off the ground via

British Airways and Air France, but there were lots of signs along the way that indicated this was never going to be a profitable venture either, including "high maintenance costs, daunting fuel bills, little passenger space, and no cargo,"[35] not to mention the project cost $2.8 billion even before operation began—a far cry from its $130 million estimate.[36] Due to these costs, the airlines were forced to charge ridiculously high ticket prices. For example, a round-trip flight from New York City to London in 1996, which would take just under three hours per trip,[37] would cost a passenger USD $7,574[38] ($13,454 adjusted for 2023 inflation). In comparison, today this trip would only cost you around USD $800 on a regular seven-hour commercial flight each way. Sure, the Concorde would save you eight hours up in the air, but at an additional $12,654? That's a little steep. No wonder the fleet was eventually grounded for good in 2003.

After 12 years to produce the Concorde, 27 years in operation, and billions of dollars spent, the term *Concorde fallacy* is now often used interchangeably with sunk-cost fallacy, because it's the perfect representation of how people's biases can make them double down on something due to what they've already invested in it, even though it is showing obvious signs of becoming a failure. On a much smaller scale, investors do this every single day when they refuse to sell a company's stock that is unlikely to recover, because they've poured too much money into it. If you're a homeowner or real estate investor, it's throwing money into more and more renovations when new problems keep popping up, just like in the 1986 movie *The Money Pit*. It could even be staying at a job too long because you've built up seniority and don't want it to be all for nothing.

To rephrase a famous quote, when the facts change, change your mind. Sometimes throwing in the towel, or at least changing tack, sooner rather than later is the best course of action. When we're making decisions for the future, it's more important to consider future costs and benefits, instead of simply fixating on past costs (there's that loss aversion again) that have already happened and can't be changed without a time machine.

HERD MENTALITY

The final cognitive bias I want to cover already came up when we looked at past market crashes. Do you remember being a kid and your parents asking you, "If all your friends jumped off a cliff, would you?" They were trying to teach you that it's important to think for yourself instead of blindly following the crowd. That blind following is called herd mentality—getting caught up in your emotions and instinctively following the herd instead of asking yourself, *Wait . . . why are we all jumping off this cliff? Isn't this sort of dangerous?* Props to our parents for trying to teach us behavioural economics at such a young age.

We see this bias all the time in daily life, and that's because it's deeply rooted in our ancestral past, when we used to live in packs and depended on that unity for our survival.[39] We hunted as one. We migrated as one. And when one of us started running because there was a predator not too far behind, we ran for our lives as one. This instinct to follow the herd is still very important for our survival even today.

Let's say you're sitting in your office's lobby, taking a phone call, when all of a sudden, you notice people running down the stairs and out of the building in a panic. Most likely, you'd hang up the phone and run out of the building with them, because crowds don't run in packs for no reason. It could be a fire or some other type of danger causing them to flee, making you instinctively want to flee, too. A similar scenario was actually captured on CCTV back in 2022. Diners at a restaurant in Brazil were seen suddenly getting out of their chairs and running down the street after they saw a woman run past them in a hurry and two men with a dog running after her. Believing she must be running away from something dangerous, the herd mentality set in and restaurant patrons started getting up and fleeing, too. But there was no danger. The woman who sparked it all was actually leading a CrossFit class on a group run.[40]

I've actually seen herd mentality be the cause of danger, with people acting irrationally for the sole reason that everyone else around them was doing the same thing. Remember the 2011 NHL Stanley Cup Final riots in Vancouver? I sure do. After watching the Canucks lose on TV, I switched to the news and saw outraged fans destroying the city, looting storefronts, and setting police cars ablaze.[41] When filmmakers Kat Jayme and Asia Youngman interviewed rioters a decade later for their documentary *I'm Just Here for the Riot*, they discovered that most people could only cite "mob mentality [and] being caught in a moment" as their reasoning for getting involved.[42] In other words, although herd mentality still has an important role to play in our lives, it can also lead you down a dark path of destruction and regret if you're not careful.

The problems with herd mentality are important to keep in mind especially when it comes to money. As I write this book, the Taylor Swift Eras Tour is in full swing, and the constant social media posts, media coverage, and marketing for it are like nothing I've seen before. When she announced she was going to do six shows in Toronto in 2024, even I thought to myself, *Should I buy tickets?* even though I haven't listened to her music in years. But everyone seemed to be either talking about it or sharing videos from the concert, and I felt oddly compelled to get in on the action and spend thousands of dollars on a show I'd normally never go see. Although I was able to snap out of it and put my credit card back in my wallet, I've succumbed to herd mentality on many other occasions. Remember, I hit pause on my investments when the March 2020 crash occurred, not just because of my overwhelming loss aversion, but because it seemed as if everyone else was getting out of the market and it was hard not to do the same.

This mentality is actually what causes market bubbles and crashes in the first place. We humans prioritize survival above all else, so we can't help but look to the crowd to see "Should we buy or sell?" instead of asking ourselves that question based on our own knowledge and research. When investors follow the herd like this, they override logic and common sense because they don't want to get left behind.[43] This fear of missing out (FOMO) is typically what causes market bubbles, which are defined as significant run-ups in prices—be it stocks, real estate, Beanie Babies, or tulip bulbs back in the 1600s—without a corresponding increase in the value of the assets themselves.[44]

What's consistent with bubbles, however, is that they go through five stages that always end in them bursting—displacement, boom, euphoria, profit-taking, and total panic. In the initial stage of displacement, people get excited about something, such as a new product or innovation (e.g., legalized cannabis or AI) or low interest rates (which make real estate more appealing). Then there's a boom, and the excitement turns into action with more people investing in businesses or industries connected to the products or innovations, or taking advantage of low interest rates by buying property. After that, there's the stage of euphoria, in which major FOMO sets in and the masses start jumping on the bandwagon, causing the assets' prices to soar well beyond their intrinsic value. The profit-taking stage is when the savvy investors of the group, who understand how bubbles work, cash in before the mania comes to a peak. And finally, there's the total panic stage, when everyone who is still invested starts noticing that the savvy investors have sold off their assets and FOMO sets in once again. Panic starts to spread, and everyone begins selling in a hurry so as not to be the last one left holding the bag.

People lose their life savings and homes because of bubbles. Unfortunately, you can only be certain that a bubble occurred after it has burst. But you can always read the signs. If you see people herding over something new and shiny (e.g., NFTs in 2021) and the price of that thing skyrockets, that should give you pause to think, *Do I actually think this is a good investment opportunity, or do I just feel the pull to follow the crowd off the cliff?* More times than not, it's the cliff. So go home, log out of your investment account, and don't look at it until your FOMO subsides.

That'll Cost You

I said I'd share only eight behavioural biases with you, but I can't end this chapter without covering some of the ways businesses are taking advantage of your reflexive reasoning and biases to get you to spend more money—more money than you intend to spend, or worse, more money than you can afford. By knowing some of the psychological tricks these companies are playing, not only can you become a more mindful consumer, but you can also do a better job of ensuring you're keeping more of your money in your pockets and putting less into the pockets of those only interested in profiting off you.

FILL 'ER UP

One day during the summer that I was writing this book, my husband and I decided to pop into the grocery store to grab a few things for dinner. But as we entered the store, we noticed something odd. Where were the baskets? We walked around for a few minutes feeling like complete idiots for not being able to find them, until my husband asked one of the cashiers where the store had moved them. The cashier looked up from her register and said blankly, "We don't have baskets anymore." When I heard this, a light bulb went off in my head. "They want us to spend more money. Those sneaky little #!@*&%!" I whispered to my husband so the cashier couldn't hear.

Considering that grocery prices have skyrocketed since the pandemic and grocery stores have raked in record profits ever since, this made my blood boil. Having done a ton of research on how to save money at the grocery store in my early days of blogging, I already knew that we humans have a tendency to fill up whatever container we have with us. If we have a basket, we'll fill it up. If there are no baskets, we're going to fill up our cart and spend even more money than if we'd just had a basket. Even when we do the smart thing and bring a grocery list with us to stay focused, often the only way we know that we're done grocery shopping is when we've run out of room to put more stuff. This feeling of being compelled to fill up our baskets, carts, closets, storage spaces, homes, and even bellies goes back once again to our ancient ancestors.

If you've ever struggled with your weight (like I have), you should know there's science that shows we tend to fill up our plate with food so we can't see any white space. The bigger the plate, the more food we'll pile on; the smaller the plate, the less food we need to pile on for it to look full. As behavioural researcher and author Brian Wansink shares in his book *Mindless Eating*, "Our bodies fight against deprivation, and our brains fight against deprivation. . . . If we don't feel deprived, we're less likely to backslide and find ourselves overeating to compensate for everything we've foregone."[45]

In other words, because we want to do everything in our power to survive, we're going to make sure we always have enough—enough food on our plates, enough food in our shopping carts, and enough stuff in our personal spaces. If we see emptiness or white space, we're going to fill it up to avoid feeling deprived. So, if you want to avoid overeating, grab a smaller plate. If you want to avoid over-shopping, grab a basket instead of a cart. It sounds simple enough, but the problem is that everything around us is big to encourage us to consume more.

Supermarket chain owner Sylvan Goldman understood this well when he invented the shopping cart back in 1937 to try to increase revenue. When it was first introduced, it was essentially the size of two shopping baskets on wheels, thus encouraging shoppers to buy twice as much.[46] As you can guess by now, it was wildly successful, and other retailers not only followed suit but also significantly increased its size to encourage even more spending, with shopping carts tripling in size from 1975 to 2000.[47] Although this was good news for grocery retailers' bottom lines, it was bad news for consumers' wallets and the environment. According to the U.S. Department of Agriculture, current food waste is between 30 and 40% of the food supply.[48] Similarly, Canada's National Zero Waste Council found that 63% of food that's thrown away by consumers could have been eaten, and Canadians spend an average of $1,300 a year on food that's wasted.[49]

Although we all do this but wish we didn't, it's a hard habit to break when there are only supersized grocery carts available, dinner plates that have increased in size by almost 23%,[50] and single-family homes that have doubled in size in both the U.S. and Canada.[51] Everything is pushing us to consume more, not less, which means we need to become experts at self-restraint. I've been experimenting on myself whenever I go to the grocery store to grab that one ingredient I'm missing for dinner. I walk right past the baskets and carts and limit myself to only how much I can carry in my arms. Despite getting some odd looks from other shoppers, I always spend less than I would have had I grabbed a basket or cart.

EVERYBODY LOVES A DEAL

I worked in retail from the ages of 15 to 22, and having seen behind the curtain how these businesses come up with promotions and "deals" for customers, well, it explains a lot about my mistrust of big business and disdain for big, splashy sales like Black Friday and Boxing Day. At the end of the day, a *really great deal* is usually code for "we want you to spend more money."

This is perfectly illustrated in a 1998 study conducted by Brian Wansink and his colleagues Robert J. Kent and Stephen J. Hoch.[52] They wanted to see how consumers decided what to buy and if marketing could influence them to deviate from their original shopping list. They knew going into the experiment that consumers tend to have certain anchors they use for decision-making, which means they already have an idea of what products they intend to buy, how many units of those products they'll purchase, and what price they are willing to pay. However, what they discovered was that stores could increase the quantity of units purchased if they used the right type of wording on in-store promotions. For example, they tested out two different displays of cans of soup. One said, "4 cans for $2," and the other said, "1 can for 50¢." The discounts were the exact same, but because of how shoppers processed the information—and likely because they already had an anchor price like one can for a dollar—getting three extra cans for only an additional dollar seemed more enticing than the one can for 50 cents. Subsequently, the stores that offered the multiple-unit pricing promotion generated 32% more sales compared to the single-unit promotion.

Anchoring bias is our tendency to "rely too much on pre-existing information or the first information [we] find when making decisions."[53] When we encounter an item that we deem is too expensive, we become pleasantly surprised when the next item we see is significantly cheaper. Picture this: You're in a clothing store going through the racks, and you see a jacket you really like. You look at the price tag and see that it's $500. That's way above your budget of $100. You keep looking and find another jacket you like and the price tag is only $200. Although it's still double your budget, you think, *Wow, this is $300 less than that other jacket. What a deal!* The same thing could happen if you were to pick up that first jacket and notice it is on sale for $500, down from $1,000. You might think it's a good deal and consider splurging on it because of how much you'll save on it, even though you're not actually saving anything; you're spending $400 above your original budget. As I like to say, "That's how they get ya!"

I'LL TAKE THE MIDDLE ONE

Along the same lines as anchoring bias, there's also a bias called the compromise effect (a.k.a. the Goldilocks effect). This is very popular among retailers who sell a range of products or services to make you think you have a variety of choices, but really they want you to choose the middle option. This is a classic technique at a car dealership. You'll notice that almost all vehicles have at least three packages available: a base model, a standard model, and a premium model. Having spent some time at a dealership recently to scope out a new family vehicle for my mom, what I gauged from the salesperson was that almost everyone chooses the standard package. You get more features than the base model, and it's significantly cheaper than the premium model, which only differs by having a few luxury features most people never use anyway.

Another bias very similar to this is called the decoy effect, in which a business selling two items will introduce a third to make it more obvious which is the "best" item for customers to choose, while getting them to spend more than they originally intended.[54] One prime example of this is when you're at the movie theatre and looking to buy some popcorn. Typically, there are three size options to choose from: small, medium, and large. Every time I frequent the cinema, I have the intention of buying just a small popcorn, and yet I almost always buy the large. Why? Because although the small popcorn is only six dollars, for a dollar more, you can get almost twice as much in a medium, and for only 50 cents more than that, you can get a large and then have enough to bring home for a late-night snack. The way the options are presented makes it seem as if it's almost irrational *not* to get the large, even though it's likely more popcorn than I actually need and $1.50 more than I wanted to spend.

JUST TRUST ME

A big reason why we decide to spend our money with certain retailers comes down to trust and feeling safe. In 1975, professor and economist Sam Peltzman wrote the paper "The Effects of Automobile Safety Regulation,"[55] which, as dry as it sounds, actually took off and established the term the *Peltzman effect* in modern psychology. What he discovered in his research was that when safety measures are in place, like the mandatory use of seat belts, people tend to increase their risky behaviours because they feel safer doing so.[56]

In terms of how this effect relates to sales and marketing, if a retailer can prove that it is trustworthy and can make consumers feel safe, those consumers will be more open to taking a risk and spending their money with that business. Retailers do this by offering free samples, offering free shipping, having liberal return policies, and providing social proof with testimonials and reviews.

This is why the rise of the influencer has exploded over the past decade. Influencers are leaning into the Peltzman effect, building trust with their audience first by providing free value such as entertainment or educational content, and then once they see their audience has been appropriately primed, they introduce a paid product or service. As someone who has stumbled into being a financial influencer myself, I can see this from both sides. On the one hand, selling and promoting products has helped me with my own business. I created free content for years (and still do) and have developed relationships with my audience, who trust me with their intimate questions about money, as well as their money when they buy one of my digital products.

I'm also a consumer and have bought services and products from influencers I follow, too. I don't think it's necessarily a bad thing when it's done in good faith, as long as you're aware of what's going on and you still do your due diligence before spending your money. I'm sure we've all been in a situation where we've trusted a brand or influencer, bought something from them, and then felt cheated on delivery. Unfortunately, this is just part of being a consumer. Sometimes you get it right, and sometimes you learn an expensive lesson about wasting money on something you saw marketed online.

THIS IS GONNA HURT

The final concept I want to cover in this chapter is called the "pain of paying." You're probably already familiar with the pleasure of shopping, wherein you get a dopamine hit when you think of buying something and anticipate taking it home or having it arrive on your doorstep, but you may be less aware of the pain of paying, which is when you experience psychological pain when you have to pay for that purchase. Because of your loss aversion, whenever you have to let go of money to pay for something, it hurts. You're effectively losing money every time you buy something, and since we humans don't like to lose things, we're going to try to find a way to bypass or delay that pain as much as possible.

With that said, we experience different levels of pain depending on what form of payment we use when making a purchase. Studies show that using cash is the most painful. If you use debit, it's slightly less painful. If you use credit, it's the least painful. Why? When you use cash, you register the loss of money instantly, because you see it going from your hands directly into the cashier's register. Ouch! With a debit card, even though it's less tangible than cash, you still know that once you check your bank account, the number inside it will have gone down. Ooof! But with credit, nothing goes down except your credit limit, which is likely sky high anyway. And the climbing total is tucked into its own account for now, while your money is "safe." Similarly, with a gift card or a different form of currency, such as chips at a casino or Starbucks rewards, the pain of loss is much lower, since you feel several steps removed from the original cash in your wallet or bank account.

Because retailers know this all too well, many encourage credit card payments above any other form of payment. Heck, some retailers don't even accept cash anymore. They know people will spend more, and spend more often, when they use credit. That's why so many retailers have also partnered with credit card loyalty programs to provide points or rewards to customers who pay with credit. It's also why you're seeing a lot more retailers offering buy-now-pay-later payment options, making it easier for you to spend money on credit with an even longer grace period to distance the joy of purchasing from that pesky pain of paying.

Takeaways

- It's not just trauma that is getting in the way of you making smart financial decisions; it's also just being human.

- In order to prevent future money mistakes, it's important to understand the different biases humans have developed over thousands of years that are likely working against you.

- Eight of the most prevalent biases we fall prey to include loss aversion, status quo bias, the paradox of choice, confirmation bias, overconfidence bias, present bias, sunk-cost fallacy, and herd mentality.

- Businesses will try a myriad of mental tricks to get you to spend more, so make sure to keep your eyes peeled for no shopping baskets (only carts), clever wording on signage and promotional materials, three comparable options to choose from with one seeming like the "obvious" choice, influencers pushing a lot of products or selling things unrelated to their brands, the lure of using credit over cash or debit, and the rise of buy-now-pay-later programs.

7.

It's Not Fair

When we identify where our privilege intersects
with somebody else's oppression, we'll find
our opportunities to make real change.
—Ijeoma Oluo

We're spoiled for choice when it comes to old adages that desperately need to be removed from our language. "There's more than one way to skin a cat." Is there, and why are we skinning cats in the first place? "An apple a day keeps the doctor away." Pretty sure it doesn't. "Kill two birds with one stone." Again, why so much talk of killing animals?

We use idioms like these on autopilot every single day because they've been embedded in our lexicon for generations. The saying about skinning a cat, for instance, dates all the way back to 1854.[1] So, in all likelihood, my great-great-grandparents were saying it, and somehow we're still saying it five generations later. Fortunately, no real cats are harmed when anyone uses this phrase, and in general, most sayings like this are fairly innocuous. But others that we may hear or even use in casual conversation are anything but.

One of them is "We all have the same 24 hours in a day." A similar version often seen on social media is "You have the same number of hours in a day as Beyoncé." On its face, it seems pretty harmless. Technically, we all do get the same number of hours per day, since time bends for no one. So, what's the problem with using this turn of phrase to illustrate the importance of using your time wisely to reach a higher level of wealth and success? Because it isn't true.

You can't say that we all have the same amount of time to improve our skills, grow in our careers, start a business, earn more money, or build wealth without acknowledging the very real fact that different people have different obligations, circumstances, barriers, and opportunities than others. Unfortunately, this fact is largely ignored when most experts are doling out their advice on how to "make it."

For instance, I don't have kids, which means I have substantially more time to focus on professional development, growing my business, and increasing my income than someone my age who's a parent, because I don't have a little human to raise. People who work from home have more time to start a side hustle outside of work or learn how to better invest their money than those who have to spend hours a day commuting to their office or work site. Someone like Beyoncé, who has childcare, personal assistants, and full-time staff to help her manage her career and home life, has more time to expand her empire than a single mom who has to work three minimum-wage jobs to support her two kids. Even though Beyoncé has undeniably worked hard to become one of the biggest pop stars in the world, you wouldn't turn to the single mom and tell her that the only things stopping her from reaching similar heights are her lack of time-management skills and work ethic, would you? Of course, you wouldn't. Because deep down, you know that there are endless reasons why someone is in the socioeconomic position they're in that have nothing to do with time management, motivation, or hustle.

A great representation of how easy it is to get stuck in a cycle of working long hours for little pay with no real opportunity to escape is Stephanie Land's memoir *Maid* or the Netflix miniseries based on her book. As much as I wish we lived in a world that mimicked the board game *Life*, where everyone enters the world under the exact same conditions and how far you get is based almost entirely on the choices you make (save for some good and bad luck from spinning the wheel), that's just not where we're at, and unfortunately, I don't think we'll get there in our lifetime.

The reality is that we don't all start at the same starting line in the race of life. One visual that always comes to mind when I'm thinking about this is a video produced by youth counsellor Adam Donyes, which went viral in 2017 and again in 2020.[2] In the video, Donyes hosts a group of teenagers on a grass field and tells them they are all going to race. To raise the stakes, he promises to award the first person to cross the finish line $100. However, not everyone is going to start at the exact same spot on the field. He tells the group they can take two steps forward every time they meet certain conditions, like their parents are still married, they got a private school education, they never had to help their parents pay the bills, or they never worried about where their next meal was coming from. What becomes strikingly obvious is how the people who grew up with this kind of privilege get a significant head start, forcing those who didn't to run twice as far to reach the same finish line and making it almost impossible for any of those kids to win the $100 prize. Although this example isn't perfect, since it fails to highlight lots of other barriers, it's nevertheless a powerful image of how inequitable things really are.

Achieving financial success doesn't just come down to knowledge or grit. As it's set up now, the system we all live in isn't fair for everyone, and no amount of money advice or manifestation can change that. Some people are born with a head start, whereas others have to run twice as far (and as fast) to reach the same finish line at the same time. I don't have the blueprint for how to dismantle this broken system so we can rebuild it, but an important start is to acknowledge the fact that some people have privilege that others don't. If we start there, we can all access more empathy and understanding and do what we can to make the future more equitable for everyone.

Why Is It So Hard to Admit Privilege?

Have you ever shared a personal struggle with someone and gotten a response like this: "Yeah, but we *all* have struggles in life" or "Sure, but life is tough on *all* of us"? You probably remember the trend of people dismissively saying, "*All* lives matter" in response to "Black lives matter," especially during the 2020 Black Lives Matter protests. What do all of these responses have in common? They are all veiled rejections of other peoples' disadvantages and hardships to mask the existence of privilege.

As we discussed earlier, when I say *privilege*, I mean having certain unearned or innate and largely unacknowledged advantages over others by simply belonging to a certain social identity group, such as being white, male, heterosexual, Christian, well-educated, or wealthy, though there are privileges outside of these groups, too.[3] Privilege doesn't mean that people who have it don't work hard or are immune to their own hardships, just that the hardships or barriers they face don't come from inherent, unchangeable aspects of who they are. You can work hard, have a tough life, and still have privilege—they aren't mutually exclusive.

This may be something you're all too familiar with because of your own life experiences, or maybe you've been doing the important work of educating yourself about this already (well done!). Nevertheless, a question I can't help but ask myself every time I see rich people credit their success to just working really hard or CEOs who earn 243 times[4] what their employees make bemoan that no one wants to work anymore is *Why do people have such a hard time admitting their privilege?*

The simple answer is that *privilege* has become a bad word, and not just for those who are shortchanged because of it. To anyone with privilege, when someone points it out, it can feel like an attack on their sheer willpower and work ethic. This was what Brian S. Lowery and L. Taylor Phillips, professors at Stanford University and New York University, sought to examine in a series of studies documented in their paper "I Ain't No Fortunate One: On the Motivated Denial of Class Privilege."[5]

Participants who were high-income earners or graduates of elite universities were broken into groups with some being presented data proving general economic inequality in the United States, and others being shown data that correlated economic inequality to privilege. Subjects were then asked to rate their own level of hardship and privilege, and what the researchers found was pretty telling.

To preserve their self-image, the participants who were shown the connection between privilege and economic inequality claimed to have suffered greater hardships and put forth more effort in their endeavours than participants in other groups. In other words, they exaggerated.

As Lowery later shared in an interview about the study, "If someone points out to you that you benefit because you're part of this group, it makes you uncomfortable," so to cope, "you try to convince yourself that you aren't benefiting," because you've had to overcome adversity in some way, too, or you've earned all of your outcomes through personal merit alone.[6] Or as personal finance educator and BuildingBread founder Kevin L. Matthews II shared with me, "People deny that privilege exists because it shatters the notion that hard work and grit are the great equalizer."

No one likes having their self-image challenged, and that's exactly what being confronted with one's privilege can do. But where does this obsession with being self-made and bootstrapping stem from?

We can look to the Puritans who migrated to the New World in the early 1600s for a start. Bringing their Calvinist values with them on the Mayflower and embedding them into American culture,[7] they believed that God blessed those who worked hard with salvation and financial prosperity.[8] With that, the Protestant work ethic was born, as well as the view that anyone who was poor or struggled financially must be lazy and thus wasn't graced with God's favour.

Obviously, through a 21st-century lens, we can see how simplistic and narrow-minded this kind of thinking is. Nevertheless, just like those idioms that have hung around even when we've forgotten their origins, many of us still carry these ingrained beliefs despite not knowing why we think this way or where these beliefs came from. Moreover, even though these values were pioneered in the U.S. and are rooted in religion, thanks to globalization, people in countries all over the world, such as Canada, the U.K., and Australia, have adopted these views and swapped out God for karma, the universe, or just pure ego.

For most of my life, I didn't truly understand the depths of my own privilege. This was partly due to me thinking that privilege was just another way of saying your family was rich (and mine wasn't), but also because, like many others in a privileged position, I fell into the same defensive trap as all those study participants. If someone told me I was privileged, my gut reaction was to prove that I wasn't born with a silver spoon in my mouth and I had worked hard for everything I achieved. I now understand that this defensiveness was sparked by my fear that if I admitted my privilege, it would diminish the things I did earn by moving the focus onto those I didn't.

As University of Bristol professor Rich D. Pancost wrote on the topic, admitting privilege can feel "like you are undermining the story of your self. And for some of us, it feels like theft," hence why many of us can feel combative when someone brings it up. But contrarily, owning our privilege "does not erase what we achieved and our associated personal narratives" but instead contextualizes it, "and by contextualizing our achievements it insists that we understand that we are part of something larger than ourselves."[9] Acknowledging our privilege is an act of self-awareness and community.

Check Your Privilege

EXERCISE

Here is a quick exercise for you to assess your privilege on your own, and then you can leave it at the door and read through the rest of this chapter with your defences down and, ultimately, more empathy and open-mindedness. Even if you've already done your own introspection, this is still a good practice in case you continue to battle feelings of discomfort and guilt when thinking about your privilege and the impact it has on others.

First, take a look at the table below and check off each social identity group that you belong to.

If you fit into even one of these categories, that is a privilege. But this is far from an exhaustive list, and these are fairly high-level categorizations of privilege. Even having a securely attached upbringing could be viewed as a privilege, since it's largely something you're born into that provides advantage. In your journal or on a piece of paper, write out any other advantages you may have experienced throughout your life that gave you a head start, especially financially. Here are some examples:

- You were gifted money from your family on birthdays or holidays.
- Your family could afford to put you in extracurricular activities for personal development or to lead to a scholarship.
- You had access to private tutors for school.
- You were given an allowance as a kid or teen.
- You were gifted a vehicle or had free access to your parents' vehicles as a teen or young adult.
- Your post-secondary education was subsidized or fully paid for by your parents or other family members.
- You were able to live at home for free while attending post-secondary and after graduation.
- A member or friend of the family helped you get an internship or job.
- You inherited money or assets or received a life insurance payout from a family member after they passed away.
- You were gifted a lump sum of money for a down payment on your first home or were gifted your first home.
- You were exposed to financial advice and education early on in life from family members.

These are just a few examples, but there are likely many other advantages you've experienced that, up until now, you hadn't realized had helped to significantly accelerate your career trajectory and financial life. Keep these in mind whenever a defensive thought pops into your mind while reading the following sections. Remember, having privilege doesn't negate your hard work or lived hardships, but denying it does dismiss the experience of others without the same advantages.

White	
Heterosexual	
Male	
Christian	
Middle to upper-class	
Private school educated	
University/college educated	
No physical or mental disabilities	
Born citizen (non-immigrant)	
Native-language speaker with regional dialect	

Living in Colour

There's a TEDx talk by Susan E. Borrego, a leadership consultant and former professor, that does a great job of addressing one of the most prevalent counter-arguments to privilege: "I grew up poor, so how could I have privilege?"[10] The first time she learned about privilege was when she was a college sophomore and her professor was discussing some of the characteristics of Black urban families, including single-mother households, high unemployment rates, and growing teenage pregnancy rates. While listening to these descriptors, she couldn't help but think, *How could she be describing the characteristics of Black urban families and me feeling like they apply to my [white] family?* She raised her hand and voiced this to her professor only to be told, "Don't you ever compare yourself to a Black family. It doesn't matter how poor you are or how under-employed you are, *you* have privilege."

As Borrego goes on to share, over time, she recognized how, despite her poor and unstable upbringing that forced her to get emancipated at 15 and go without health insurance or a permanent address to call home as a young adult, because of the colour of her skin, she still had inherent privilege that people of colour don't. Her hardships were real, but they weren't *because* of her skin colour whereas Black people do experience disadvantage and unequal treatment simply because of theirs. This only became clearer when she eventually witnessed the marginalization that her Black son-in-law and grandchildren face every day.

LET'S TALK ABOUT WHITE PRIVILEGE

As we explored in the previous exercise, privilege comes in many different forms, such as class and gender, but one that often gets challenged still is white privilege.

In a continent that was born out of oppressing people of colour, starting with Indigenous people, then enslaved African people and their descendants, and in more recent history non-white immigrants and citizens, is it so unbelievable that if you're poor and white, you still have certain advantages over people of colour, even if they're in a better socioeconomic position than you?

As activist and women's studies scholar Peggy McIntosh described it in her foundational 1989 paper on the topic, white privilege is like having "an invisible weightless knapsack of special provisions, maps, passports, codebooks, visas, clothes, tools and blank checks."[11] Being born white automatically grants you more access, opportunities, safety, and freedom than non-white people have simply because of the colour of your skin.

She then went on to list 26 of these invisible privileges that white people have over people of colour, including the following (which I've updated slightly to better reflect the times we now live in):

· not being denied a home to rent by a landlord because of your skin colour
· not worrying about being followed or harassed by employees when out shopping

- feeling confident that if the CRA or IRS audits your tax return or you apply for a loan at the bank, you're not being singled out because of your race
- not being labelled a "diversity hire" or having to prove that you were hired for any other reason than your qualifications

GUILTY OF BEING NOT WHITE

The example of not worrying that you'll be targeted while shopping reminds me of a story Elizabeth Leiba recounted in her book *I'm Not Yelling: A Black Woman's Guide to Navigating the Workplace.* While in college, she was racially profiled and arrested because she couldn't prove that the $2.49 pack of batteries in her bag weren't stolen. She was taught at a young age to always keep her receipts handy just in case a situation like this ever arose, but when pressured to provide proof of payment, she couldn't find it anywhere. It was only after she had posted bond and was released from jail that she discovered the receipt tucked into one of her school folders.[12] I don't know about you, but I've never thought, *I should keep this receipt on hand just in case I'm wrongfully accused of stealing.* And that's likely because if this same scenario happened to a white student, the outcome would have been vastly different, with the student receiving no more than a simple warning.

Even though Leiba was able to prove her innocence, this event not only traumatized her but gave her a criminal record, and because Florida is a state in which you can only seal and expunge your criminal record once, her attorney urged her not to in case she was ever targeted again and needed to use her one chance for a more serious offence in the future. She wrote, "Later, I would be grateful that [my lawyer] gave me that advice after additional negative encounters with the police in my adulthood. I was glad to have that insurance."[13]

This goes way deeper than a traumatic experience. Unless you're able to get it sealed, a criminal record can cause some severe and long-term financial consequences, even if the charges are dismissed. For example, upon doing a background check, lenders can deny your mortgage application and employers can choose not to hire you.[14] Owning property and being employed so you can save and invest a portion of your income are the two main ways to build personal and generational wealth. And Black and Indigenous people are the two largest populations in the American[15, 16] and Canadian[17] prison systems, and they are both more likely to be wrongfully accused or convicted of a crime and given harsher sentences than white people.[18, 19, 20] Add those facts together, and it's clear why Black and Indigenous people are also the two poorest communities in both countries.[21, 22, 23]

BY PROFESSIONAL, DO YOU MEAN "WHITE"?

Leiba eventually found justice and even won a civil lawsuit, but this event had a major impact on her future. Seeing her blackness as a target on her back, she began a transformation that many other people of colour make to become a version of themselves that comes off as less "threatening" in white spaces. From then on, she strived to be quiet, work twice as hard as her white peers but take fewer risks, and do everything she could to look like she was "not someone who could cause any problems." This also included code-switching in school and at work by adopting a Valley Girl way of speaking, as well as hairstyles, mannerisms, and styles of dress more in line with those of her white counterparts.[24] If you're not familiar with code-switching, two great representations of it can be found in the 2018 film *Sorry to Bother You*[25] and Season 1, Episode 3, of the TV show *Insecure*.[26]

As disturbing as it is that many people of colour have to change[27] who they authentically are to make white people more comfortable and avoid stereotype threat[28]—the risk of confirming negative racial stereotypes like being lazy or aggressive—studies sadly show that code-switching works. One study confirmed that when people of colour code-switch, they are perceived as more professional in the workplace,[29] thus reinforcing the idea that if they want to increase their odds of being hired, getting promoted, and reaching the coveted C-suite to raise their socioeconomic status, they have to act white.

With that said, there's a cost to doing this. Psychologically, the effort required to code-switch can "deplete cognitive resources,"[30] which could lead to increased stress, anxiety, and, eventually, burnout. But even if you don't have an unjust criminal record holding you back or you code-switch flawlessly, you can still experience discrimination because of your skin colour, which can have a big impact on your financial future.

DISCRIMINATION EVERY STEP OF THE WAY TO WEALTH

In *Seen, Heard & Paid: The New Work Rules for the Marginalized*, author Alan Henry shares an all-too-common story of a high school teacher telling him he'd never finish college and implying that it was because of his race.[31] To prove him wrong, Henry got two bachelor's degrees and a master's degree. But for students of colour without the same self-confidence and willpower as Henry, this act of racial discrimination could discourage them from closing the college race gap,[32] which has been steadily widening over the past decade.[33] As statistics show, having a degree is not only advantageous (it can increase your earning potential by 74% or more[34]) but also necessary (three in four jobs require one[35]). This "paper ceiling" is a big barrier for people of colour, preventing them from attaining higher lifetime wealth compared to their white counterparts.

Even when a student of colour does seek higher education, they may encounter other gatekeepers who impede their ambitions along the way. Akin Taiwo, associate professor at King's University College at Western University, almost couldn't pursue his master's degree in social work because of one racist professor who clutched the keys to the castle. Originally hailing from Nigeria, Taiwo arrived in Canada with one bachelor's degree and two master's degrees on his resumé. Wanting to switch careers, he applied to a master's degree program in social work and even made an appointment to visit the head of the department to put a face to a name and improve his chances by making his application more memorable. Unfortunately, it had the opposite effect. When he arrived at the office of the department head, who was an older white man, Taiwo recalls, "He just took a look at me and continued working." Taiwo tried to interrupt and offer to come back at a better time, but the department head said that wouldn't be necessary. What followed a few months later was a rejection letter in the mail.

Taiwo knew something seemed off, so he contacted the school about his application. After he connected with the department's secretary, a Black woman, incidentally, she was able to uncover that his application had never even been opened. The secretary encouraged Taiwo to submit a letter of appeal, but feeling dejected, he started thinking that maybe he should reconsider going back to school or pursue a different career entirely. Luckily, during this time, the department head responsible for his rejection left his post to teach at a different school. The gatekeeper was gone. With a new department head in place, his application was finally reviewed and he was admitted into the program right away. Although there's a happy ending to this story, just think of how many other students of colour were rejected by that one department head simply because of their non-European first and last name, their skin colour, or because they earned degrees from a foreign country.

But even after Henry and Taiwo achieved higher education, the discrimination didn't stop there. Taiwo shared stories with me of how he's heard students question his credentials under their breath when they think he can't hear them. Henry continued to face similar racial discrimination in the workplace in the form of microaggressions—veiled acts of racism that can be so subtle, they often appear invisible and are hard to prove to others.[36] Racially motivated microaggressions can take many forms, such as being left off email chains, excluded from meeting invitations "by accident," or passed over for promotions, negatively affecting the person's career trajectory.

Sometimes the aggressions aren't so micro. Toronto visual artist Melissa Falconer decided to take a big leap after university and become a full-time painter, largely because of the racism she experienced as a Black woman at every part-time job she held throughout high school and college. She told me, "My first ever job was working at a Tim Hortons, and I'd have older white men outright refuse to have me take their order. After that, I worked at Swiss Chalet, then Mr. Sub, and it was the same thing. Because of those negative experiences, I promised myself I'd never work for someone ever again." Although today Falconer's art business is thriving, no one should ever feel like self-employment is their only option to feel safe and avoid racism at work.

Besides school and the workplace, another important space that gets less attention but has proven to still be very discriminatory to people of colour is the financial industry—both as a place of work and as a place to obtain financial services. Let's first take a look at the financial industry as a whole, where traditionally, white people have been overrepresented. A 2018 report by McKinsey & Company[37] found that, from entry-level to C-suite roles, white people made up the majority of all positions. As a quick side-by-side, here's the difference in terms of race representation at each level of the financial services industry.

Position	White	People of Colour*
Entry-level	61%	39%
Manager	64%	36%
Senior manager or director	76%	24%
Vice president	81%	19%
Senior vice president	88%	12%
C-suite	90%	10%

* "People of colour" is a collective term used in this study to represent American Indian or Alaska Native, Black, Latinx, Native Hawaiian, Pacific Islander, and mixed-race people.

As you can see, the gap widens at the top with 80 to 90% of the executive roles—which have the most authority and influence to make change in the industry, not to mention the highest pay—occupied by white people. As we all know, the tone at the top influences everybody below it. But if the top is predominantly white, how can we expect anything but more of the same? Executives will simply continue to lean into their unconscious (or conscious) biases and recruit and hire more people who look and sound just like them, because they'll mistake racial familiarity for being the "right fit" for the company.[38]

Besides biased hiring practices, another reason for the diminishing representation of people of colour through this pipeline is the rates at which employees leave the industry and the rates at which they get promoted. What the numbers show is that people of colour who are on track to reach the top either choose to leave the industry early on, often due to micro- or macroaggressions in the workplace, or experience job stagnation, because promotion rates are higher for white employees.

Because of this racial imbalance inside the industry, there's discrimination on the client side, too. In a report conducted by Edelman,[39] researchers found that the financial services sector ranked last in terms of addressing racism compared to other industries. Moreover, non-white survey respondents also reported experiencing discrimination across all types of financial services, such as mortgages, auto lending, banking, credit cards, asset management, and insurance, with some participants saying they have needed to code-switch to get better service, were given higher interest rates on loans or were made to pay higher fees compared to white clients, were asked to provide more proof of employment than the norm, or were denied service altogether.[40]

For some real-life examples, in April 2022, a class-action lawsuit was filed against Wells Fargo for discriminatory mortgage policies and lending practices. The court found that Wells Fargo approved more white mortgage applicants compared to Black applicants, despite them having equivalent creditworthiness, and Black borrowers with high credit scores were given interest rates that were 0.11% higher than the rates white borrowers received.[41] Similarly, Los Angeles–based City National Bank was forced to pay $31 million in 2023—the largest redlining settlement in history—for "refusing to underwrite mortgages in predominantly Black and Latino communities."[42] In Canada, there is less publicly available data showing mortgage discrimination, as made evident in the 2002 report "Housing Discrimination in Canada: The State of Knowledge."[43] However, it very much exists and is one of the biggest financial barriers for people of colour, since home ownership has historically been a key vehicle for long-term wealth creation.

The last issue I want to touch on is the biases and racism that banks exhibit when dealing with business owners of colour. As we saw with artist Melissa Falconer, oftentimes the safest space to earn a living away from racism is one that you create yourself and can control. However, one important element of starting a business is getting financing through a loan or line of credit, and as you may guess, people of colour are more often refused credit, given higher borrowing rates, and faced with worse customer service than white people. In a piece for the CBC, Black business owner Tanya Reddick was profiled, and she shared how she tries to conduct all her business banking on the phone instead of in person, because "she gets better customer service when the representative on the other end thinks she's white."[44] Moreover, data from the Federal Reserve System showed that businesses "by people of color were half as likely as white-owned [businesses] to report that they received all the traditional financing they sought," even when they proved to have high credit scores.[45]

Hearing these stories and reading these data points makes it clear that even if you're poor and white, you still have more advantages inside your invisible weightless knapsack than someone with more money in the bank with a different skin colour. Race is one of the biggest barriers to wealth, and so is being a woman.

The Plight of Women

I was pretty sheltered growing up when it came to gender discrimination. Besides living in a household of mainly women, with my mom and two sisters, I had a very special dad. He was an artist who taught me how to sketch with charcoal and bake muffins when I was younger (he was a baker's son, after all). He made me feel like I could be anything I wanted to be as long as I worked hard enough. So, when I decided to pursue a degree in film, I wasn't concerned that the film industry is a male-dominated field. Instead, I felt confident that things would soon change and I shouldn't let mere demographics stop me from following my passion.

Once I entered film school, I continued to live in a protective bubble of liberalism and gender neutrality. Even though my program was made up of fewer than 40 students, 85% of whom were male, I can't remember a space since in which I felt so safe to be authentically me. I wasn't judged by my gender, only by my art. But that all changed when I got my first taste of the real world.

CHOOSING A SAFE WORKPLACE ISN'T WITHOUT ITS PRICE

My uncle is an assistant director in the film and TV industry in Vancouver, and knowing that I was about to graduate soon, he invited me to be a production assistant on a TV movie he was working on so I could see what the industry was really like (another example of privilege). And I sure did.

As one of the only women crew members and only 22 years old, not only did I feel significantly younger than everyone around me, but for the first time in a work environment, I felt vulnerable. At the end of my shift, as I was heading to my car to drive home, some male crew members in one of the equipment trucks waved me over to chat. They asked me if I was new, and I shared that my uncle had just gotten me the job. They then invited me to join them in the back of their truck to have a drink to celebrate a hard day's work. I almost said yes. I was so used to the safety I felt with my male classmates, my defences were down and I didn't immediately register the danger signs all around me. I didn't know these men, their names, or whether my uncle could vouch for them. They were all at least 10 to 20 years older than I was. And they invited a young, unworldly college student into their van to drink alcohol with them. After a split second, I had a premonition of what would happen if I stayed, got drunk, didn't know where I was or how to contact my uncle, and wasn't sober enough to drive myself home. It chilled me to the bone. Just in case you're thinking, *Come on, they could have been totally harmless,* all I can say is that women's intuition is a real thing, and you can check out Gavin de Becker's book *The Gift of Fear* to see what I mean.

So, I politely made an excuse as to why I couldn't stay, drove home with my hands shaking at the wheel, and decided from that moment on I could never go back. Being on a film set did not feel safe to me, and I couldn't imagine having my defences up like that for the rest of my career. That's the real reason why I never pursued a career in film after getting my degree. I've never told anyone that story before. Instead, I told a different story about how I didn't want to work 15-hour days in the cold rain. But the truth is, I knew that if I continued down that path, I'd be putting myself in harm's way.

That was obviously a very personal experience, and I'm not saying that women should avoid working in the film industry because it isn't a safe space. In fact, I know a number of women who graduated from my program and went on to have very successful careers in film, and it makes me so proud to see more female representation behind the lens so we can have more accurate depictions of women on screen. With that said, my experience isn't unique. A survey conducted by *USA Today* found that 94% of women "have experienced some form of sexual harassment or assault during their careers in Hollywood."[46]

The reason I'm sharing my story is to highlight a factor that doesn't often get brought up in discussions of the gender pay gap. Just as many people of colour choose careers based on whether they are safe spaces from racism, many women choose careers based on whether they are safe spaces from sexual predators and harassment. This notion is supported by research Catalyst did that found that women are more likely to experience sexual harassment in male-dominated industries, with 47% of women reporting they've experienced inappropriate sexual behaviour when working in trades, transportation, equipment operations, and other related occupations. These factors could contribute to why only 5% of women work in trades in Canada and only 6.5% of women work in male-dominated industries in the U.S.[47] For a woman, it's safer to work in a female-dominated industry, because the odds are that you won't have to exert as much or any energy fearing or evading unwanted harassment and can just focus on the job at hand.

But there's always a cost to choosing safety. As one report explained, "female-dominated occupations pay less than male-dominated occupations. The average median weekly pay of all workers (male and female) in occupations with more than 50% female workers ($827) is about 15% lower than the average median weekly pay for all workers in occupations with more than 50% male workers ($974)."[48] When I made the switch from film to a career in marketing, I had no idea I'd be potentially giving up a higher future income. After working various jobs over the course of seven years surrounded by female co-workers and bosses, it wasn't until I made the switch to the male-dominated field of finance that I saw my income skyrocket, allowing me to reach financial milestones that would have taken me years if I'd stayed where I was.

With that said, I should point out that women choosing female-dominated fields for safety isn't the only reason for the gender pay gap, which stood at 93 cents on the dollar for Asian women, 83 cents for white women, 70 cents for Black women, and 65 cents for Hispanic women as of 2022.[49] As one study found, when women in large numbers moved to jobs that were traditionally male, "those jobs began paying less even after controlling for education, work experience, skills, race and geography [because] employers placed a lower value on work done by women." When women started becoming biologists, wages fell by 18%. When they started becoming designers, wages fell by 34%.[50] Another research paper corroborated this by finding evidence that "the presence of women in an occupation results in declines in average wages for both men and women in that occupation."[51] In contrast, when men started taking traditionally female roles, like computer programming, which was once considered a "menial role done by women," the job began paying more and gained prestige.[52]

ARE YOU SURE YOU'RE IN THE RIGHT PLACE?

Let me be clear: women in general have made strides in many ways, and many women have been able to advance and make strides in male-dominated fields. When I got my first post-grad job as a sales assistant, my boss, Donna, not only held her own in a department of male sales executives who would often exclude her or try to steal her clients, but eventually rose through the ranks to become the sales director before starting her own company. She was a force of nature and inspired me to never back down in the face of gender discrimination. Nevertheless, I also learned that no matter how strong you are, barriers for women in the workplace still very much exist.

For me, the transition from being surrounded by women in the workplace to often being the only woman in the room wasn't an easy one. Even though I now work for myself from home, it's when I venture out to speak at an event or network with industry professionals that I remember what I gave up by switching careers. Like many women, I've struggled with imposter syndrome for most of my adult life. Looking back at the confident girl I used to be growing up, I can say without a doubt that imposter syndrome has been one of my biggest wealth-killers, holding me back from asking for more money from employers and clients, taking risks in my career, and taking control of my investments.

Although there were glimmers of the syndrome in university and my early career, it began to intensify after I'd been blogging for a few years. At the start, my blog was my private escape from the stresses of my nine-to-five, while filling a creative void left after saying goodbye to filmmaking. What I wasn't prepared for was opening myself up to sexist comments, criticism, and judgment for years to come.

I started to feel as if no matter what I did, it was never good enough compared to my male counterparts, who were getting lots of praise and adoration for the content they were creating. Even though we had equivalent education and experience, I faced substantially more criticism, usually more personal in nature, too. To give you an idea of what I mean, just check out some of my podcast reviews. Although there are more positive reviews than negative, it's hard to forget the nasty ones saying things like I sound like a little girl interviewing her dad when speaking with male guests, I speak too much, I speak too fast, I'm not professional or credible enough to listen to. And then there are the more explicit ones (which I try to get taken down) calling me names and using abusive language. I've even experienced this criticism in person, which is as awful as you can imagine. After finishing a 45-minute presentation on the foundations of investing several years ago, one of the first audience questions I got during the Q & A afterwards was "Why should we listen to you?" That one is burned in my brain for eternity, let me tell you. So, it's no surprise why this feeling of being a fraud in the face of people pointing their fingers at me, yelling, "You don't belong here!" persists to this day.

Imposter syndrome was something I internalized as a "me" problem and thought I'd have to live with for the rest of my life. Then I read a part in Leiba's book that made me pause. She'd experienced imposter syndrome, too, but it usually reared its head only when she was in white spaces. Over time, she realized that the feeling of not being good enough wasn't something within herself, which is often what imposter syndrome is described as—an internal belief that you're undeserving of your achievements despite your qualifications. Instead, maybe it was something *outside* herself.

You don't just start feeling like an imposter out of nowhere. Someone or something makes you feel that way. In Leiba's case, it was spurred on by being the only Black woman in the room and being judged by her skin colour and all the stereotypes and false narratives attached to it. For me, and many other women, it gets triggered by being the only woman in the room and being judged by my gender.

When you think about it, it makes a lot of sense why imposter syndrome is so prevalent among women (although other genders can experience it, too). Up until recent history, we weren't allowed to share many of the same spaces as men, were confined to the home, and were barred in many ways from building a career or achieving any form of financial independence. For example, you may have never heard the term *coverture* before, but it was a British law that spilled over to Britain's American and Canadian colonies when they were being established that made women give up any legal rights to enter contracts, own real property, or own or work in a business once they got married. Laws based on this precedent continued until the 1950s.[53] That's only 75 years ago! Not only that, but there were numerous marriage bars[54] that existed for many occupations, such as teachers, nurses, and secretaries from the early 20th century to the mid-1950s, that prevented women from working after they got married. In 1921, for example, married women were restricted from being hired to public service in Canada, and women who already held a permanent position in public service were forced to resign if they decided to get married. This restriction wasn't abolished until 1955.[55]

But women weren't just restricted in their careers; they were also prohibited from holding on to their own money. It wasn't until 1964[56] that women in Canada were allowed to open up a bank account without their husband's signature, and not until the Equal Credit Opportunity Act was passed in 1974 that women were allowed to "open bank accounts, apply for credit and commit to a mortgage without needing a male co-signer" in the U.S.[57]

Women feel like imposters in their careers and, in turn, avoid taking risks or opportunities to reach the next level because for centuries, women weren't even allowed to have long-term careers. Women avoid working in male-dominated fields, which could lead to earning higher incomes, because they are made to feel as if they shouldn't be there and it isn't safe. Women question their financial skills and put off learning how to invest or buy property because it's only been in the last few decades that they've had any financial autonomy whatsoever. Imposter syndrome isn't a "me" or "you" problem. It's a natural response to the oppression women have had to endure for hundreds of years. And it's a major wealth-killer for women. So is being a mother.

THE MOTHERHOOD PENALTY

Like many women, I was asked when I was going to start having kids right after my wedding. I was 26 and had zero desire to start a family. *Maybe when I turn 30 I'll change my mind*, I thought. Then I turned 30, then 35, and at 38 I can say I'm 99% sure having kids is not in my future. It seems ridiculous when you think about it, but being a woman in her 30s who is vocal about not wanting kids is still considered controversial in some circles today. But I'm of the belief that I get to decide what my life looks like, not anyone else.

I'd be lying if I said that money wasn't one of the many factors that influenced my decision not to have children. According to Statistics Canada, raising one child until they are 17 could cost a middle-income two-parent household $375,500.[58] Do you know how many trips around the world my husband and I could go on for that kind of money? Or we could retire years earlier. That figure from Statistics Canada only includes things like food, clothing, housing, health care, child care, education, and transportation. It doesn't factor in the financial setbacks mothers experience when going on maternity leave and exiting the workforce, even if temporarily.

Eligible mothers can take up to 15 weeks of paid maternity leave, plus up to 35 weeks for standard or 61 weeks for extended paternity leave in Canada. Maternity leave is available only to people who are pregnant or have recently given birth (it can't be shared between parents), whereas paternity leave can be used on top of maternity leave, is available to parents of a newborn or newly adopted child, and can be shared between parents.[59]*

Since these taxable benefits are paid through Employment Insurance (EI), as of 2024, you can take home 55% of your average insurable earnings up to a maximum of $668 a week for maternity leave, then 55% of your earnings up to $668 a week for standard paternity leave or 33% of your earnings up to $401 a week for extended paternity leave (though some employers provide a top-up).

Let's say you're a consultant who normally earns $80,000 a year and qualifies for the maximum amount of benefits. If you were to take your 15 weeks of maternity leave plus 35 weeks of standard paternity leave, totalling 50 weeks (almost a full year), you'd be bringing in only $33,400. That means you'd be taking home only 41.75% of your regular income (50 weeks of paid and 2 weeks of unpaid leave) before any potential top-ups provided by your employer. To frame it differently, you'd be missing out on $46,600 by going on leave to have a child. That's a lot of money. Not only that, just think if you had two to four children. You could be sacrificing between $93,200 and $186,400 in lost wages.

---

* If you share paternity leave with your partner, you can share up to 40 weeks for standard parental leave or 69 weeks for extended leave. However, one parent cannot receive more than 35 weeks of standard benefits or 61 weeks of extended benefits.

If you live in the U.S., unfortunately, there's no paid maternity leave unless your state or employer offers some form of benefits. Otherwise, the only thing you're eligible for thanks to the Family and Medical Leave Act (FMLA) is 12 weeks of unpaid leave. Using the same example, if you were to take 12 weeks off from your $80,000-a-year job, you'd be losing $18,461.54 in wages to take that time off work. And then you're going to have to pay for child care when you return to work. That's some substantial money that could have gone toward the mortgage to build equity, been invested to compound over time, or just helped with the astronomical cost of raising children today.

But the loss in wages isn't the only consequence of going on maternity leave. Simply being absent from the workplace can severely stall your career growth, too. Studies have shown that office decision-makers consider women who take maternity leaves of 12 months or more as being less career-driven and committed to their jobs. Because of this bias, women who take paid leave may be passed over for promotions and career advancement opportunities in favour of men or childless women.[60] And when they do return to the workforce, they are encouraged more often than men to "take accommodations, such as going part-time and shifting to internally facing roles" even though by doing so, they may be stigmatized and see their careers derailed.[61]

You may be wondering why, if this is the case, couples don't just split paternity leave so mothers can go back to work sooner, aside from their desire to be home with their child in the early months. The "State of the World's Fathers 2019 Report"[62] found that 40% of fathers in Canada took zero time off work when their child was born. And since there's no mandated paternity leave in the U.S., less than 0.1% of fathers there took any time off. Why such a reluctance to balance out paternity leave with their partners? Unsurprisingly, it comes down to money. Survey respondents' rationale for these numbers was that because men typically earn higher salaries, it makes more financial sense for the women to stay home, to reduce the family's overall loss in income.[63]

Although this does make financial sense, it also continues to perpetuate the gender pay gap. How can women ever hope to catch up to men's incomes if they are always the ones who have to stay behind when having children? Especially when recent research has found that when men take paternity leave, they either experience no negative effects[64] to their career or may even experience positive effects by unlocking a "family provider premium"[65] by being perceived as more likeable and overall more employable than women who are mothers. The double standard is clear as day: When women have children, their careers and financial prospects suffer. When men have children, it actually helps them thrive.

This is why economist Claudia Goldin, who won the 2023 Nobel Prize for her research on the gender pay gap, said, "We're never going to have gender equality until we also have couple equity." This should look like evenly shared paternity leave, even if it means a loss of income, and evenly shared household responsibilities, since women "have less time to dedicate to their careers" because they are often tasked with more child care and household chores than men.[66]

With all of this information, you may think that choosing to be childless like me means that you can avoid the motherhood penalty and end up in a better financial situation for it. Although yes, you won't have to worry about the cost of raising children or the loss in wages from being on maternity and paternity leave, that doesn't mean you won't be affected by the motherhood penalty in some way.

As evidenced by Pew Research,[67] when controlling for education level, mothers earn about the same wages as women without children, whereas both groups earn less than fathers. This could be for a number of reasons, such as women's output being valued less than men's, whether they're a mother or not. But it could also be due to employers discounting women's wages in anticipation of them going on leave or exiting the workforce in the future. Just because a woman is childless today doesn't mean she won't have children or become the default caretaker for her elderly parents later on. These possibilities could undermine the perception of women's potential within a company, making the employer less likely to invest in her through either higher wages or advancement opportunities.

The Cost of Ableism

I experienced debilitating back pain for the second time in my life while writing this chapter. The first time it happened, I was in my early 30s and discovered it was because my office chair had zero back support and my old mattress desperately needed an upgrade—an easy fix. This time, in my late 30s, the only solution was to see a physiotherapist after no amount of walking, yoga, ice packs, or Robaxacet would help relieve the excruciating pain. At the peak, it was literally all I could focus on, making it hard to sleep, work, or get into a creative headspace to keep writing. I remember thinking to myself, *How does anybody live like this and get anything done?* I still don't have an answer for that. And 20%[68] of adults live with chronic pain and go to work every day.

The last barrier we're going to cover is how living with pain or a disability can make it almost impossible to reach the same financial heights as those without it because doing just about anything is that much harder. Yet almost no one is talking about it. I've read countless personal finance books at this point, and the one thing they all seem to have in common is that their advice is clearly meant for the non-disabled. Their advice is built on the assumption that you don't have any physical or mental barriers, and thus the only thing stopping you from improving your finances is your lack of financial literacy, an action plan, and self-motivation. But as you know by now, we don't live in a perfect world, so advice that assumes we do isn't that helpful for those of us living in reality.

VISIBLE DISABILITIES

So, what does the real world look like? Well, 22%[69] of Canadians (6.2 million) and 27% of Americans (61 million)[70] have one or more physical, sensory, cognitive, or mental health–related disabilities for starters. Because of this, activities like working a full-time job, keeping up with bills, financial decision-making, and saving for the future are much harder to do, which is why statistics show that people with disabilities are more likely to be under- or unemployed and more likely to live in poverty, with women being disproportionately affected.[71]

But it's not just the actual disabilities that make things harder. It's also how employers unfairly discriminate against people living with them. For example, the employment rate for Canadians with disabilities is 49% compared to 79% for those non-disabled. In the U.S., those numbers are 35% compared to 76%.[72] These gaps are largely because employers tend to lean into their biases and choose not to hire people with disabilities for fear of legal liability and concerns over the costs for accommodation, the reduction in productivity, and the negative impact on their workplace culture.[73] But even when they do hire employees with disabilities, employers often practise what's called "occupational segregation," a form of discrimination in which they cluster people with disabilities into certain low-skill, low-wage jobs with limited or no benefits.[74]

So, it's hard for people with disabilities to find employment, and even when they do, chances are they'll still wind up earning less than someone without a disability. Luckily, there are plenty of government-funded disability support programs to bridge the pay gap, right? Not exactly. Most disability programs barely make a dent and have an inordinate number of restrictions to eligibility. In my home province of Ontario, for example, in 2023, the maximum amount you could get from the Ontario Disability Support Program was $1,308 a month.[75] This amount is meant to help you cover your basic needs and shelter costs. Considering the average cost of rent in Ontario was $2,496 a month as of September 2023,[76] that money sure isn't going to go far. Not to mention that if you are earning money, after the first $1,000 a month, support payments are clawed back by 75% of every dollar. So, if you want and need to receive the full benefits, you're capped at a total income of $2,308, which is *still* below the average rent. On top of that, you become ineligible for benefits if you have more than $40,000 in assets, such as having savings or investments, and can have your benefits suspended until you get back under the threshold.

In other words, you won't get enough support to pay for a roof over your head, and if you find work, you'll have to carefully limit your earnings; otherwise, you're penalized by having your benefits reduced or taken away completely. Moreover, if you try to save any money you receive or earn, you get penalized again if you accrue "too much" wealth. As disability advocate Andrew Pulrang so aptly put it, "limits on monthly earning and saving to maintain eligibility for benefits . . . [make it so millions] of disabled people exist in a vast gray area between total financial self-sufficiency and complete reliance on benefits. . . . It's a poverty trap."[77]

INVISIBLE DISABILITIES

Not all disabilities are the same. Some are more visible than others, which is why most employers underestimate how many disabled employees they actually have. Many people choose not to disclose their disabilities to avoid facing discrimination, losing out on opportunities, or having their job terminated. Employers may never find out if their employees have an invisible disability, such as mental illness, so it may not directly block a stable income. Five million Canadians have a mood, anxiety, or substance use disorder[78] and one in every eight people globally (970 million) live with a mental illness, many of which go undetected by the naked eye. Nevertheless, these disorders can still have a big negative impact on people's finances.

When I interviewed Gabe Dunn, podcast host and author of *Bad with Money*, they shared how it wasn't until their bipolar diagnosis that they started to better understand why they had made some not-so-good financial decisions in the past. For example, they had a habit during certain manic episodes of selling all of their possessions or booking a spontaneous trip to Paris without thinking about the financial consequences, like how they would buy back everything they'd sold or pay off their maxed-out credit card.

Similarly, Ellyce Fulmore, a financial content creator and author of *Keeping Finance Personal*, explained how her ADHD diagnosis helped her determine why, despite the piles of instructional personal finance books she'd read, she still struggled with impulse spending and sticking to a budget. She said, "Once I got diagnosed with ADHD, I started to learn more about how it affects people and put the puzzle pieces together to understand that my brain just thinks differently and thus needs different systems and different motivation than neurotypical people. Making those tweaks and changing how I approached my finances was how I was finally able to achieve the most success with my financial stability."

If you're one of the millions of adults who suffer from depression or anxiety (or both), then you likely know first-hand how much money and mental health are intrinsically linked. According to a study by the Money and Mental Health Policy Institute,[79] 46% of people in debt have a mental health issue and 86% of survey respondents said their financial situation worsened their mental health problems and led to increased stress and anxiety. Similarly, 18% of people with mental health issues fall into debt, with 72% of respondents saying their mental health issues worsened their financial situation. It's basically the worst kind of never-ending cycle, in which your mental health problems make it harder to earn and manage your money, leading you into financial difficulty, which exacerbates your mental health issues, and so on.

A Starting Point

I'll be honest: this was one of the hardest chapters for me to write because I know how important these issues are, and I knew that I wouldn't be able to fully address every type of financial barrier or form of discrimination that people experience in their lives every single day. But my hope is that this discussion can be a great starting point for all of us to view money and people's different financial situations with more empathy and understanding—including our own. With that said, despite all of the barriers we've discussed up until now, there is a way to break through to the other side. There is a path forward for you to get on a better financial footing, which is what we'll explore next.

Takeaways

- Privilege can take many forms, and those with it can still experience other disadvantages.

- Life isn't fair, but one step to make things more equitable is for us to start admitting our privilege when we have it.

- Do an inventory of all the privileges you had growing up that have had an impact on your career and finances up until now. Acknowledging the advantages you have had doesn't diminish hardship or barriers you have faced. But it is an act of community that will help you become more self-aware and empathetic to those who haven't had those same advantages.

- People of colour face racial discrimination in school, the workplace, and at the bank, which contributes significantly to the increasing racial wealth gap.

- We haven't broken the glass ceiling and gender-equity is still years away, so it's important to understand some of the financial barriers still in place that prevent true pay parity.

- Personal finance education has historically been ableist, and having a disability, invisible or not, has statistically meant earning lower wages with little governmental support. We all need to be more aware of these barriers so we can make change for everyone in the future.

PART IV

The Road to Recovery: How to Heal, Pivot, & Design a Financially Fulfilled Life

8.
A Path Forward

You may not control all the events that happen to you,
but you can decide not to be reduced by them.
—Maya Angelou

It's funny how life can imitate art sometimes, isn't it? When I first sent my book proposal to my publisher, it was a very different book than the one you're reading now, let me tell you. There was only one line briefly mentioning the impact that trauma and systemic injustice have on our finances, but to my surprise, that one line was what stuck out the most. I was subsequently asked to pitch a new proposal for a book exploring those topics in-depth and, well, here we are.

When I was writing that second proposal, I was definitely leaning into the mantra "fake it till you make it," because I felt well outside my wheelhouse. What could I say about trauma when I thought I had none? How could I speak to the financial hurdles that marginalized people face every day when I come from a place of privilege? How could I talk about unpacking your feelings when I couldn't even bring myself to cry at my grandparents' funerals and hated my own vulnerability? How could I write a book about discovering why almost all of us have a complicated relationship with money when I was terrified to uncover my own, despite my years of writing about and working in personal finance? Well, it's because of those years of working with clients and talking with people about their struggles with money that I recognized the need for this book that up until now didn't exist on bookshelves. Nevertheless, the prospect of putting it all out there and diving deep was daunting.

The truth was that although I'd been seeing a therapist for a number of years at that point, I withheld a lot because I was ashamed of some of the things that caused me pain, the biggest one being that, deep down, I was lonely. From the outside looking in, it sure didn't look that way. After all, I have a loving family, a wonderful husband, and people I call friends from my hometown of Vancouver, my new home in Toronto, and all over the world, thanks to the internet. Heck, I've even been part of the same book club for over a decade. How could I possibly be lonely?

All I can say is something shifted inside me when I moved to Toronto in 2013. It's true what they say about it being hard to make friends as an adult, but for me, it was especially so. After a number of failed friendships that left me hurt and questioning my own personal worth, I just didn't have it in me to be as open or trusting as I used to be. So, I made the subconscious decision to never go that deep with friends in the future. Whatever new friendships I made or old ones I kept, I'd have my armour securely fastened. This meant keeping each friend at arm's length, limiting what I'd share about myself for fear of it being weaponized against me, and playing it "cool" by never being the first one to suggest plans or send a text, to avoid coming off as needy.

If the feeling of loneliness ever crept back in, I always had the perfect solution to get rid of it: keep busy. I'd start a new project, make plans for the future, or set a new lofty goal to tack onto my vision board. I'd fill every possible empty moment with work so I never had time to feel—or heal.

Then I caught COVID right before Christmas in 2022, and all my armour fell apart. Because my husband hadn't caught the virus yet, we quarantined in different rooms until I tested negative so he wouldn't get sick. This meant a lot of time alone with my thoughts, because apparently, there *is* a limit to how much Netflix you can watch. For the first time in years, I had to sit still and take a good look at myself—and I didn't like the person I saw. She was hard, judgmental, and mistrustful, and lived a life hyperfocused on proving others wrong and getting noticed. There was very little space for joy or peace, or simply doing things for any reason other than being productive or reaching a new milestone. But as I saw 40 on the horizon, I realized I didn't want to bring that person with me into the next decade. I wanted to like myself again, just as I did when I was a kid full of hope and magic. I wanted to try out *real* self-care, not just throw on a face mask in the bath and call it a day. I wanted to let out a cry I'd been holding in for the past 10 years.

Writing this book pushed me to finally open up those wounds I'd been putting Band-Aids on for so long. I didn't just need to heal for myself; I needed to heal for my clients and for you to prove that you can get to the other side, too. If, like me, the weight of your unhealed trauma and hurt has been holding you back from living your most authentic life and adopting a healthier relationship with money, it's not too late. I was 36 when I started doing the work, and although I wish I'd started sooner, as the saying goes, the second-best time is now.

With that said, although I'm going to share different methods for how you can heal in this chapter, just know that there is no such thing as a one-and-done solution. Healing is a process and takes time. You have to dig into the dark places to heal them, and no one is saying that's easy. To move forward with your personal and financial life, unburdened and healed, it's a long road and there are going to be moments when you'll want to quit. And you might quit. You may go to one or two therapy sessions and not go back for years, thinking, *Yup, that did the trick* or *What a waste of money*. But what you'll eventually realize is that a few sessions likely didn't fix everything, and it wasn't a waste of money. Maybe you just weren't ready and needed to pump the brakes until you were. Maybe you need to find the right professional to work with. Or maybe you haven't tried the form of treatment yet that will finally lead to your breakthrough.

Because Getting Help Isn't Cheap

Before diving in, I need to address the elephant in the room. It's one thing to admit, "I need help," but it's quite another to afford it. As several studies have found, the biggest barrier to accessing mental health care is affordability.[1, 2, 3, 4] Even if you do have mental health benefits, whether they are through work or through a private health care plan, they can still have their limitations. Most plans typically don't cover the entire cost, or they restrict the number of sessions you can have within a calendar year.

Which leads to an interesting question: What comes first? Sorting out your finances so you can afford mental health care, or getting mental health care so you can sort out your finances? I used to think it was the former, but what the research and personal stories in this book have shown is that it's actually the latter. Here's the thing: You can learn how to budget, get out of debt, and invest for your future fairly easily these days. There are hundreds of books you can read and thousands of websites, podcasts, and YouTube channels you can learn from for free. But it's likely you've already tried that, which has brought you to this book so you can figure out "Why is nothing I've learned working on me?" If that's the case, it's time to take a different approach. If affordability is what's in your way, the approach should be to take advantage of the mental health resources that are within your reach right now, and at the same time, take small steps to improve your finances so you can eventually get to a place where you can afford to pay your own way with ease.

FREE OR LOW-COST MENTAL HEALTH RESOURCES

So, what kinds of resources are out there? The good news is that there are plenty of free or low-cost resources you can use if you don't have workplace benefits, you're in between jobs, or you can't yet afford to subscribe to a private health care plan or pay out of pocket. Here is a list of some of the resources available in Canada, the United States, and globally for you to consider.

Canada

- mental health support and crisis lines by province or territory (canada.ca/en/public-health/services/mental-health-services/mental-health-get-help.html)
- Suicide Crisis Helpline (988.ca)
- eMentalHealth.ca mental health database (ementalhealth.ca)
- Hope for Wellness (hopeforwellness.ca)

- Togetherall (togetherall.com)
- MindShift CBT (anxietycanada.com/resources/mindshift-cbt)
- Healthy Minds (hminnovations.org/meditation-app)
- BounceBack (cmha.ca/bounce-back)
- TELUS Health MyCare App (telus.com/en/health/my-care)
- Maple (getmaple.ca)
- MindBeacon (mindbeacon.com)

United States

- Therapy Aid (therapyaid.org)
- E-Therapy Cafe (e-therapycafe.com)
- National Alliance on Mental Illness (nami.org)
- Mental Health America (mhanational.org)
- The National Association of Free and Charitable Clinics (nafc-clinics.org)
- WeAreMore (wearemore.life)
- Supportiv (supportiv.com)

Global

- Online-Therapy.com (online-therapy.com)
- Talkspace (talkspace.com)
- Bliss Free Online Therapy for Depression (cimhs.com/bliss-free-online-therapy-for-depression.html)
- 7 Cups (7cups.com)
- Open Path Collective (openpathcollective.org)

FREE WAYS TO KEEP CALM TO CARRY ON

You can learn how to use some free tools to help with your emotional regulation. Triggers that push you into fight or flight (sympathetic) or freeze or fawn (dorsal vagal) can pop out anywhere, and we can't completely avoid them. Staying at home with the blinds closed and the internet disconnected is not a good long-term strategy and would lead to new problems anyway. So, what are some ways that you can teach yourself to return to a place of safety and connection (ventral vagal) so you won't resort to any harmful money behaviours to soothe yourself?

I already discussed some grounding techniques in Chapter 4 that can come in handy, but it's important to understand other ways to self-regulate and co-regulate. Self-regulating means managing your own emotional state by using a number of different practices, such as self-compassion (e.g., positive self-talk, mindfulness) or self-containment through self-holding exercises like placing one hand under your left arm on the side of your heart and the other wrapped around your right shoulder (it will look like you're hugging yourself).[5] But if you've got a partner, close family members, or even a pet, you can use them to co-regulate, which means using their calm energy to calm yourself down. My husband and I do this all the time when one of us is having a bad day or feeling anxious about something. We hug each other or soothe the other with comforting words like "Everything's going to be okay," or "It'll get better." Or we use no words at all and just offer an empathetic ear. I know these suggestions sound simple, but hey, they work!

Another simple technique I've found to be incredibly effective is called the physiological sigh.[6] You inhale through your nose to 100%, pause, inhale again to get to 110% (which sounds impossible, but it's not), then exhale slowly through your mouth. This particular technique has gained popularity over the years thanks to neuroscientist Andrew Huberman's podcast the *Huberman Lab* as well as his research that found that the physiological sigh is more effective for emotional regulation than other techniques like box breathing or even mindfulness meditation.[7]

Ultimately, the goal of doing any of these practices is to find your anchor back into the ventral vagal, and as Deb Dana shares in her book *Anchored*, you can also do this by finding what she calls glimmers. Because we humans have a natural propensity for seeing only the negative, Dana says, "We have to actively look for, take notice of, and keep track of these [positive] moments, or micro-moments, of safety and connection that are our glimmers."[8] And what's really exciting is that the more we look for glimmers, the more frequently we'll see them, making emotional regulation easier as we practise. I envision glimmers to be like the personal totems that the characters in the movie *Inception* had in their dream worlds so they could always find their way back to reality. For Leonardo DiCaprio's character, Cobb, the totem was a spinning top. The glimmers that help me are the fluffy squirrels that run rampant in my neighbourhood, the sight of mountains or big bodies of water, and the smells of lemongrass, lavender, and coffee. Start taking note of some of your glimmers, which you can turn to when you need a quick path back to your happy place.

Finally, if you have a smartwatch that tracks your heart rate, check it before you make any type of purchase or financial decision. It's a great tool to use if you have trouble detecting whether you're emotionally dysregulated or not. As psychologist John Gottman discovered in his research on managing conflict in relationships, if your heart rate goes above 100 beats per minute, you've likely entered fight or flight mode, or as he calls it, emotional and physiological flooding.[9] When you're in that state, logic gets thrown out the window and you're running on pure adrenalin. So, try out some of the calming exercises we just went through to get your heart rate back down so you can think clearly once again.

There are so many other techniques and exercises out there besides the ones I've just shared, such as journaling, meditation, and physical activity, just to name a few, but something you'll soon discover is that some will work for you and some won't, or some will work in certain contexts and not in others. That's why it's important to try one, stick with it for a bit, and if you're not getting any results, try something else. As an example, for the life of me I just can't meditate. But that physiological sigh has come in very handy over the past year.

Setting Up Your Financial Foundation

Once you've started to heal, you'll not only feel more hopeful about the future, but you'll be in an all-around better headspace to tackle some small issues in your financial life that previously seemed impossible.

When you open yourself up to receiving help, whether it be from a support group, helpline, or professional, you'll start to see things with a very different perspective and recognize you're not alone in this world, people do care about you, and you're stronger and more resilient than you think.

I've got to admit that I only started making real progress with my own mental health when I was in a better financial position. When I wasn't worrying about how to stretch my next paycheque to pay all my bills and have money left over for my barely-there emergency fund, my psychological burdens became less amplified. If we think back to Maslow's hierarchy of needs, this makes a lot of sense. That's why I recommend starting with free or low-cost mental health alternatives first to get the ball rolling, then trying to undertake a few key tasks that will help you lay a more solid financial foundation.

MAKE A SPENDING PLAN

The cornerstone of that foundation is a spending plan. I'm not going to use the word *budget* because it can be triggering if you've tried sticking to one a million times before with no success. I prefer to call it a spending plan, since that's what it really is—a plan for how you'd like to spend your money. Feel free to come up with your own name for it that makes you feel excited and hopeful for the future, not anxious or boxed in.

Although there are literally thousands of templates online you can choose from, a spending plan is actually very simple in nature. The first fully functioning one I ever developed was an Excel spreadsheet that had only three tabs: the plan, the spending tracker, and the net worth tracker. I wanted one tab to outline what I wanted to happen with my money, one tab to show me what I was actually doing with my money, and one tab to tell me what my progress was over time—that's it. Although over the years I've added some charts and a spouse and taken self-employment into account, I've been using the same spreadsheet for close to a decade and, no exaggeration, it has been the biggest game-changer in my financial life and the lives of thousands of others who've downloaded it from my website.

Instead of simply describing it to you, let me show you what it looks like. Let's pretend you're a single employee who works as a marketing coordinator in Toronto, Ontario.

THE PLAN

To start, write out your current job title, your income type (e.g., salaried or hourly), and how frequently you get paid. This is so when you make a new plan at the start of each year, you'll have a record of what stage you were at in your life and career. It may not sound important now, but cut to 5, 10, or 20 years later, and you'll be glad you saved your old spending plans to see the proof of what you were able to accomplish over time. I've been keeping mine from the past eight years, and they've been a big source of motivation for me to keep going.

Job Title	Income Type	Payment Frequency
Marketing Coordinator	Salaried	Bi-weekly

Next, include how much you make in a year before income taxes and other deductions are taken off your pay (gross income) and then how much you actually take home after taxes and other deductions (net income). Some of those other deductions could be these:

- employee benefits (health plan or insurance premiums)
- Canada Pension Plan (CPP) or Quebec Pension Plan (QPP) contributions, or Social Security contributions
- Employment Insurance (EI) contributions
- pension plan, group RRSP, or 401k contributions
- union dues

All of these deductions should be listed on your pay stub, so if it's been a while since you've taken a good look at it before feeding it to the shredder, make a point of doing that now.

After that, divide your annual net income number by 12 to find out how much you take home each month. Then divide your annual net income number to find out how much you take home each pay period. If you get paid semi-monthly, divide it by 24; if it's biweekly, divide by 26; if it's weekly, divide by 52. This calculation will help you get a clear idea of how much money gets deposited into your bank account yearly, monthly, and every payday.

Annual Gross Income	Annual Net Income	Monthly Net Income	Bi-weekly Net Income
$56,000	$43,627	$3,635.58	$1,677.96

Once you know how much money you're bringing in, I suggest you use the pay-yourself-first method, which is simply a strategy to make sure you prioritize your savings goals before your expenses. That way, each month, you'll always be a little further ahead with your money. Note down all of your different savings goals and how much of your income you'd like to allocate to each. These numbers will likely have to change after you allocate funds to your expenses, but that's okay. The point is to make sure all of your income isn't just going toward expenses, because if it is, that means you either have to cut back or earn more (or both). Moreover, your goals will likely be a combination of short (one to two years), medium (two to five years), and long-term (more than five years) goals. It's important to categorize your goals from the outset so you can get a better idea of what account you should use for that money (e.g., a savings account, a TFSA, or a Roth IRA) and what you should do with that money (e.g., keep it in cash or invest it). Different savings goals might include these:

- emergencies
- home maintenance (e.g., money for replacing the roof, appliances, or other fixtures that are coming to the end of their lifespan)
- travel
- retirement
- kids' college fund

- home down payment
- wedding
- new vehicle
- new baby
- pet adoption
- education/tuition
- birthdays
- holidays (e.g., Thanksgiving, Christmas, Hanukkah, Valentine's Day)
- starting a business

You can also save up throughout the year to pay your annual car or home insurance, pay property taxes, make lump sum charitable donations, or even have a special shopping fund for your irregular shopping trips. I had a friend who would save up for a yearly trip to the U.S. with her family to shop for new clothes.

Savings Goals	Account Type	% to Save	Yearly	Monthly	Bi-weekly
Emergencies	High-interest savings account	5%	$2,181.35	$181.78	$83.90
Retirement	RRSP	15%	$6,544.05	$545.34	$251.69
Travel	High-interest savings account	5%	$2,181.35	$181.78	$83.90
Shopping	High-interest savings account	3%	$1,308.81	$109.07	$50.34

You may be looking at these numbers and thinking, *Wow, it's going to take a long time to save up for a decent trip or have enough for retirement!* Don't forget, this is your first spending plan that you're actually going to make part of your routine and stick to long-term. You need to start small, but you can build on it over time. As you earn higher pay or get raises or bonuses, you'll be able to allocate more of your income to your savings goals to reach those goals sooner. Patience is your best friend. For your long-term goals, you shouldn't just be saving that money; you should be investing it so it can grow over time.

After you've allocated money to your savings goals, you need to see how much is left over. With some simple calculations, in this example you'll discover that you're putting 28% of your income into savings, leaving you with 72% of your net income for expenses. Although there are plenty of general guidelines out there, like you should aim to save at least 20% of your income, what I don't love about them is how people tend to follow them as if they're written in stone. They can be great starting points, but ultimately, it's your money and you get to set the rules based on your own goals and needs.

Total Amount for Savings	28%	$12,215.56	$1,017.96	$469.83
Amount Left Over for Expenses	72%	$31,411.44	$2,617.62	$1,208.13

The last part of the spending plan is the least fun part, unfortunately. The proper way to do this is to take a look at your bank and credit card statements from the past three to six months to gauge how much you spend each month on average on different expenses. I prefer doing this manually as opposed to using a financial app that does it automatically, because the manual approach forces you to pause and really absorb the information in front of you. This can be tedious, I know, but when you get it over with, later on you'll only have to make a few tweaks to your spending plan maybe once per year.

If this is the first time you've ever done a deep dive into your spending, I won't lie, it might hurt and stir up a bunch of negative feelings inside you. If this happens and you start to feel yourself spiralling, go back to the grounding techniques we explored in Chapter 4 or refer to one of the mental health resources you've been using to get back into a good headspace to move forward. Another practice I do with myself and when working with financial counselling clients is to remember to be kind to the past you. When you look at your old spending, it's a snapshot of what was going on with you emotionally three to six months ago. You might be surprised by how much just looking at your spending will tell you.

I remember when I was at my wits' end at one of my past jobs and wasn't sure whether I should quit or stick it out. During those last few months before I handed in my notice, my spending was out of control. I was spending more money on bagels (my comfort food of choice), wine (to numb my pain), and clothes (for that quick boost of dopamine) than I ever had in my life. I was spending money on things that gave me temporary pleasure to mask my anguish. But after I quit, the fog I was living under lifted. No longer in a toxic work environment, I felt lighter and more capable of taking care of myself. This, in turn, made it easier to get my spending habits back under control, as well as my drinking and bagel-eating (no joke, after the whole ordeal, I didn't touch a bagel for two years).

No matter what you've been dealing with the past several months, forgive yourself. That's sometimes easier said than done, but you can't change the past; you were doing your best with what you had at the time. Hopefully, this book and the exercises in it have helped you see that making mistakes and learning are a big part of being human. You're a different person now who's walking a very different path, so show some kindness and empathy to the you of yesterday, try not to judge or criticize them, and remember, this spending plan is meant to lift you up and bring you to a better place with your money.

When it comes to expenses, I like to divide them into two distinct categories: fixed expenses and variable expenses. This makes it easier to figure out what to cut or reduce when your expenses leave little room for saving. Variable expenses are generally easier to adjust than fixed expenses. Fixed expenses are roughly the same amount every month. Variable expenses fluctuate every month, so the number you input is an average, even though in practice, some months you may spend more and some you may spend less.

I also like to include the payment method you typically use for each type of expense, so you can either optimize it to get more out of your spending (e.g., use a credit card to get rewards or cash back and build your credit score) or strategize to prevent overspending (e.g., switch to debit or a prepaid credit card because the temptation of a high credit limit is too great). For example, if you've had trouble controlling your spending when using credit cards in the past, what I've found to be successful with my clients is to use credit cards only for fixed expenses or big purchases you've saved up cash for in advance. This way, you will always have the money to pay off your credit cards, while at the same time earning rewards or cash back and building your credit score. For variable spending, stick to using debit or a prepaid credit card, so you're only spending money you have.

Fixed Expenses	Payment Method	Yearly	Monthly	Bi-weekly
Rent + utilities	Chequing account automatic withdrawal	$15,600	$1,300	$600
Student loan	Chequing account automatic withdrawal	$2,400	$200	$92.31
TV + music subscriptions	Credit card #1	$360	$30	$13.85
Cell phone	Credit card #1	$720	$60	$27.69
	Total	**$19,080**	**$1,590**	**$733.85**

Variable Expenses	Payment Method	Yearly	Monthly	Bi-weekly
Groceries	Prepaid credit card	$7,200	$600	$276.92
Dining out/ takeout	Credit card #2	$2,040	$170	$78.46
Public transit	Debit	$960	$80	$36.92
Fun money (guilt-free spending on whatever you want)	Debit	$2,100	$175	$80.77
	Total	**$12,300**	**$1,025**	**$473.07**

With your savings goals and expenses accounted for, let's see how you did. First, you want to make sure you're not spending more than you're earning (this would mean you'd be getting yourself into debt every month). Second, you want to make sure you're not spending more than the 72% (based on this example) of your net income allocated for expenses. It looks like you've actually got a surplus of $2.62 each month (or $1.21 bi-weekly), which means this plan is ready to be set in motion!

If you're wondering whether you should allocate that $2.62 somewhere so there's no surplus, you absolutely can do that, but you don't have to. You could also let it stay as some buffer money in your chequing account. Saying that, I'd also suggest having a few hundred dollars or more as a buffer in your main bank account where bills are paid from, to prevent you from accidentally going into overdraft or getting charged a non-sufficient funds (NSF) fee when money for a bill is automatically withdrawn from your account before your paycheque is deposited. Having some buffer money is a great way to reduce financial anxiety. If you don't have it yet, that can be one of the savings goals you make in your first spending plan.

	Yearly	Monthly	Bi-weekly
Total Fixed and Variable Expenses	$31,380	$2,615	$1,206.92
Amount Over or Under Net Income*	$12,247	$1,020.58	$471.04
Amount Over or Under Spending Plan	$31.44	$2.62	$1.21

* If the number is positive, it means there's a surplus (your expenses aren't exceeding your income or spending plan). If the number is negative, that means there's a deficit (your expenses are exceeding your income or spending plan).

Now it's time for my secret sauce to make this plan really stick. The best way to ensure your plan will be successful is to automate as much as possible. You can do this by designing a cash flow framework like the one shown here, so you can have a visual for how all of your bank accounts and credit cards flow together. As you can see, on payday, your paycheque is automatically deposited into your chequing account. From there, you can set up e-transfers through your bank (if it enables this) so money automatically flows into your different savings accounts, investment accounts, and credit cards. You can even use this strategy if you bank with multiple financial institutions through e-transfer or e-bill payments. But the point is, the less manual work you have to do, the better chance you'll have of actually adhering to your plan.

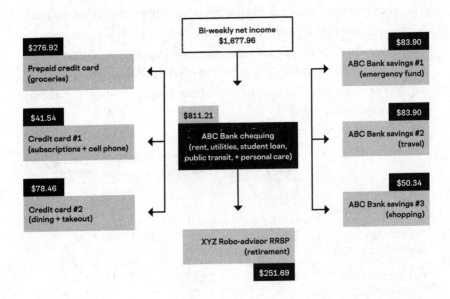

THE SPENDING TRACKER

When I work with financial counselling clients, the task of setting up their spending plan in the first session usually takes up to a full hour, but it may take longer for you (which is why using a template helps). In our second session together, we move on to their spending tracker, which is a spreadsheet where they can input all of their fixed and variable spending each month. It enables them to categorize each purchase and see the total to gauge if they spent more or less than what they expected.

I'm going to be honest with you: almost all of my clients (and even me, for that matter) are rarely on target with their spending consistently each month. You can make the best plan in the world, but sometimes life just happens. Unexpected costs, exciting opportunities, and expenses you forgot to plan for (it's their birthday *this* month?) come up. That's okay. The point of having a spending plan isn't to be perfect; it's to be better. There will always be room for improvement, but the only way to get results is to never give up. I'm talking specifically to you, my fellow perfectionists.

Besides allowing you to compare your spending to your plan to see how on or off target you were, tracking your spending keeps you accountable to yourself. How can you discover the problem areas in your spending if you don't take a good look at where your money is going each month? The answer is, you can't. You've got to take the blindfold off at some point, and as I've seen with countless clients, it's usually not as bad as you think. It's always 100% fixable, and it gets easier and less painful with time and practice.

I've been doing it for eight years now, and how I get through it (because even I don't love doing it) is I put on a comfort TV show I can watch passively without getting distracted (my go-tos are *The Office* or *Downton Abbey*), make a nice cup of tea (or pour a glass of wine if it's called for), download all of my bank and credit card statements into Excel documents, then get to work copying and pasting the numbers into my spreadsheet. Every month, it probably takes me about an hour to get it all done. If you're not convinced, time yourself the first few times you do it. You may be surprised at how little time it actually takes you.

THE NET WORTH TRACKER

The last part of the spending plan is my favourite—the net worth tracker. This is how you are going to prove to yourself that you are, in fact, good with money and can reach heights you never thought possible. Your net worth is a reflection of your overall financial health. You get it by calculating your total assets (e.g., cash, investments, real estate, vehicles, or anything that holds value) minus any liabilities (e.g., debts like student loans, credit card and lines of credit balances, car loans, or mortgages).

Tracking my own net worth over many years and seeing clients do the same has been such a rewarding experience. I've witnessed innumerable clients start with a negative net worth, feeling like they were a hopeless case, and go on to reach five- or six-figure net worths in just a few years of hard work and consistency. This could be you! With that said, if this is your first time tracking your net worth, you likely won't love your starting point—nobody really does. I think it's largely because we often compare the start of our personal finance journeys to the middle or end of someone else's while completely disregarding context or the fact that we don't actually know what's going on in other people's financial lives. Or we just get hyperfocused on all our past financial failures and missed opportunities and retreat back into a place of negativity and despair.

The only way to cut through all that crap is to, once again, be kind to and forgive the past you, and remember that this is a journey and you can't quit before you've even gotten started. Your hard work will pay off if you keep at it, and I promise you, after 12 months of sticking to your plan, tracking your expenses, and tracking your net worth, you will be able to see the fruits of your labour. Also, it's math, and math doesn't lie! If you're saving and investing your money and paying down your debts, your net worth will go up every month (save for any fluctuations in the stock market or new debts you accrue).

To show you what I mean, here's an example of what your net worth would look like if you were that marketing coordinator we created a plan for earlier.

Liquid Assets	Amount	Investment Assets	Amount	Personal Assets	Amount
Chequing Account	$500	RRSP	$1,500	Collectibles (Rare baseball cards)	$2,000
Savings #1 (Emergencies)	$1,200			Jewellery	$1,000
Savings #2 (Travel)	$780				
Savings #3 (Shopping)	$500				
	$2,980		**$1,500**		**$3,000**

Short-term Liabilities	Amount	Long-term Liabilities	Amount
Credit card #2	$100	Student loan	$10,500

Assets	$7,480
Liabilities	$10,600
Net Worth	-$3,120

When we do the magic net-worth formula of assets - liabilities = net worth, you'll see that you're starting off in the red with a negative net worth. Don't panic! Almost every client I've ever worked with has started in the negative. But guess what can happen after staying consistent with your plan for 12 months?

Liquid Assets	Amount	Investment Assets	Amount	Personal Assets	Amount
Chequing Account	$431.44	RRSP*	$8,409.71	Collectibles (Rare baseball cards)	$2,000
Savings #1** (Emergencies)	$3,450.78			Jewellery	$1,000
Savings #2 (Travel)	$3,018.01				
Savings #3 (Shopping)	$1,841.34				
	$8,741.57		**$8,409.71**		**$3,000**

---

* Assuming an 8% annualized rate of return.

** Assuming a 3% interest rate for all of the savings accounts.

Short-term Liabilities	Amount	Long-term Liabilities	Amount
Credit card #2*	$0	Student loan**	**$8,581.43**

Assets	$20,151.28
Liabilities	$8,581.43
Net Worth	$11,569.85

---

* You decided to use $100 from your chequing account to pay off your credit card balance.

** Assuming a 5% fixed interest rate for the student loan.

As you can see, you were able to turn things around fairly quickly. Your net worth increased by $14,689.85 by saving and investing money and paying down debts—as a percentage, it increased by 470.83%! It's important to note that when you spend the money you saved on travel and shopping, or if you have to dip into your emergency fund, your net worth may drop again, but that shouldn't make you feel bad. All money is saved to eventually be spent, and if you continue with your plan, you'll be able to get back up to where you left off in no time. The best part is that compounding really works. There's a certain tipping point with your finances that really does feel like magic. When you're first getting started, it can feel like everything is moving at a snail's pace. But then all of a sudden (and by that, I mean after a few years of doing the work), you'll start to see your net worth grow by bigger amounts each month. It's really quite astonishing.

IN CASE OF EMERGENCY

Besides following through with your spending plan, one of the most significant things you can do for yourself is to save up an emergency fund. I talk about this all the time when people ask me, "Where should I start with my money?" because having worked one-on-one with so many clients, I've seen first-hand how an emergency fund can be the difference between dodging a major financial setback and stalling progress with your finances for years to come.

The general advice that you may have come across before is to save up three to six months' worth of your living expenses (the sum total of your fixed and variable expenses) in a high-interest savings account, which like any other guideline, is a decent starting point. That amount of money can go a long way when the unexpected happens, like losing your job, having to take unpaid time off work to take care of a sick family member, having to pay an expensive repair bill for your car, or having to pay for your pet's surgery.

Sometimes even six months of expenses saved up isn't enough for your needs, which is why it's important for you to determine how much would be. For example, if you're self-employed like me, six months' worth of expenses may not be enough savings for a personal emergency or business emergency (e.g., your clients are late paying you, or a vital piece of equipment breaks and needs to be replaced).

What I see too often when people are making their spending plans is they are preparing for the best-case scenario instead of remembering that life rarely plays out that way. This is largely due to another type of behavioural bias we all have called optimism bias,[10] which means we tend to overestimate good things happening to us while underestimating the potential pitfalls.

Optimism bias is a contributing factor to why 26%[11] of Canadians and 57%[12] of Americans are unable to afford an unexpected expense of $1,000 or less because they didn't save up an emergency fund. It's also why a high percentage of Canadians[13] and Americans[14] are underinsured. We just don't think something catastrophic will happen to us, because, likely, up until this point it's always happened to the other guy. But unless you have a crystal ball, don't count yourself out. It's good to have a positive outlook, but it's also important to be prepared for rainy days.

Just ask Keisha Blair, author of *Holistic Wealth*.[15] When I had her on my podcast, she shared how she experienced the unthinkable in 2009. Eight weeks after giving birth to her second child, her husband told her that he didn't feel well and needed to see a doctor. They didn't think it was anything too serious, but as a precaution they checked into the emergency room to get him looked at. Three hours later, Blair left the hospital alone with a plastic bag with her husband's belongings inside. At only 34 years old, her husband had died suddenly from pheochromocytoma, a rare tumour that affects two to eight people out of every million.[16] On top of the emotional weight of that traumatic loss, Blair was now responsible for supporting her family on her own. One financial saving grace was that they had gotten a life insurance policy a year prior, just in case anything were to happen to either of them. Receiving that death benefit money not only helped Blair to continue paying her bills and avoid getting into debt, but it also gave her some crucial breathing room to grieve and slowly restructure her spending plan for her now single-income family instead of being forced to go right back to work to start earning.

Blair's story just goes to show that although an emergency fund is essential, so is being properly insured. This means you need to review what type of insurance you have through your employer to see how much coverage you have, and fill in any gaps, since most employers' plans are insufficient. If you don't have any insurance through work, shop around and make sure you get enough coverage privately. You may need policies for these different kinds of coverage:

- life insurance
- critical illness insurance
- disability insurance
- health insurance
- tenant/rental insurance
- home insurance
- auto insurance
- pet insurance

As well, consider making an estate plan. According to some recent reports, 70% of Canadians[17] and 67% of Americans[18] don't have an estate plan, which is an outline for how you'd like your assets to be distributed after your death through a will, assigns power of attorney to someone who will make financial and health decisions on your behalf if you become incapacitated, and assigns guardians to any dependants or pets. One argument I hear from people who put creating an estate plan low on their priority list is "What's it matter anyway? I'll be dead." But the truth is, an estate plan isn't actually about you; it's about your loved ones and your legacy. Having your wishes clearly recorded and a plan in place will make things so much easier for your loved ones. We discussed in Chapter 5 how generational wealth can have a big impact on how easy or difficult your life is. As history has shown, if your family has money that gets passed down to you, you'll get a major head start in life that can open doors that would otherwise be closed to you. You could perhaps afford to go to a prestigious university, take an expensive degree program, live in a higher cost city with better career opportunities, take more risks since you have a bigger financial cushion, and even retire early. Wouldn't you want to give your dependants a head start if you could?

I find that most people think estate planning is more complicated than it really is. The most traditional way to do it is to hire a financial planner as well as an estate lawyer to help you create a solid plan from start to finish. But there is obviously a higher cost to going that route. A more affordable option is to simply use one of the many do-it-yourself will kits now available online, such as Willful.co, LegalWills.ca, or EpilogueWills.com in Canada; and WillMaker.com, USLegalWills.com, RocketLawyer.com, or TotalLegal.com in the U.S. Although holographic wills—handwritten wills without any witnesses—are legal and valid in most of Canada and the U.S., they aren't in British Columbia, Prince Edward Island, and many of the states. Moreover, they may still be rejected by the probate court, which is why using a will kit and having witnesses is an overall better route to take. Then when you accrue more assets and your estate needs become more complex, you can hire professionals to update your plans as needed.

Maybe You Should Talk to Someone

There are so many other areas of personal finance I'd love to explore here, but if you're able to create a spending plan, stick to it for at least a year (then, hopefully, years to come), save up an emergency fund, get properly insured, and create an estate plan, you'll be in a much better financial position than you are now, as well as most people in the world. This should give you some much-needed confidence and peace of mind, which will be helpful when you tackle your mental health. So, with that, let's talk therapy.

First, I want to point out that there is actually a practice called financial therapy, though it's relatively new (the Financial Therapy Association was founded in 2009) and is a designation currently available and recognized only in the U.S. Professionals with this designation either have a background in finance, psychology, or social work, but they do not need to be a licensed therapist to become a certified financial therapist.

If you're based in the U.S., you may want to investigate this further to see if it's the right fit for you. Otherwise, an alternative is to work with an accredited advice-only financial professional in addition to a licensed therapist.

But what exactly *is* a therapist? Therapists have various titles, and it's important to understand whom to hire (and whom to avoid). In 2023, the popular singer SZA made headlines for thinking she was working with a therapist to help with her anxiety, only to discover months later, after her anxiety had worsened, that she was actually working with a life coach. Although life coaches can be helpful if you're looking for guidance on setting and reaching personal or career goals, they are not therapists, even though I've seen many market themselves as such. I've also seen the same thing in the personal finance space. Technically, anyone can call themselves a money or financial coach without any formal training, but these titles are not recognized by any financial regulatory body. That's why it's important, before signing on to work with any kind of mental health or financial professional, to ask them what their credentials are.

Finding the right qualified professional to work with you will really depend on where you live. In Canada, for example, each province is responsible for regulating the profession and thus uses different titles, such as psychotherapist, counselling therapist, registered clinical counsellor, or Canadian certified counsellor. Similarly, the regulation of counsellors and therapists in the U.S. is at the state level, and titles may vary, too. Confusing, right? Again, this is why it's so important that before you hire a professional to work with, you look up the regulations for therapists in your province or state first.

There's a big difference between a therapist, psychologist, and psychiatrist. In general, a therapist is someone who has at minimum a master's degree in psychology or social work, has passed a registration exam, and has completed a minimum number of client hours, but they are not a doctor and cannot assess or diagnose mental health disorders. A psychologist, on the other hand, has a Ph.D. in psychology, has passed required regulatory exams, and has completed a minimum amount of clinical work, and although they can diagnose mental health disorders, they cannot write prescriptions. A psychiatrist is a medical doctor (M.D.) who has passed regulatory exams and completed clinical work, and they can write prescriptions.

As you might guess, working with a psychologist or psychiatrist is typically more expensive than working with a therapist (though in Canada, these sessions might be covered by provincial health care plans), but that doesn't necessarily mean they are better to work with. Unless you need to see a doctor to get a diagnosis for a mental health disorder or need medication for treatment, a therapist may be a better fit for you, especially in regards to what we've discussed in this book thus far.

WHAT KIND OF THERAPY SHOULD YOU DO?

If all of this wasn't complicated enough, when you start researching therapists, what you'll soon discover is there are as many as 400 different forms of therapy.[19] This may come as a big surprise if you've never gone to therapy before or have tried only one kind. When people mention therapy, people tend to think of either two things: The first could be the classic image of you sitting on a couch with a therapist across from you, asking how you feel. That's traditional talk therapy. The other is cognitive behavioural therapy (CBT). As Toronto psychotherapist Suzanne Wiseman describes it, "CBT is a structured therapeutic protocol where individuals are taught to question irrational thoughts or beliefs and learn new strategies to be more flexible in their thinking." Not only is CBT becoming one of the most common forms of therapy recommended by doctors and insurance companies, it is also considered to be the "gold standard of the psychotherapy field."[20]

Although I'd been doing CBT for a cumulative four years, it actually wasn't until I tried different types of therapy that I started making some major breakthroughs. This, of course, is just my personal experience, and I still believe that CBT is a great place to start, and it could be the right fit for you. But if you don't feel like you're making progress after some time with CBT, there are other options as well. With that said, I want to go over two types of therapy that are becoming increasingly more popular because of their effectiveness. I can also personally attest to them being absolutely life-changing in terms of processing and healing your trauma. They are eye movement desensitization and reprocessing (EMDR) and internal family systems (IFS).

EYE MOVEMENT DESENSITIZATION AND REPROCESSING (EMDR)

After years of CBT, the first new type of therapy I tried was one I initially saw demonstrated by Prince Harry in the 2021 documentary *The Me You Can't See*,[21] but is now the "highest recommendation across most clinical practice guidelines," including those of Veterans Affairs and the Department of Defense in the U.S., the U.K.'s National Institute for Health and Care Excellence, and Australia's National Health and Medical Research Council.[22] It's called eye movement desensitization and reprocessing (EMDR). EMDR's focus is to help you process trauma and ease its symptoms by recalling trauma-related memories during bilateral stimulation so you can "repair" the mental injury from that memory. In other words, when you talk through your trauma while stimulating both sides of your brain by performing rapid eye movements, tapping, or having pulses buzz through each hand one after the other through an EMDR machine (which was my experience), your brain will learn to reprocess the trauma to make its related feelings much more manageable and, ultimately, desensitize you from it.[23]

Interested to see how it would work in real life, I looked up EMDR therapists in my area and booked a session with one, simply with the intention of trying it out once so I could better describe it for this book. I ended up doing eight sessions and confronted some deep childhood trauma I'd never understood or vocalized before, including how I transformed from a loud and bubbly child to one who preferred to be quiet and invisible when my younger sister was born and I became a middle sibling at six years old.

Remember when I said I wanted to release a cry I'd been holding in for 10 years? EMDR was what finally got it out of me, and it was so liberating. But like any therapy, it can also be uncomfortable and painful, mainly because sometimes you're required to heal with others or let go if that's not possible. For me, this meant having some very vulnerable conversations with my parents for the first time so we could start to heal together and strengthen our relationship moving forward. Although it was difficult to have those conversations, it was absolutely worth it and has brought my parents and me closer than we've ever been.

INTERNAL FAMILY SYSTEMS (IFS)

After those sessions (and taking a pause for several months so I could digest everything), the next form of therapy I tried was internal family systems (IFS). I couldn't put down IFS founder Richard C. Schwartz's book *No Bad Parts*[24] and craved a similar experience to the session he recorded with *Voices of Esalen* host Sam Stern (which I highly recommend you listen to).[25] But there was also a part of me that was resistant to doing it—which is funny, because IFS is all about the parts of you. I had every intention of booking my first session with an IFS therapist in the fall, but I kept putting it off until December arrived and I was running out of time to try it before my manuscript's deadline in January. So, just a few days before I boarded a plane to visit my family in Vancouver for the holidays, I did a double session with an IFS therapist, and it was as if I picked up right where I left off from my EMDR sessions. I also realized afterwards what had been holding me back from making an appointment sooner.

The premise of IFS is that we are all made up of parts that play important and distinct roles in our lives. Similar to how all families have systems and roles within those systems, so do each of us on an internal and individual level. When you're mentally healthy, the parts inside you work in harmony with each other, like a flock of birds that exist as a unit, while also maintaining their full autonomy, like when a bird leaves the flock to go off on its own.[26] Problems arise when some of your parts become burdened due to an experienced trauma, forcing them to take on an extreme role to protect against further hurt but also causing inner conflict in the process.

Within IFS, there are four parts that are the focus: the self, exiles, managers, and firefighters. The self is simply you in your truest form and the "core governing entity" of all your other parts.[27] Exiles are the parts of you that have been hurt, typically because of a childhood trauma, that your protector parts (managers and firefighters) have exiled into your unconscious mind for safety. Much as in an office setting, managers run the day-to-day operations of your life and help with things like following social norms, keeping deadlines, prioritizing, and keeping organized. But when they are burdened with protecting exiles, they can react in extreme ways in order to safeguard the exiles from becoming triggered and feeling pain again. For instance, burdened managers typically manifest as harsh inner critics, both rigid and non-conforming, with a mindset of "Never again." They can be incredibly controlling and often take the form of perfectionism, workaholism, and people-pleasing. Firefighters, on the other hand, only come out when managers can no longer protect exiles from being triggered. They manifest as explosive, disorganized, and emotionally charged reactions, such as substance abuse, self-harm, overeating, aggression, sex, gambling, over-spending, or extreme risk-taking to distract from and numb the pain.

What makes IFS different from many other forms of therapy is that the therapist really only serves as a mediator between you and your parts. They are there to guide you to heal yourself by giving you the script to speak to your parts, and find out who they are, what they do, what has been burdening them up until this point, and how you can liberate them.

To give you an idea of how this could look, I'll walk you through my session. You know how I had such a hard time booking an appointment in the first place? That was my manager's fault. What I didn't know was that my manager was in the background trying to prevent me from booking a session because it wanted to avoid anyone getting access to my exile. It also felt like it had everything under control and IFS could potentially ruin all of its hard work. But much to my surprise, it was actually my firefighter who presented itself first in the session. I had a really tough time exploring my feelings at the start, and I wasn't sure why. That is, until my therapist asked me if there was a part that was there to prevent me from opening up. What I discovered was that my firefighter was right there, standing guard like a big, burly bouncer of sorts, and it was not interested in opening the door to anyone. Luckily, after speaking with it to get to know it a bit more and build trust, it finally allowed me in so I could, no pun intended, speak to the manager.

Once in the same "room" as the manager, I was able to uncover what I was looking for. And it all started with me asking it a very simple question: "What's your name and how old are you?" The manager responded, "the Parent" and "18." My next question was directed toward my exile, who was slowly coming out from hiding. I asked it the same question, and it said "the Child" and "six." I immediately burst into tears, because finally, the pieces of my puzzle were coming together. Once I became a middle child at six years old, my whole world and outward personality changed. As all the attention shifted to my younger sister, instead of trying to get some attention back or voicing my needs to my parents, I retreated. Later, I went through another big transformation at 18. After graduating from high school and starting university, I was desperate for a new life, a new me. I wanted to be someone who was strong, could take care of herself, and was meant for bigger things. I wanted to be someone who would eventually become so rich and successful that she'd get all the attention she'd secretly been pining for ever since she got stuck in the middle. At the end of the session, I was able to introduce my adult self to both parts. At 37, my self could relieve the Parent from its protective duties, and let the Child know that I was stepping in to take care of it so it could now properly heal.

Thirty-one years—that's how long I'd been letting this wounded part inside me drive my biggest life decisions such as going to film school, starting a blog, moving away from my family and friends for bigger career opportunities, becoming a media personality and influencer, and starting a business centred on money. I wanted to be loved and seen, and I believed that outward attention and wealth would get me there. I know that, on the surface, none of those things sound bad. After all, every one of those moves helped me get to where I am today, which is in a career I love with financial stability. But as we'll explore in the final chapter, money and attention only get you so far, and I can't help but wonder how much happier or more fulfilled my life could have been if the path I took hadn't been paved with pain. If I'd felt loved and seen, and truly loved myself throughout my entire journey, where would I be today? *Who* would I be?

It's Not Easy Being You

There's a lot therapy can do, but unfortunately, there's also a lot it can't. For example, it can't undo the thousands of years of programming ingrained in you that no longer works in your modern context. It also can't create a protective bubble around you to shield you from the discrimination you may face in school, the workplace, or just minding your own business as you go for a walk because of who you are or what you look like. But there are other tools you can use to slowly try to reprogram some of your unhelpful money behaviours. Similarly, there are methods you can use to lift yourself back up when you keep getting pushed down that you can, in turn, use to lift others up and start to see the change in the world that you'd like to see.

REWRITING YOUR USER'S MANUAL

Although most of our behavioural biases are unconscious, even if we become aware of them, we can still fall prey to them. But you can learn how to manage your biases so they don't end up controlling you. The most effective way of doing this is to follow a rules-based strategy when you feel like your biases are taking over. In psychologist and behavioural finance expert Daniel Crosby's book *The Laws of Wealth*, he shares that the best approach to managing your biases is to follow the four Cs—consistency, clarity, courageousness, and conviction.[28]

Consistency involves being consistent with your financial decision-making, instead of letting gut feeling or market sentiment lead the way (and astray). This requires you to make a structured financial plan based on your goals, values, and risk level, with alternate plans you can pivot to if something in your life, the financial markets, or the economy changes. Remember that spending plan? I promise you, it's going to come in handy, because it will serve as a clear outline of what you want to happen with your money and how to achieve it.

As Crosby explains in his book, although you don't need a checklist for straightforward tasks in life, "you're awfully glad that your airplane pilot uses one and you should expect no less from the person managing your money (whether that's you or a professional)."[29] So, start thinking of managing your money like flying a plane. There are ups, downs, good weather, bad weather, and a lot of buttons you shouldn't touch without a good reason. The only way to make sure you can safely take off and land is to have a plan, especially when you feel the pull of your biases encouraging you to press that big red button that's only meant for emergencies.

Besides sticking to a plan, you need clarity. There's a lot of noise and nonsense around you, and you need to put your noise-cancelling headphones on to silence it all. If you're ever feeling agitated because of something you read in the financial news or because you saw some influencer claim that you're an idiot for not buying crypto, because all of the banks are going to collapse at any moment—headphones on! You need to be able to hear *yourself* think and not allow any external element to cloud your judgment.

Courageousness is one of my favourite Cs, because it's the hardest one to do, but it gets easier with practice and experience. To be courageous with your money means to be a contrarian. You need to do nothing or keep investing when everyone is pessimistic and cashing out. You need to start liquidating and realizing your profits when everyone is optimistic, and invest in things that are good long-term investments or undervalued. You need to stay calm when everyone is panicking or getting overly excited. You need to question those who are adamant they are right or can claim to see the future. All of this sounds simple, but actually doing it, time and time again, is difficult in practice.

The final C is conviction, which is really about knowing yourself, your personal beliefs and values, and what works best for you. Everyone has an opinion, after all, but oftentimes we forget that the most important opinion we should heed is our own. Don't make financial decisions based on what other people are doing or think you should be doing when they know nothing about you. Make decisions because they're what you want to do. At the end of the day, you're the only one who will have to live with the rewards or consequences of your actions.

Besides following these four Cs, another habit to get into is keeping a journal for when you're about to make a big financial decision. When we don't write things down, we humans have a tendency to rewrite history or forget some key details. Note down the time and date, how you're feeling at that moment, and your rationale for the decision. Six months to a year later, check back to the entry and make a note about how you feel after the fact. This journal can be a great resource to see if there are any patterns you've previously been unaware of, so you can learn not to repeat past mistakes in the future.

Lastly, having someone in your financial corner is key. This could be a mentor, such as a family member, friend, or colleague with a wealth of financial knowledge whom you look up to. But ideally, it would be a financial professional whom you could consult for support and advice when you don't feel as if you have the emotional regulation, expertise, or bandwidth to do it on your own. After all, there's a reason why studies have shown that people who work with financial planners end up making better financial decisions than those who don't.[30, 31]

NEVER GIVE UP YOUR FIGHT FOR FINANCIAL FREEDOM

When I interviewed Akin Taiwo (from Chapter 7) about the discrimination he faced after moving to Canada, I couldn't help but ask how he persevered in the face of so much intolerance and prejudice. He told me a story I'll never forget. Unfortunately, after he started his master's, he continued to experience discrimination in the classroom.

One day, he just couldn't take it anymore and let the tears roll down his face. This caught the attention of one of the Black professors who was an advocate for him getting into the program. She came up to him to ask what was wrong. Taiwo told her that he was fed up learning about social justice while having the same department discriminate against him. He just couldn't see a path forward and wanted to quit. After hearing what was distressing him, she looked at him and asked, "What's your name?" A bit confused, Taiwo said, "You know what my name is. It's Akin." The professor smiled and then asked, "And what does that name mean?" Taiwo paused before giving his answer: "It means warrior." The professor said, "So, where's your fighting spirit?" Taiwo not only persevered but became a leader and mentor to make positive change for future students following in his footsteps.

In the face of societal injustice, discrimination, and everything else that is trying to keep us down, we need to keep fighting. We need to be resilient, not just for our own financial well-being, but so we can set the standard for future generations and ensure they won't have to face the same economic barriers we did. I often wonder what kind of world we'd be living in today if it weren't for the women's suffrage movement, the four waves of feminism, the civil rights movement, and the gay rights movement. I know for a fact I wouldn't be allowed to run my own business, be as financially independent as I am, or be allowed to write a book like this.

It's because of the resilience of these activists that we all have this freedom and opportunity to improve our financial prospects, no matter where we're starting from or what obstacles still lie ahead. It's for that reason, and to lift up generations to come, we must never let others extinguish our fighting spirit.

Takeaways

- Mental health and financial health are often related. Improving your mental health might be the first step you need to take to get your financial life on track.

- Start your journey to a more solid financial foundation by setting up a spending plan, tracking your spending and net worth, becoming properly insured, and making an estate plan.

- When you're ready to find a mental health professional, make sure they are properly licensed and certified to help you.

- Choose what type of therapy is the best fit for you, such as CBT, EMDR, IFS, or the many others available, stay open, and stick to it, because it usually takes several sessions to reach a breakthrough. If you don't feel like you're making any progress, maybe that's a sign that you need to try a different provider or form of therapy.

- To better control your biases, follow the four Cs, start a financial journal to track past and future financial decisions, and find a money mentor to guide you.

- In the face of injustice and discrimination, never let anyone extinguish your fighting spirit.

9.
At the Heart of Money

We're all just walking each other home.
—Ram Dass

How much money would make you happy? I know we've all got a number in mind. In my early 20s, that number was $100,000. With a fresh diploma in my hands and a student loan to pay off, $100K seemed like an impossible amount of money to me. But by working multiple jobs, saving, investing, and living extremely frugally, compounded by my privilege being white, university-educated, without disabilities, with no dependants, I was able to save that amount and more by the time I celebrated my 30th birthday. But I wasn't happy.

So, I bumped that number up to $1 million. If my husband and I could reach a combined million-dollar net worth by the time I reached 35, I'd be happy. More than happy, we'd be frickin' millionaires! With some strategic budgeting, my business taking off and quadrupling my income, some good luck with our investments and home purchase, and my husband unexpectedly receiving an employer-provided life insurance payout when a close relative passed away, we reached that milestone, too. But I still wasn't happy.

You'd think by that point I would have learned an important lesson, but no. I just assumed I'd got the math wrong, so I moved the goalpost up once more to $2 million by 40. That is, until I started this journey to confront and mend my broken relationship with money. Although I still have that goal in the back of my mind, it's not because I think amassing that amount of money will finally make me happy. I know it won't. Instead, I just want to see if we can do it. The ambitious part of me will always be there. Plus, I like having a specific number to work toward to give my spending plan a clear sense of direction. I also know that if we don't achieve it, and there's a very high likelihood we won't, that's okay, too. Because throughout all the hours of therapy, expert interviews, personal stories, and research I've done, there's one thing I've never been more certain of: You are not your money and your money is not you. Your net worth is not your self-worth.

The Money vs. Happiness Debate

As author Jason Vitug pointed out in his book *Happy Money Happy Life*, "[w]hile money can buy happiness" in the form of housing, food, clothing, health care, necessities, and a few luxuries, too, "money *isn't* happiness."[1] Sadly, I think that's something most of us have lost sight of.

Let that sink in for a moment: money is not happiness. Why are these four little words so significant? Because they are contrary to everything social media, advertising, and Hollywood is trying to make you believe. From seemingly all angles, we are being convinced that money is the path to never-ending bliss—if only you buy these clothes, this car, that house, and have a certain amount of money in the bank. But that's just not true. The joy you get from making a purchase or seeing multiple zeros in your account only lasts for a moment. There's a limit to how much happiness money can provide.

For example, a 2018 study[2] out of Purdue University found that for individuals, "the ideal income point is $95,000 for life satisfaction and $60,000 to $75,000 for emotional well-being."[3] Since inflation has increased the cost of living dramatically since this study was published, that would look like $113,000 and $71,000 to $89,000 respectively in 2023 dollars.[4] However, because this study took data from 1.7 million individuals around the world, it also acknowledges that depending on your particular city's cost of living, your satiation point may be different from these numbers.

Nevertheless, what I thought was most interesting about this study was it found that if you surpass these thresholds, your life satisfaction and emotional well-being can actually start to decline. Once you hit your ceiling, you start to fixate on things like making social comparisons (i.e., how you stack up next to the Joneses) and acquiring more material gains (e.g., more money, more stuff). In other words, you become propelled by the belief that others are doing better than you, so you need to get more to keep up, making your life satisfaction recede.

In a related 2023 study, psychologists Daniel Kahneman and Matthew Killingsworth pitted their opposing theories against each other in an adversarial collaboration to see if happiness did, in fact, plateau at a certain income level. In 2010, Kahneman famously theorized that emotional well-being did not increase above an income of $75,000 a year,[5] whereas a decade later, Killingsworth argued that it could.[6] After surveying a new crop of participants, they ended up discovering together that although happiness could increase with more money, there was a ceiling for fending off *un*happiness.

If you're already unhappy because of heartbreak, bereavement, clinical depression, or "other miseries" such as trauma or experienced discrimination, money can diminish your suffering only up to $100,000 a year but not much beyond that.[7] As Killingsworth shared about these findings, "this suggests that for most people larger incomes are associated with greater happiness . . . [but the] exception is people who are financially well-off but unhappy. For instance, if you're rich and miserable, more money won't help. For everyone else, more money was associated with higher happiness to somewhat varying degrees."[8]

Here's what all these studies tell me: First, no matter what, if you don't have enough to cover your basic needs, more money is undeniably the solution to that problem. This always reminds me of a classic *Friends* exchange where Ross says, "I just never think of money as an issue," to which Rachel responds, annoyed, "That's because you have it."[9] When you have enough money, it stops being an issue. It can, however, move the spotlight over to your other issues. As Vitug put it in his book, "money fixes money problems, but it isn't *the* answer to life problems."[10]

As I said at the start of this book, there's a reason why there are so many miserable millionaires and billionaires out there. There's also a reason why I've met so many people in the FIRE community who successfully amassed a seven-figure nest egg, only to realize they were still unhappy after they retired early. If you're already unhappy, money alone can't fix you. No wonder my level of happiness (or unhappiness) remained unchanged despite how much my income or net worth grew over the years. Like so many others, I was under the illusion that money was some magic cure for all my emotional problems, and I just needed a little bit more for the medicine's effects to kick in. Unfortunately, just as hordes of people discovered after buying miracle tonics from charlatans in the 1800s, there's no cure in that bottle—just a bunch of mineral oil, animal fat, turpentine, and red pepper.[11]

As life-changing as money can be, what it can't do is erase your pain and hurt on its own. Only you can make that change, not only by trying some of the healing practices we explored in the previous chapter (which money can help pay for) but also by taking your life into your own hands. This requires you to rid yourself of the idea that happiness is a number and realize that it's something you must define for yourself. That's why we need to stop asking ourselves questions like "How much money would make me happy?" and instead start asking, "After all my basic needs are met, what would make me happy?"

That's what we'll be exploring in this last chapter. The final step to letting go of your toxic relationship with money so you can replace it with a much healthier one is to define your personal happiness outside of money. Only then can you figure out how money can help you achieve it. This is what financial fulfillment is all about: using money as a means of finding fulfillment in all aspects of your life, body and soul. Money is just a tool, after all. You're the hand that wields it.

What Will Actually Make You Happy

One of my favourite quotes by Pulitzer Prize–winning satirist Art Buchwald is "The best things in life aren't things." This is a truth I wasn't able to fully grasp until the year I wrote this book. If you remember, I was in a very dark place at the end of 2022. Cut to a year later, having gone on the deepest emotional journey of my life, I can confidently say that I was able to pull myself out and back into the light again. More than that, 2023 was unequivocally one of the happiest years I can remember. I feel bad saying that, since there are other years that should probably take that title, like the year I got married, but in the past, I was never able to be fully happy. Or maybe a more accurate way of putting it is that I never *allowed* myself to be fully happy. This was largely because I put too much importance on what other people thought, and attached happiness to things like material possessions, accolades, and financial success, feelings that lasted only a few hours, or days if I was lucky, before vanishing. I was surprised to discover that others have struggled with this. One of the most common regrets people have on their deathbeds is not letting themselves be happier.[12]

What's funny is that nothing outwardly substantial happened to me in 2023. Compared to other years, this one was pretty slow and uneventful. All the same, most of my happiness came from the simplest things, like going for walks, taking naps, trying out new recipes, reading, watching TV, working out, and going out for dinner—all pretty normal stuff that I previously didn't appreciate or would feel guilty about because it was time used "unproductively."

Then I learned about psychologist Martin Seligman's PERMA+ model, which explains a lot about why my happiness improved so much. It's because I was finally funnelling my energy into things that are known to increase well-being and happiness over the long term. Seligman, regarded as the father of modern positive psychology, breaks these things down into the five building blocks of flourishing: positive emotion, engagement, relationships, meaning, and accomplishment.[13]

POSITIVE EMOTION

Positive emotion means allowing yourself to experience and embrace emotions like love, compassion, pride, hope, gratitude, amusement, and joy. In the past, I'd never let myself sit with these emotions for very long, likely because they made me uncomfortable or I just didn't know what to do with them. Now I give myself permission to savour them for as long as I can and actively practise this to continue to strengthen this muscle.

ENGAGEMENT

Engagement is being fully present, losing self-consciousness, and entering a flow state where time stops and nothing else matters besides what you're doing then and there. Picture this as being absorbed in a puzzle, video game, or book, or doing something like painting, knitting, or gardening. It can also be described as when your skill set matches the challenge at hand, like when you fill out a crossword puzzle with just enough difficulty to make it fun and interesting.[14]

RELATIONSHIPS

Relationships, as you might guess, refers to engaging in positive relationships with family and friends and feeling loved, supported, and appreciated by others. I'd also add that it means feeling like a valuable member of a community or group. This was one of the biggest additions to my life. After years of having my walls up, I finally started tearing them down and deepened friendships I already had, renewed connections with friends I hadn't nurtured enough, and even made some new ones, too. My relationships are hands-down what brought me the most joy in 2023, which corroborates what the longest scientific study of happiness found: relationships are what make our lives more meaningful and satisfying.[15] To explore this concept further, I highly recommend reading *The Good Life* by study directors Robert Waldinger and Marc Schulz.[16]

MEANING

Meaning is feeling that your life has a clear purpose and that you're part of or are serving something bigger than yourself. This can look like having religion or spiritual belief as part of your life, participating in social or political causes, or simply determining "Why am I here and what do I stand for?" I remember reading *The Purpose Driven Life*[17] when I was 18, and although it's a Christian-based book and the religious aspects don't resonate with me, the one thing that stuck with me was to make sure I've got some sort of guiding light in my life. The idea that I have a purpose for being alive, or that I'm here for a specific reason, has given me a lot of happiness and comfort these past two decades.

ACCOMPLISHMENT

Accomplishment represents the importance of feeling like you've accomplished something. Whether that's achieving a goal you've set for yourself, like finishing a 10-k race, or mastering a skill, like baking a loaf of sourdough bread, we gain happiness when we complete things and do them well. Since most of what I've been driven by has been setting and achieving goals over the years, I'd also add that accomplishment can only truly make you happy if you make sure to enjoy the process and the outcome.

But that's not all. The plus sign (+) after PERMA wasn't a typo. It was added later on to include four more elements that have a big impact on well-being, too: optimism, nutrition, sleep, and physical activity.[18]

OPTIMISM

I think people too often mistake optimism for being unrealistic or naive, like Kenneth from *30 Rock* or Ted Lasso. But in fact, when you cultivate this emotion that makes you feel confident and hopeful about the future, it can, in turn, help you build resilience in the face of life's hardships. And who doesn't want that? Plus, data shows that being an optimist can make you live up to 15% longer, so that's a bonus, too.[19]

NUTRITION

In terms of nutrition, sleep, and fitness, I know what you're probably thinking. This information isn't new. We've known about the importance of these for years. Still, I can't help but think of my five-year-old niece when bringing these up. Whenever she's unhappy, the reasons are almost always that she's hungry, tired, or needs to run around to burn off some energy. These may seem like pretty basic things to improve your happiness, and they are, but the reason we need to be reminded of them is that we are really bad at getting adequate amounts of them.

Take nutrition, for example. It sounds simple enough to eat healthy meals on a set schedule, but it's hard to do when life gets busy and you miss a meal, get hungry, and the easiest thing to do is grab some processed food you can pop into the microwave. Believe me, I know. I used to be notorious for forgetting to eat during a busy workday, and I still have a habit of keeping a few frozen pizzas in the freezer as "emergency meals" for when it's nine at night, I'm hangry, and I have zero energy (or desire) to cook something healthy. But as research shows, keeping regular mealtimes[20] and eating a healthy diet by consuming whole foods like fruits, vegetables, grains, and lean meats can not only improve your well-being and mood, but also help minimize mental health issues like depression.[21, 22]

SLEEP

When it comes to sleep, I really do get it. I *love* sleep, hence why incorporating 20-minute naps into my week has been a game-changer for me. When I don't get enough sleep, I'm a totally different person. I become moody, I have a shorter fuse, and I can feel my stress and anxiety levels go way up. It's not just me who gets like this; studies have shown that lack of sleep can increase your odds of mental distress and make emotional regulation much more difficult.[23, 24, 25] So, just like that bluntly titled parenting book I giggle at whenever I see it on bookshelves, one simple pathway to happiness is to go the f—— to sleep!

PHYSICAL FITNESS

Finally, there's physical fitness. Like half of Canadian[26] and American[27] adults, I struggled to stay active, despite there being so much evidence that proves it helps with depression[28] and improves life satisfaction and happiness.[29] For two to three months, I'd get the motivation to work out regularly, usually because of some factor like new-year-new-you January or summer would be rapidly approaching and I wanted to fit into my shorts again. But then my drive would wane, and I'd fall off the wagon for the next six to eight months. The cycle would repeat, but it would get harder every time to get the motivation back, which is why the breaks in between would stretch longer and longer.

But just like I was able to make significant strides with my mental health in 2023, I was also able to make a big change on the physical side. I joined a spin class in addition to a group fitness program, and this is the first time in my adult life that I've been able to stick to any type of physical activity consistently for over a year, largely because of their community-based formatting. Not only do I feel better in my body, but it's also helped my mental health. You just can't beat those endorphins, let me tell you!

THE BEST THINGS IN LIFE AREN'T THINGS, BUT MONEY CAN STILL HELP

Fitness classes aren't cheap, and eating a healthy diet can be expensive. One study found that a healthy diet can cost $1.50 more per day than an unhealthy diet (and that adds up).[30] You could even argue that getting a good night's sleep has a price tag, since it's a lot easier to get your recommended seven to nine hours[31] when you can afford to work only one job, work from home or within a short commute, and have hired help to make sure tasks like child care, laundry, meal preparation, and household upkeep don't cut into your bedtime. This is how the element of money comes into play. You can check off every main PERMA building block without money being a big issue, but aside from optimism, money sure can help with the +. Just like with Maslow's hierarchy of needs, although money won't do much to fulfill the top three tiers of love and belonging, esteem, and self-actualization needs, it's still essential to satisfy your physiological and safety needs.

This again reinforces the fact that although most things that make you happy are free, having money can definitely help.

Money Well Spent

Now that you know the secret to happiness, we need to talk about your spending. Aside from spending money on necessities, most of us are spending our money on things we think will make us happy, but they often fall short. It's not your fault. Blame living in a capitalistic society in which every business is fighting for your attention and dollars, promising that all your dreams will come true if you just take out your credit card and buy its shiny new object.

Thankfully, there is a science to happier spending, which professors Elizabeth Dunn and Michael Norton distill into five principles in their book *Happy Money*:[32]

- buy experiences
- make it a treat
- buy time
- pay now, consume later
- invest in others

Let's walk through each principle, so you can start spending your money to achieve optimal happiness.

EXPERIENCES OVER MATERIAL GOODS

When you think of something you spent money on recently that made you happy, was it an experience or something material? Although there are no wrong answers, chances are it was an experience that came to mind. Here's the thing: there's no denying that possessions make us happy, because they can provide us with comfort, convenience, and pleasure. For instance, my Nespresso brings a smile to my face every morning, since I'm one press of a button away from a delicious brew to wake me up, not to mention that coffee is one of my glimmers.

But overall, material purchases provide a different type of happiness than experiences. As one study found, "Material purchases provide more frequent momentary happiness over time, whereas experiential purchases provide more intense momentary happiness on individual occasions."[33] What this means is that both purchases can make us happy. However, buying a new couch, for example, will "bring repeated doses of happiness over time in the weeks" that follow before that happiness starts to dissipate, whereas going to a concert you paid for will "offer a more intense but fleeting dose of happiness."[34] It's fleeting because the act of going to the concert will end after the show, whereas you'll sit on your couch repeatedly for years to come.

Nevertheless, even though the concert ends but the couch stays, several studies have also shown that we are happier in anticipation, in the moment, and in retrospect when we spend money on experiences rather than material goods.[35, 36] When we think about a positive past experience we paid for, we get an extra boost of happiness when we reminisce about it.[37] Although I love my couch and use it every day, I can't say that I've ever reminisced about all the good times I've spent sitting on it. I do, however, reminisce about all the awesome concerts I've gone to, especially that time my roommate and I saw Robyn in 2010, when she'd just released "Dancing on My Own." That $25 ticket has given me way more hours of happiness in my lifetime than my much-loved Urban Barn sofa ever will.

TREAT YOURSELF (BUT PACE YOURSELF)

You know the saying "Too much of a good thing"? It makes a lot of sense. Just think of the last time you went to a buffet. At the time, it seemed like a good idea. But at a certain point in your dining experience, you started to have regrets, especially that last egg roll and piece of cake you ate that really tipped the scales. As Dunn and Norton explain, "If abundance is the enemy of appreciation, scarcity may be your best ally."[38] When it comes to happiness (and buffets), less is more.

In 2023, there was a big shortage of the original Sriracha sauce due to poor weather conditions and water supply issues.[39] I like the sauce just fine, but I was never obsessed with it like the legions of hardcore Sriracha fans out there. But as soon as I stopped seeing it at the supermarket, I couldn't stop searching for it at every grocery store I went to thereafter. For months, it was nowhere to be seen, and then one fateful day, I went to my neighbourhood market to grab a few things for dinner, and while perusing the Asian foods aisle, I spotted it. Eight bottles were sitting on the bottom shelf. I couldn't believe my eyes. I think I actually gasped. Knowing friends who would want some, too, but not wanting to be greedy, I bought three bottles, one each for me and two friends who were also on the hunt for it. I'd never appreciated Sriracha as much as at that moment. And boy, did finding those bottles of hot sauce make me and two others very happy.

It's not uncommon for us to think that if we have more of something, we'll be happier. Again, blame capitalism. But what the science shows is that we are happier when we don't always have access to something (e.g., Sriracha or Girl Guide cookies), temporarily give up something (e.g., for Lent or Sober October), or simply don't overindulge (it's all fun and games until you need to unbutton your pants at the table).

Something I remember doing in my early 20s, when I was living on a very tight budget, was to treat myself to an English Toffee coffee from Tim Hortons every payday. I got paid bi-weekly, and I'm telling you, I looked forward to that ultra-sweet drink from one payday to the next. Cut to several years later, when I was in my late 20s and making almost double my previous salary, and I'd buy a latte or caramel macchiato from Starbucks almost every other day without an extra thought. Guess which drinks brought me more happiness?

When you make something a once-in-a-while treat, it not only gives you time to anticipate the coming reward but also makes you savour the thing when you get it. Although my sensitive teeth can't handle those sugary drinks from Tim Hortons anymore, I'll never forget how much happiness they brought me when I was younger.

BUYING TIME BUYS HAPPINESS

Speaking of my most frugal years, I had an ample supply of time in my 20s but very limited money. Every dollar really did count, and I'd do almost anything to save a dollar here and a few cents there—including telling my husband the morning after our wedding night, which we spent at the Fairmont Pacific Rim in Vancouver as a wedding present, that we would not be taking a cab home; we'd be taking the bus. He still hasn't let me live that down, by the way. I think it's kind of funny though.

Talking with my friend Kara Perez, author of *Green Money*, I learned that she was much the same as me in her 20s. To trade time for money, she routinely fixed a pair of two-dollar Forever 21 leggings every three weeks when they got holes in them instead of just replacing them. She also stood in line for someone once to make an extra $150. Standing in line doesn't sound that bad, but considering it was from nine o'clock at night until six in the morning in the dead of winter in Austin, Texas—let's just say she never did it again.

As both of us got older and our lives became busier, we started realizing how precious time is and how we'd much rather sacrifice money to get more of it. And we seem to be in the majority about this. After researchers in one study looked at large samples of working adults from Canada, the U.S., Denmark, and the Netherlands, they found that participants reported "greater happiness after spending money on a time-saving purchase than on a material purchase."[40] This could look like buying a Roomba to save time cleaning, using Instacart to save time shopping, or subscribing to Goodfood to cut down on your cooking time.

We can also look at the pandemic to see how gaining more time can improve people's happiness. In May 2020, 37% of the Canadian workforce and 35% of the U.S. workforce transitioned into working from home, eliminating hours of commuting.[41] And they were a lot happier for it. A survey from Tracking Happiness found that workers were 20% happier working from home, whereas their happiness decreased the longer their commute was.[42] No wonder 63% of respondents to a FlexJobs survey said they'd be willing to take a pay cut of 20% or more to work remotely.[43]

I can definitely relate, because my happiness went way up after I quit my nine-to-five to work for myself at home. I was able to shave off at least 1.5 hours of daily commuting, which calculates to 7.5 hours per week, 30 hours per month, and 360 hours per year. Just think of all the PERMA+ building blocks you could do instead, like socializing, sleeping, playing, or working out, by gaining an additional 360 hours in free time. Although I get that we all need to trade some time for money to earn a living, it's important to remember that, as a resource, time is finite. Money isn't.

IT PAYS TO BE PATIENT

Last year, I went to an all-inclusive resort in Cancun with my husband, and the concept of delaying consumption to increase happiness was never more apparent than when we were talking with the other guests. On our last night, we joined three other couples for a hibachi dinner and went around the circle to share how our stay had been so far. When it was my turn, I couldn't help but say, "I love it here, but my shorts sure don't fit as well as they did on day one of our trip!" At that, the 25-year-old newlywed sitting across from me piped up and said, "I get that. It's hard not to keep eating and drinking when everything's free!" But nothing in the resort was free. Unlimited, sure, but not free. We had all paid thousands of dollars to be there.

Remember when we discussed the pain of paying in Chapter 6? Well, one way to minimize that pain is to separate the payment from the purchase with time.[44] Although the initial payment transaction is still painful, it's practically painless from then on. So painless that you might even forget all the hard work it took you to save up for a five-night vacation in Mexico after you book your stay.

Additionally, by paying in advance and delaying your consumption, you also make room for the joy of anticipation. Because we paid for our trip eight months before we went on it, we effectively bought eight extra months to excitedly fantasize about our trip by looking up reviews and photos, looking at people's posts in the resort's Facebook group, and planning out what activities and restaurants we would try when we got there.

This type of experience can also be attributed to other things you pay for in advance, like subscription boxes, wine-of-the-month clubs, or a pre-sale on a limited-edition bag. Still, it's important to remember that even in anticipation, we gain more happiness with experiences than with material goods.[45] So, if you're not sure whether to spend $5,000 on a future vacation or $5,000 on a designer bag that won't be shipped to you for a few more months, you'll get a lot more happiness miles out of that holiday.

PAYING IT FORWARD

When I was growing up, giving back was always an important part of how my mom managed the family finances. No matter how tight the budget was, she'd always make sure to contribute money to the church and buy a few extra food items to donate to the food bank at our local grocery store. I also have fond memories of participating in our church's Christmas donation program, in which we got to buy presents for children in need. Honestly, just thinking about it makes me feel really happy, and that's because as humans, we are actually happier spending money on others than on ourselves.

To prove that this is true, *Happy Money* authors Elizabeth Dunn and Michael Norton, as well as Simon Fraser University professor Lara Aknin, conducted an experiment that involved giving participants $5 or $20 to spend by the end of the day. They "instructed half of the participants to spend the money on themselves (personal spending) and half to spend the money on someone else (prosocial spending)." What they discovered was that the people who spent the money on someone else reported feeling happier throughout the day than those who spent it on themselves.[46]

This rings true for my own personal experiences with prosocial spending, and there are many other studies to confirm this, too. So why is it that charitable donations have gone down in recent years? For instance, the Fraser Institute found that from 2011 to 2021, Canadian tax filers donating to charity fell from 23% to 17.7%.[47] Similarly, according to a Giving USA report, in 2022, Americans gave the "lowest percentage of their disposable incomes to charity" since 1995, giving only 1.7% of their personal disposable income to charity.[48] Why is this? It could be partially due to the recent pandemic and financial crisis that saw many people lose their jobs or live on a reduced income. But it could also be due to the fact that when we think about money, we become less inclined to part with it.[49]

When we are reminded of money, we start behaving with more self-sufficiency and adopt a mindset of "I don't depend on anyone and I don't want anyone else to depend on me." Because of this, we feel more protective toward our money and thus more resistant to helping others by giving money or possessions away, or even donating our time through volunteering.[50]

So how do we solve this? We know that prosocial spending brings us happiness, but when we think about money, we become less charitable. As Dunn and Norton suggest in their book, in order for us to feel primed to give, we need to feel like it's our choice and not be forced into it, have a deep connection to the receiver (e.g., a close friend's GoFundMe or cancer research because family members have been affected by it), and feel like our gift or donation is going to make a positive impact.[51] In effect, if you want to increase your happiness by investing in others, you have to take money out of the equation and instead focus on how your actions can bring happiness outside of you.

I always like to remind my financial counselling clients that money is meant to be spent, not just saved or invested. We are not meant to keep it all for ourselves; it's supposed to circulate. That's why it's called currency. The term originates from the Latin word *currere*, which means "to run" or "to flow."[52] As Lynne Twist so eloquently describes it in her book *The Soul of Money*, "money is like water. Money flows through all our lives, sometimes like a rushing river, and sometimes like a trickle. When it is flowing, it can purify, cleanse, create growth, and nourish. But when it is blocked or held too long, it can grow stagnant and toxic to those withholding or hoarding it."[53]

When you think of money in those terms and then think of the happiest people you know, it's likely that those people are also the most generous.

With that, I want to offer a few suggestions on giving. In terms of giving within your own circle, whether it be a birthday present or gifts during the holidays, I always recommend making that a line item in your budget. Save up for those gifts throughout the year so you always have enough to make those purchases guilt-free. Outside of that, also carve out room in your budget to donate money monthly or set up a special account to save up money for more lump-sum charitable giving throughout the year. This way, when a friend launches a GoFundMe or a world event occurs that you want to donate to (e.g., the Australian bush-fires of 2020 or the war in Ukraine), you won't feel the pain of paying as much, but you will feel really good giving to a cause you want to support.

With thousands upon thousands of charities around, it can be over-whelming to choose the "right one." Here are some organizations that can help you find a charity or cause that will deliver the highest impact:

- GivingMultiplier.org
- GiveDirectly.org
- RCForward.org
- GiveWell.org
- CharityNavigator.org
- CharityIntelligence.ca
- UniteforChange.org

Rewriting Your Money Story

EXERCISE

We've arrived at the final exercise of the book: rewriting your money story. If you refer back to the exrcise you did at the end of Chapter 3, you should have a very clear outline of what money story you've been telling yourself up until now, and what parts of it have been holding you back all these years. But after looking inside yourself and diving into your past, it's now time to move forward into a new chapter of your story.

In this final exercise, I want you to take out your journal or a piece of paper one final time and answer the following questions. The an-swers you provide will now serve as your new financial blueprint. This is who you want to be, where you'd like to go, and what kind of relation-ship with money you'd like to have from now on.

1. Considering the income thresholds we went over at the start of this chapter, what is the ideal annual income you'd like to reach if you haven't already reached it?

2. Talking about money can help weaken its power over you. Who are some people you trust whom you could feel comfortable talking about money with? Name two or three people and then make it a goal to have some conversations with them in the coming days or weeks. Use this book as a way to break the ice.

3. What are some of your current financial struggles? Are they monetary or emotional or mental in nature? List specific steps you intend to take to resolve them.

4. What are some financial goals you'd like to achieve in the future and why? (Remember, money isn't happiness, but it can help you access some of the PERMA+ building blocks.)

5. How do you wish to view poverty, wealth, and money in general as you move forward, and what are the mindset shifts you need to make to get there?

6. What money lessons or behaviours do you want to let go of for good that you previously held on to?

7. What money lessons or behaviours do you want to keep with you?

8. How would you like to characterize yourself in connection with money?

9. What does money mean to you now that you've read this book?

Takeaways

- Allow yourself to savour emotions connected to happiness.

- Be present and engage in activities that absorb you.

- Foster your social connections and put in the effort to stay in touch through meet-ups, phone or video calls, emails, texts, and DMs.

- Never give up on your search for meaning in life.

- Set goals you can reach, and learn and improve your skills.

- Practise being an optimist.

- Prioritize getting enough sleep, eating well, and staying physically active.

- Spend your money on experiences, treats, buying time, pre-paying for purchases, and never stopping the flow of money to others.

More Than Your Money

If there's one thing I hope you take away from this book, it's this: no matter what's happened to you, what your upbringing was like, what behaviours you adopted or mistakes you made, you are more than your money. You are *so* much more than that. This may not have been something you fully understood or could accept before, but it's the truth. It is never too late to become the person you always knew you could be and start living a life of happiness, connection, and wholeness. So, forgive yourself, love yourself, and most of all, congratulate yourself for taking this huge next step into the rest of your life.

Acknowledgements

I'd be lying if I said writing these acknowledgements wasn't just as difficult as writing this entire book, because there are so many important people I want to thank and I don't want to miss a single person.

First, I want to thank everyone who allowed me to interview them for this book. By giving me permission to share your money stories with the world, in turn you will help so many others unearth their own money stories so they can start to heal. This goes for the many individuals whose stories didn't make it into the book. You were so generous with your time and unbelievably brave for opening up to me. Your stories matter, and I thank you for trusting me with them.

I want to express my immense gratitude to those who have supported me from the beginning, when I was still blogging and podcasting on nights and weekends, dreaming of the day when I could turn my little side hustle into a career that I feel so fortunate to have now. Thank you for being my cheerleaders every step of the way. I don't think I could have finished this book without all of your kind messages these past two years telling me that you can't wait to read it. This book is for you!

Along the same lines, thank you to all the authors who let me pick their brains for five minutes after we finished our podcast recordings together. Your advice and words of wisdom for a first-time author have been invaluable.

To my agent, Jeff Lohnes: one of the best things I ever did was send you a cold email in 2021 asking you to be my agent. You've helped me reach career heights I never knew possible, not to mention realize one of my biggest dreams of becoming an author. I can't wait to see what exciting opportunities are up next!

To my amazing editor, Julia McDowell, whom I immediately clicked with in that first meeting at HarperCollins Canada's headquarters.

Thank you for championing me and this book, and taking my writing to the next level. This book needed to be written and I thank you for believing that I should be the one to write it. A big thank you also to my production editor, Natalie Meditsky, and copyeditor, Stacey Cameron, for giving my book's punctuation, word choices, and sentence structure what I can only describe as a *Princess Diaries* makeover.

Thank you to the many experts and consultants I had review this book, including psychotherapist Suzanne Wiseman and sensitivity consultant Alicia Chantal, as well as those who wished to remain anonymous. Your feedback and advice helped make this book go from good to great.

This book may never have seen the light of day if not for the support of my amazing friends in the personal finance space. Paulette Perhach, thank you for helping me craft my first book proposal and making me believe that a publisher would actually say yes one day. Kara Perez, I'll miss our Monday accountability sessions when we were both in the thick of writing our first books. Cait Flanders, thank you for being an author I could look up to as well as a great friend who's always been supportive of my own literary aspirations. Alyssa Davies, thank you for being such a bright and positive supporter throughout this entire journey. Jordann Brown, thank you for being one of the first bloggers I connected with over a decade ago and whom I'm still so lucky to call a friend (even though we've never lived in the same city!).

To my friends outside of the personal finance space, Gina, Andréane, Tahnya, and Michelle, thank you for letting me vent, trauma-dump, and workshop ideas with you. To my friends and book club ladies, Stephanie, Amy, Sarah, and Rose, thank you for your support and introducing me to books I'd likely never read on my own. I can't tell you how much my writing has improved because of it.

To my family, Mom, Dad, Anna, and Sarah, thank you for your unconditional love and support. Mom, you're the reason I was always smart with money right out of the gate and are the main inspiration for my career in financial literacy. Also, I have no idea how you raised a family of five on such a tight budget for so many years. You're a miracle worker! Dad, if it weren't for you instilling in me the importance of dreaming and pursuing my passion, I would have given up the idea of writing a book a long time ago. Anna, we all know you're the real writer in the family, and I thank you for being someone I could always look up to. Thank you for introducing me to my first personal finance blog back in 2010. Unknowingly, you set me on a path to my current career and ultimately writing this book! Sarah, you'll always be my baby sister who I want to help and protect, but it's been the biggest joy for me to see you come into your own these past few years. I can't wait to see what's next for you. I hope I've made you all proud.

To my grandparents, Audrey, Columbe, and Jacques: Your determination to provide a better life for your children and grandchildren is what's allowed me to be in the privileged position I am today. Thank you!

And last but not least, to my husband, Josh: In the almost two decades we've been together, you've always encouraged me to take risks and never stop trying to achieve my dreams. You've always believed in me, even when I didn't believe in myself. You're the best life partner I could have ever asked for. I dedicate this book to you.

Notes

1. WE'RE ALL DOING THE SAME THING

1. "Americans Would Rather Talk about Anything besides Money, Capital Group Survey Finds," Capital Group Newsroom, last modified December 6, 2018, https://www.capitalgroup.com/about-us/news-room/americans-would-rather-talk-about-anything-besides-money-capital-group-survey-finds.html/.
2. Armand Domalewski (@armandadoma), tweet, August 20, 2021, https://twitter.com/ArmandDoma/status/1428900898449756163?/.
3. Itamar Shatz, "The Ostrich Effect: Why and How People Avoid Information," Effectiviology, accessed April 15, 2023, https://effectiviology.com/ostrich-effect/.
4. "Mindfulness," National Health Service, last modified September 14, 2022, https://www.nhs.uk/mental-health/self-help/tips-and-support/mindfulness/.
5. John Koenig, *The Dictionary of Obscure Sorrows* (New York: Simon & Schuster, 2021), 257.
6. University of California—Los Angeles. "Putting Feelings into Words Produces Therapeutic Effects in the Brain." *ScienceDaily*, June 22, 2007, https://www.sciencedaily.com/releases/2007/06/070622090727.htm/.

2. AND HOW DOES THAT MAKE YOU FEEL?

1. Tchiki Davis, "Shame: Definition, Causes, and Tips," Berkeley Well-Being Institute, last modified January 2022, https://www.berkeleywellbeing.com/shame.html/.
2. Brené Brown, *Daring Greatly: How the Courage to Be Vulnerable Transforms the Way We Live, Love, Parent, and Lead* (New York: Avery, 2012), 69.
3. Julie Corliss, "Want to Feel More Connected? Practice Empathy," *Harvard Health Publishing*, February 22, 2021, https://www.health.harvard.edu/blog/want-to-feel-more-connected-practice-empathy-2021022221992/.
4. Kristin Keffeler, *The Myth of the Silver Spoon: Navigating Family Wealth and Creating an Impactful Life* (Hoboken: Wiley, 2023), 48.

5.   Joe Pinsker, "Who Actually Feels Satisfied about Money?" *The Atlantic*, July 21, 2019, https://www.theatlantic.com/family/archive/2019/07/who-feels-rich /594439/.

6.   Norman Vanamee, "Meet the Rich Kids Who Want to Give Away All Their Money," *Town and Country*, Sept. 27, 2019, https://www.townandcountrymag .com/society/money-and-power/a29008841/rich-kids-revolution-resource -generation/.

7.   Joe Pinsker, "The Reason Many Ultrarich People Aren't Satisfied with Their Wealth," *The Atlantic*, December 4, 2018, https://www.theatlantic.com/family/ archive/2018/12/rich-people-happy-money/577231/.

8.   Elana Klein and Taylor Borden, "The Hiltons Turned a $5,000 Investment into a Global Empire—Meet the Family Behind the Hotel Brand Worth Billions," *Business Insider*, March 2, 2023, https://www.businessinsider.com/how-the-hilton -family-got-so-rich-2014-10/.

9.   Emma Mudge, "What Causes Guilt and How to Overcome It," *AXA Health*, July 12, 2023, https://www.axahealth.co.uk/health-information/mental-health/resilience /what-causes-guilt-and-how-to-overcome-it/.

10.   Robert Taibbi, "Irrational Guilt: How to Put It to Rest," *Psychology Today*, February 19, 2016, https://www.psychologytoday.com/ca/blog/fixing-families/201602 /irrational-guilt-how-put-it-rest.

11.   Carlos Tilghman-Osborne, David A. Cole, and Julia W. Felton, "Inappropriate and Excessive Guilt: Instrument Validation and Developmental Differences in Relation to Depression," *Abnormal Child Psychology*, 40 (May 2012): 607–20, https:// www.ncbi.nlm.nih.gov/pmc/articles/PMC4119797/.

12.   Ralph Adolphs, "The Biology of Fear," *Current Biology* Vol. 23, Issue 2 (January 21, 2013), PR79-R93, https://doi.org/10.1016/j.cub.2012.11.055.

13.   "What Are Anxiety Disorders?" American Psychiatric Association, last modified June 2023, https://www.psychiatry.org/patients-families/anxiety-disorders/what -are-anxiety-disorders/.

14.   "Mood and Anxiety Disorders in Canada: Fast Facts from the 2014 Survey on Living with Chronic Diseases in Canada," Public Health Agency of Canada, last modified June 3, 2015, https://www.canada.ca/en/public-health/services/publications /diseases-conditions/mood-anxiety-disorders-canada.html/.

15.   Sean Fleming, "This Is the World's Biggest Mental Health Problem—and You Might Not Have Heard of It," *World Economic Forum*, January 14, 2019, https:// www.weforum.org/agenda/2019/01/this-is-the-worlds-biggest-mental-health -problem/.

16.   "What's the Difference between Anxiety and an Anxiety Disorder?" Here to Help, last modified 2015, https://www.heretohelp.bc.ca/q-and-a/whats-the -difference-between-anxiety-and-an-anxiety-disorder.

17. "Understanding Anxiety: What's Normal and What's Not," Houston Behavioral Healthcare Hospital, last modified January 9, 2018, https://www.houston behavioralhealth.com/blog/understanding-anxiety-whats-normal-whats-not/.

18. "The Facts: What You Need to Know," Money and Mental Health Policy Institute, last modified June 2, 2017, https://www.moneyandmentalhealth.org/money -and-mental-health-facts/.

19. "Envy," APA Dictionary of Psychology, last modified April 19, 2018, https:// dictionary.apa.org/envy/.

20. Jens Lange and Jan Crusius, "Dispositional Envy Revisited: Unraveling the Motivational Dynamics of Benign and Malicious Envy," *Personality and Social Psychology Bulletin* 41(2) (2015): 284–94, https://doi.org/10.1177/01461672 14564959/.

21. Lilly Shanahan, Sherika N. Hill, et al., "Does Despair Really Kill? A Roadmap for an Evidence-Based Answer," *American Journal of Public Health* 109(6) (June 2019): 854–58, https://doi.org/10.2105%2FAJPH.2019.305016.

22. "Despair," APA Dictionary of Psychology, last modified April 19, 2018, https:// dictionary.apa.org/despair.

23. Elisabet Beseran, Juan M. Pericàs, et al., "Deaths of Despair: A Scoping Review on the Social Determinants of Drug Overdose, Alcohol-Related Liver Disease and Suicide," *International Journal of Environmental Research and Public Health* 19(19) 12395 (September 29, 2022), https://doi.org/10.3390/ijerph191912395.

24. Samuel H. Fishman and Iliya Gutin, "Debts of Despair: Education, Financial Losses, and Precursors of Deaths of Despair," *SSM Popular Health* 28, 14 100759 (February 2021), https://doi.org/10.1016/j.ssmph.2021.100759.

25. "The Feeling Wheel," All the Feelz, accessed April 26, 2023, https://allthefeelz .app/feeling-wheel/.

3. WHAT'S YOUR MONEY STORY?

1. Brad Klontz and Ted Klontz, *Mind over Money: Overcoming the Money Disorders That Threaten Our Financial Health* (New York: Broadway Books, 2009).

2. Klontz, *Mind over Money*, 151.

3. Denise Albieri Jodas Salvagioni et al., "Physical, Psychological and Occupational Consequences of Job Burnout: A Systematic Review of Prospective Studies," PLoS ONE 12(10) e0185781 (October 4, 2017), https://doi.org/10.1371/journal .pone.0185781.

4. "Hoarding: The Basics," Anxiety & Depression Association of America, last modified October 19, 2023, https://adaa.org/understanding-anxiety/obsessive -compulsive-disorder-ocd/hoarding-basics.

5. "Your Brain on Shopping—A Look at Compulsive Buying Disorder," McGill University Health Centre, last modified December 7, 2016, https://muhc.ca/news room/article/your-brain-shopping-look-compulsive-buying-disorder.

6. Donald W. Black, "A Review of Compulsive Buying Disorder," *World Psychiatry* 6(1) (February 2007): 14–18, https://www.ncbi.nlm.nih.gov/pmc/articles/PMC 1805733/.

7. Robert Hinojosa, "What Is Financial Infidelity? Common Signs & Examples," Choosing Therapy, January 4, 2023, https://www.choosingtherapy.com/financial -infidelity/.

8. Sharon Martin, "Why Do We Repeat the Same Dysfunctional Relationship Patterns Over and Over?" *PsychCentral*, July 13, 2018, https://psychcentral.com /blog/imperfect/2018/07/why-do-we-repeat-the-same-dysfunctional-relationship -patterns/.

9. "Reactance Theory," Decision Lab, last modified July 29, 2021, https://thedecisionlab .com/reference-guide/psychology/reactance-theory/.

4. IT'S NOT YOU, IT'S YOUR TRAUMA

1. Bruce D. Perry and Oprah Winfrey, *What Happened to You?: Conversations on Trauma, Resilience, and Healing* (New York: Flatiron Books, 2021), 17.

2. "Trauma," *Merriam-Webster*, last modified April 5, 2024, https://www.merriam -webster.com/dictionary/trauma/.

3. "Trauma," Centre for Addiction and Mental Health, accessed April 15, 2023, https://www.camh.ca/en/health-info/mental-illness-and-addiction-index /trauma/.

4. Bessel van der Kolk, *The Body Keeps the Score: Brain, Mind, and Body in the Healing of Trauma* (New York: Penguin Books, 2014), 53–54.

5. Perry and Winfrey, *What Happened to You?*, 115.

6. "Secondary Traumatic Stress," National Child Traumatic Stress Network, last modified January 30, 2018, https://www.nctsn.org/trauma-informed-care/secondary -traumatic-stress/.

7. "What Is Vicarious Trauma, and What Are Its Long-Term Effects?" BetterHelp, last modified April 2, 2024, https://www.betterhelp.com/advice/trauma/what -is-vicarious-trauma-and-how-is-it-treated/.

8. "What Is ADHD?," American Psychiatric Association, last modified June 2022, https://www.psychiatry.org/patients-families/adhd/what-is-adhd/.

9. Guifeng Xu, Lane Strathearn, et al. "Twenty-Year Trends in Diagnosed Attention-Deficit/Hyperactivity Disorder among US Children and Adolescents, 1997–2016," *JAMA Network* 1(4): e181471 (August 31, 2018), https://doi.org/10.1001%2 Fjamanetworkopen.2018.1471.

10. The Diary of a CEO Clips, "World Leading Physician View on ADHD: Gabor Maté," YouTube Video, 12:07, November 7, 2022, https://www.youtube.com/watch?v=itcD7f0H64A/.

11. Rebecca Ruiz, "How Childhood Trauma Could Be Mistaken for ADHD," *The Atlantic*, July 7, 2014, https://www.theatlantic.com/health/archive/2014/07/how-childhood-trauma-could-be-mistaken-for-adhd/373328/.

12. Todd E. Elder, "The Importance of Relative Standards in ADHD Diagnoses: Evidence Based on Exact Birth Dates," *Journal of Health Economics* 29(5) (September 2010): 641–56, https://doi.org/10.1016%2Fj.jhealeco.2010.06.003.

13. Janna N. Vrijsen, Indira Tendolkar, et al., "ADHD Symptoms in Healthy Adults Are Associated with Stressful Life Events and Negative Memory Bias," *ADHD Attention Deficit Hyperactivity Disorder* 10 (2018): 151–60, https://doi.org/10.1007/s12402-017-0241-x.

14. Wes Crenshaw and Jordan Mayfield, "The Relationship between PTSD and ADHD Diagnosis, Treatment," *ADDitude*, February 5, 2024, https://www.additudemag.com/ptsd-symptoms-adhd-diagnosis-difficult/.

15. "Adverse Childhood Experience Resources," Centers for Disease Control and Prevention, last modified June 29, 2023, https://www.cdc.gov/violenceprevention/aces/resources.html/.

16. "The Original ACE Study," Administration for Children and Families, accessed May 5, 2023, https://nhttac.acf.hhs.gov/soar/eguide/stop/adverse_childhood_experiences/.

17. "About," Stephen Porges, last accessed May 27, 2023, https://www.stephenporges.com/.

18. Deb Dana, *Anchored: How to Befriend Your Nervous System Using Polyvagal Theory* (Boulder: Sounds True, 2021), 13.

19. Dana, *Anchored*, 13.

20. Pete Walker, *Complex PTSD: From Surviving to Thriving* (Lafayette: Axure Coyote Publishing, 2014).

21. Dana, *Anchored*, 14.

22. "How to Help Your Clients Understand Their Window of Tolerance," National Institute for the Clinical Application of Behavioral Medicine, last modified November 21, 2022, https://www.nicabm.com/trauma-how-to-help-your-clients-understand-their-window-of-tolerance/.

23. Mary D. Ainsworth, Mary C. Blehar, et al., "Patterns of Attachment: A Psychological Study of the Strange Situation" (1978), https://psycnet.apa.org/record/1980-50809-000.

24. "What Is Attachment Theory?" Attachment Project, last modified December 8, 2023, https://www.attachmentproject.com/attachment-theory/.

25. Amir Levine and Rachel Heller, *Attached: The New Science of Adult Attachment and How It Can Help You Find—and Keep—Love* (New York: TarcherPerigee, 2010), 8.

26. Levine and Heller, *Attached*, 8.

27. Levine and Heller, *Attached*, 118.

28. Levine and Heller, *Attached*, 8.

29. Xiaomin Li, Melissa A. Curran, et al. "Romantic Attachment Orientations, Financial Behaviors, and Life Outcomes among Young Adults: A Mediating Analysis of a College Cohort," *Journal of Family and Economic Issues* 41 (2020): 658–71, https://doi.org/10.1007/s10834-020-09664-1.

5. BLAME YOUR ANCESTORS

1. "Intergenerational Trauma," American Psychological Association, last modified November 15, 2023, https://dictionary.apa.org/intergenerational-trauma/.

2. Gwendolyn Scott-Jones, "The Traumatic Impact of Structural Racism on African Americans," *Delaware Journal of Public Health* 6(5) (November 2020): 80–82, https://doi.org/10.32481%2Fdjph.2020.11.019/.

3. Martha Henriques, "Can the Legacy of Trauma Be Passed Down the Generations?" BBC, March 26, 2019, https://www.bbc.com/future/article/20190326-what-is-epigenetics/.

4. "PTSD: National Center for PTSD," U.S. Department of Veterans Affairs, last modified April 11, 2023, https://www.ptsd.va.gov/understand/what/history_ptsd.asp/.

5. Lisa Fritscher, "Advantages and Disadvantages of the Diagnostic Statistical Manual," *Verywell Mind*, January 17, 2023, https://www.verywellmind.com/dsm-friend-or-foe-2671930/.

6. "What Is Epigenetics?" Centers for Disease Control and Prevention, last modified August 15, 2022, https://www.cdc.gov/genomics/disease/epigenetics.htm/.

7. Mariana Brait and David Sidransky, "Cancer Epigenetics: Above and Beyond," *Toxicol Mech Methods* 21(4) (May 2011): 275–88, https://doi.org/10.3109%2F15376516.2011.562671/.

8. "Canada and the Dutch Hunger Winter," *Canadian Encyclopedia*, last modified April 29, 2020, https://www.thecanadianencyclopedia.ca/en/article/canada-and-the-dutch-hunger-winter/.

9. Peter Ekamper, Govert Bijwaard, et al., "Prenatal Exposure to Famine Heightens Risk for Later Being Overweight," *Columbia Mailman School of Public Health*, May 10, 2021, https://www.publichealth.columbia.edu/news/prenatal-exposure-famine-heightens-risk-later-being-overweight/.

10. Carl Zimmer, "The Famine Ended 70 Years Ago, but Dutch Genes Still Bear Scars," *The New York Times*, January 31, 2018, https://www.nytimes.com/2018/01/31/science/dutch-famine-genes.html/.

11. Bastiaan T. Heijmans, Elmar W. Tobi, et al., "Persistent Epigenetic Differences Associated with Prenatal Exposure to Famine in Humans," *Proceedings of the National Academy of Sciences U.S.A.* 105(44) (November 4, 2008): 17046–49, https://doi.org/10.1073/pnas.0806560105/.

12. Brian G. Dias and Kerry Ressler, "Parental Olfactory Experience Influences Behavior and Neural Structure in Subsequent Generations," *Nature Neuroscience* 17 (2014): 89–96, https://doi.org/10.1038/nn.3594/.

13. Henriques, "Legacy of Trauma."

14. "Study Finds Epigenetic Changes in Children of Holocaust Survivors," U.S. Department of Veterans Affairs, last modified October 20, 2016, https://www.research.va.gov/currents/1016-3.cfm/.

15. Tori Rodriguez, "Descendants of Holocaust Survivors Have Altered Stress Hormones," *Scientific American*, March 1, 2015, https://www.scientificamerican.com/article/descendants-of-holocaust-survivors-have-altered-stress-hormones/.

16. Tom Wien and Suzanne Gousse, "Filles du Roi," *Canadian Encyclopedia*, February 24, 2015, https://www.thecanadianencyclopedia.ca/en/article/filles-du-roi/.

17. "The Future of New France: The Filles du Roi (Daughters of the King)," CBC, accessed on May 25, 2023, https://www.cbc.ca/history/EPCONTENTSE1EP2CH7PA5LE.html/.

18. Mark Wolynn, *It Didn't Start with You: How Inherited Family Trauma Shapes Who We Are and How to End the Cycle* (New York, Penguin Books, 2016), 148.

19. Wolynn, *It Didn't Start with You*, 135.

20. Resmaa Menakem, *My Grandmother's Hands: Racialized Trauma and the Pathway to Mending Our Hearts and Bodies* (Las Vegas, Central Recovery Press, 2017), 59.

21. Menakem, *My Grandmother's Hands*, 59–60.

22. Menakem, *My Grandmother's Hands*, 72.

23. "The Dawes Act," National Park Service, last modified July 9, 2021, https://www.nps.gov/articles/000/dawes-act.htm/.

24. "The Dawes Act," National Park Service.

25. "Native Americans and the Homestead Act," National Park Service, last modified November 29, 2021, https://www.nps.gov/home/learn/historyculture/native-americans-and-the-homestead-act.htm/.

26. Donald L. Fixico, "When Native Americans Were Slaughtered in the Name of 'Civilization,'" *History*, July 11, 2023, https://www.history.com/news/native-americans-genocide-united-states/.

27. Eli Yarhi, T. D. Regehr, and Andrew McIntosh, "Dominion Lands Act," *Canadian Encyclopedia*, August 11, 2023, https://www.thecanadianencyclopedia.ca/en/article/dominion-lands-policy/.

28. Kory Wilson and Colleen Hodgson, "The Indian Act," *Pulling Together: Foundations* (Victoria, BCcampus), Section 2, September 5, 2018, https://opentextbc.ca/indigenizationfoundations/chapter/the-indian-act/.

29. Annette Sorensen and Scott van Dyk, "The Indian Act, Residential Schools, and the White Paper," *Indigenous Perspectives on Business Ethics and Business Law in British Columbia* (Victoria, BCcampus), 7th ed., Part 2, Chapter 3, September 21, 2022, https://opentextbc.ca/indigenouperspectivesbusiness/chapter/the-indian-act-residential-schools-and-the-white-paper/.

30. Becky Morgan, "Native Households Make 8 Cents for Every Dollar a White Household Has," *National Indian Council on Aging*, April 5, 2021, https://www.nicoa.org/native-households-make-8-cents-for-every-dollar-a-white-household-has/.

31. "Poverty in Canada," Canadian Poverty Institute, accessed on June 5, 2023, https://www.povertyinstitute.ca/poverty-canada/.

32. "Stress & Trauma Toolkit," American Psychiatric Association, accessed June 20, 2023, https://www.psychiatry.org/psychiatrists/diversity/education/stress-and-trauma/indigenous-people/.

33. "Slave Trade: International Day of Remembrance of the Victims of Slavery and the Transatlantic Slave Trade," United Nations, accessed on June 13, 2023, https://www.un.org/en/observances/decade-people-african-descent/slave-trade/.

34. Daina Ramey Berry, "American Slavery: Separating Fact from Myth," *The Conversation*, June 19, 2017, https://theconversation.com/american-slavery-separating-fact-from-myth-79620/.

35. Thomas Lewis, "The Middle Passage," *Encyclopaedia Britannica*, February 29, 2024, https://www.britannica.com/topic/transatlantic-slave-trade/The-Middle-Passage/.

36. "The Enslavement of African People in Canada (c. 1629–1834)," Parks Canada, last modified July 31, 2020, https://www.canada.ca/en/parks-canada/news/2020/07/the-enslavement-of-african-people-in-canada-c-16291834.html/.

37. J. David Hacker, "From '20. and Odd' to 10 Million: The Growth of the Slave Population in the United States," *Slavery & Abolition* 41(4) (May 13, 2020): 840–55, https://doi.org/10.1080/0144039X.2020.1755502/.

38. Vanessa Williamson, "Closing the Racial Wealth Gap Requires Heavy, Progressive Taxation of Wealth," Brookings Institution, December 9, 2020, https://www.brookings.edu/research/closing-the-racial-wealth-gap-requires-heavy-progressive-taxation-of-wealth/.

39. Joy DeGruy, *Post Traumatic Slave Syndrome: America's Legacy of Enduring Injury and Healing* (Portland: Joy DeGruy Publications Inc., 2017), 9.

40. DeGruy, *Post Traumatic Slave Syndrome*, 137.

41. "Japanese Internment Camps," History, last modified October 29, 2021, https://www.history.com/topics/world-war-ii/japanese-american-relocation/.

42. Matthew McRae, "Japanese Canadian Internment and the Struggle for Redress," Canadian Museum for Human Rights, May 19, 2017, https://humanrights.ca/story/japanese-canadian-internment-and-struggle-redress/.

43. "The Internment of Ukrainian Canadians," Canadian War Museum, accessed on July 6, 2023, https://www.warmuseum.ca/firstworldwar/history/life-at-home-during-the-war/enemy-aliens/the-internment-of-ukrainian-canadians/.

44. Andrew McIntosh, "Ukrainian Internment in Canada," *Canadian Encyclopedia*, June 5, 2018, https://www.thecanadianencyclopedia.ca/en/article/ukrainian-internment-in-canada/.

45. Mélanie Morin-Pelletier, "Unearthing Canada's First World War Internment History," Canadian Museum of History, June 27, 2022, https://www.historymuseum.ca/blog/unearthing-canadas-internment-history/.

46. "Children of the Camps: Internment History," PBS, accessed on July 21, 2023, https://www.pbs.org/childofcamp/history/health.html/.

47. Valerie Rein, *Patriarchy Stress Disorder: The Invisible Inner Barrier to Women's Happiness and Fulfillment* (Austin: Lioncrest Publishing, 2019).

48. "Gender Earnings Ratio and Wage Gap by Race and Hispanic Ethnicity," Women's Bureau–U.S. Department of Labor, accessed on August 8, 2023, https://www.dol.gov/agencies/wb/data/earnings/earnings-ratio-wage-gap-race-ethnicity/.

49. Nicole Torres, "Closing the Gender Wealth Gap," *Harvard Business Review*, October 3, 2019, https://hbr.org/2019/10/closing-the-gender-wealth-gap/.

6. YOU'RE ONLY HUMAN

1. Liz Frazier, "The Coronavirus Crash of 2020, and the Investing Lesson It Taught Us," *Forbes*, February 11, 2021, https://www.forbes.com/sites/lizfrazierpeck/2021/02/11/the-coronavirus-crash-of-2020-and-the-investing-lesson-it-taught-us/?sh=5a52d95f46cf/.

2. Bob Pisani, "One Year Ago Stocks Dropped 12% in a Single Day. What Investors Have Learned Since Then," *CNBC*, March 16, 2021, https://www.cnbc.com/2021/03/16/one-year-ago-stocks-dropped-12percent-in-a-single-day-what-investors-have-learned-since-then.html/.

3. Jean-Sébastien Fontaine, Guillaume Ouellet Leblanc, and Ryan Shotlander, "Canadian Stock Market Since COVID-19: Why a V-Shaped Price Recovery?" Bank of Canada, last modified January 3, 2023, https://www.bankofcanada.ca/2020/10/staff-analytical-note-2020-22/.

4. C. Gonzalez, "Decision-Making: A Cognitive Science Perspective," *The Oxford Handbook of Cognitive Science*, S. E. F. Chipman (Ed.) (2017): 249–63, https://doi.org/10.3389%2Ffpsyg.2017.01335/.

5. Martie G. Haselton, Daniel Nettle, and Damian R. Murray, "The Evolution of Cognitive Bias," *The Handbook of Evolutionary Psychology: Integrations*, 2nd ed. (2016): 968–87, https://doi.org/10.1002/9781119125563.evpsych241/.

6. Daniel Kahneman, *Thinking Fast and Slow* (Toronto: Anchor Canada, 2013), 20–21.

7. Shane Frederick, "Cognitive Reflection and Decision Making," *Journal of Economic Perspectives* Vol. 19, No. 4 (2005): 25–42, https://doi.org/10.1257/0895330057 75196732/.

8. Daniel Kahneman and Amos Tversky, "Prospect Theory: An Analysis of Decision under Risk," *Econometrica* Vol. 47, No. 2 (March 1979): 263–92, https://doi .org/10.2307/1914185/.

9. "Why Do We Buy Insurance?" Decision Lab, last modified August 15, 2019, https://thedecisionlab.com/biases/loss-aversion/.

10. John E. Grable, "Financial Risk Tolerance and Additional Factors That Affect Risk Taking in Everyday Money Matters," *Journal of Business and Psychology* 14(4) (2000): 625–30, https://psycnet.apa.org/doi/10.1023/A:1022994314982/.

11. William B. Riley Jr. and K. Victor Chow, "Asset Allocation and Individual Risk Aversion," *Financial Analysts Journal* Vol. 48, No. 6 (Nov.–Dec. 1992): 32–37, https://www.jstor.org/stable/4479593/.

12. Johannes Haushofer and Ernst Fehr, "On the Psychology of Poverty," *Science* 344(6186) (May 23, 2014): 862–67, https://doi.org/10.1126/science.1232491/.

13. Tomomi Tanaka, Colin F. Camerer, and Quang Nguyen, "Risk and Time Preferences: Linking Experimental and Household Survey Data from Vietnam," *American Economic Review* Vol. 100, No. 1 (March 2020): 557–71, http://dx.doi.org /10.1257/aer.100.1.557/.

14. Chris Kolmer, "26 Average Salary Increase When Changing Jobs Statistics [2023]," Zippia, February 7, 2023, https://www.zippia.com/advice/average -salary-increase-when-changing-jobs/.

15. Ian Tam, "More to Funds Than Fees: Keep an Eye Out for These Attributes," Morningstar, January 31, 2023, https://www.morningstar.ca/ca/news/231310/more -to-funds-than-fees-keep-an-eye-out-for-these-attributes.aspx/.

16. "The Real Cost of ETFs—Not Just the MER," Provisus Wealth Management, last modified February 13, 2024, https://www.provisus.ca/the-real-cost-of-etfs-not -just-the-mer/.

17. Kevin Voigt, "Mutual Fund Calculator: Calculate Investment Growth and Fees," NerdWallet, March 20, 2024, https://www.nerdwallet.com/article/investing /mutual-fund-calculator/.

18. "Report Provides Data, Analysis of Canadian Mutual Fund and ETF Assets and Sales, and Investor Trends," Investment Funds Institute of Canada, January 31, 2024, https://www.ific.ca/en/news/ific-releases-2023-investment-funds-report/.

19. Ian Bickis, "How Big Banks Dominate Canada's Financial Landscape," The Canadian Press, April 19, 2023, https://globalnews.ca/news/9634933/canada-big-banks-analysis/.

20. Nora Dunn, "What Is a Credit Union?" NerdWallet, February 23, 2024, https://www.nerdwallet.com/ca/banking/what-is-a-credit-union/.

21. Sheena S. Iyengar and Mark R. Lepper, "When Choice Is Demotivating: Can One Desire Too Much of a Good Thing?" *Journal of Personality and Social Psychology* 79(6) (2000): 995–1006, https://doi.org/10.1037/0022-3514.79.6.995/.

22. Eugene Malthouse, "Confirmation Bias and Vaccine-Related Beliefs in the Time of COVID-19," *Journal of Public Health* Vol. 45, Issue 2 (June 2023): 523–28, https://doi.org/10.1093/pubmed/fdac128/.

23. Ola Svenson, "Are We All Less Risky and More Skillful Than Our Fellow Drivers?" *Acta Psychologica* Vol. 47 (1981): 143–48, https://api.semanticscholar.org/CorpusID:16310850/.

24. Brian C. Tefft, "Drowsy Driving in Fatal Crashes, United States, 2017–2021 (Research Brief)," *Foundation for Traffic Safety—AAA*, March 2024, https://aaa foundation.org/category/driver-behavior-performance/.

25. "2016 Traffic Safety Culture Index (Technical Report)," *Foundation for Traffic Safety—AAA*, February 2017, https://aaafoundation.org/2016-traffic-safety-culture-index/.

26. Rita De Ramos, "New FINRA Foundation Research Examines Changing Investor Demographics, Preferences and Attitudes," FINRA Investor Education Foundation, December 15, 2022, https://www.finra.org/media-center/newsreleases/2022/new-finra-foundation-research-examines-changing-investor-landscape/.

27. "SPIVA," S&P Dow Jones Indices, accessed on August 3, 2023, https://www.spglobal.com/spdji/en/research-insights/spiva/.

28. "Self-Confidence," American Psychological Association, accessed on June 2, 2023, https://dictionary.apa.org/self-confidence/.

29. "Present Bias," Behavioral Economics, last modified February 20, 2023, https://www.behavioraleconomics.com/resources/mini-encyclopedia-of-be/present-bias/.

30. Gopi Shah Goda, Matthew R. Levy, et al., "The Role of Time Preferences and Exponential-Growth Bias in Retirement Savings," *National Bureau of Economic Research Working Paper Series* No. 21482 (August 2015), https://doi.org/10.3386/w21482/.

31. "What Is the Life Expectancy in Canada?" Canada Protection Plan, March 14, 2023, https://www.cpp.ca/blog/what-is-the-life-expectancy-in-canada/.

32. "Life Expectancy in the U.S. Dropped for the Second Year in a Row in 2021," Centers for Disease Control and Prevention, last modified August 21, 2022, https://www.cdc.gov/nchs/pressroom/nchs_press_releases/2022/20220831.htm/.

33. "Why Are We Likely to Continue with an Investment Even If It Would Be Rational to Give It Up?" Decision Lab, last modified September 9, 2020, https://thedecisionlab.com/biases/the-sunk-cost-fallacy/.

34. "Concorde Takes Off," History, last modified January 19, 2024, https://www.history.com/this-day-in-history/concorde-takes-off/.

35. John Tagliabue, "A Role for the Concorde, Even with Its High Costs," *The New York Times*, August 5, 2000, https://www.nytimes.com/2000/08/05/business/international-business-a-role-for-the-concorde-even-with-its-high-costs.html/.

36. Justin Hayward, "How Much Did a Single Concorde Plane Cost When New?" Simple Flying, January 8, 2023, https://simpleflying.com/concorde-cost-new/.

37. Jack Mitchell, "20 Years Ago, the Supersonic Passenger Jet Concorde Flew for the Last Time," NPR, November 24, 2023, https://www.npr.org/2023/11/24/1211551109/concorde-last-flight-2003/.

38. "How Much Was a Ticket on the Concorde?" *Britannica*, last modified September 15, 2020, https://www.britannica.com/question/How-much-was-a-ticket-on-the-Concorde/.

39. Robert D. Hormats, "Born to Herd," *Harvard Business Review*, December 2004, https://hbr.org/2004/12/born-to-herd/.

40. Carly Bass, "Terrified Diners Flee Busy Restaurant—But Not All Is as It Seems," Yahoo News, September 27, 2022, https://au.news.yahoo.com/runners-mistaken-robbers-terrified-diners-run-080038477.html/.

41. Susan Lazaruk, "Stanley Cup Riot of 2011 Cost $9 Million, Says Report," *Province*, January 19, 2016, https://theprovince.com/news/local-news/stanley-cup-riot-of-2011-cost-9-million-says-report/.

42. Chris Dart, "A New Doc Asks: What Was Really behind Vancouver's 2011 Stanley Cup Mayhem?" CBC, May 4, 2023, https://www.cbc.ca/arts/vancouver-stanley-cup-2011-i-m-just-here-for-the-riot-1.6830921/.

43. Michael Pompian, "How Herding Leads to Market Bubbles," Morningstar, June 15, 2017, https://www.morningstar.com/financial-advice/how-herding-leads-market-bubbles/.

44. Jeremy Bowman, "What Is a Stock Market Bubble?" Motley Fool, November 20, 2023, https://www.fool.com/terms/s/stock-market-bubble/.

45. Brian Wansink, *Mindless Eating: Why We Eat More Than We Think* (New York: Bantam Books, 2007), 28 29.

46. Nathaniel Meyersohn, "Why People Hated Shopping Carts When They First Came Out," *CNN*, May 14, 2022, https://www.cnn.com/2022/05/14/business/grocery-shopping-carts-history/index.html/.

47. Steven E. Landsburg, "Attack of the Giant Shopping Carts!!!" *Slate*, April 27, 2000, https://slate.com/culture/2000/04/attack-of-the-giant-shopping-carts.html/.

48. "Food Waste FAQs," U.S. Department of Agriculture, accessed on September 17, 2023, https://www.usda.gov/foodwaste/faqs/.

49. "Making Every Bite Count, Our First Three Years—2018–2021," Love Food Hate Waste, last modified June 24, 2022, https://lovefoodhatewaste.ca/about/lfhw -canada/.

50. Koert Van Ittersum and Brian Wansink, "Plate Size and Color Suggestibility: The Delboeuf Illusion's Bias on Serving and Eating Behavior," *Journal of Consumer Research* Vol. 39, No. 2 (August 2012): 215–28, https://doi.org/10.1086 /662615/.

51. Darrin Qualman, "Home Grown: 67 Years of US and Canadian House Size Data," Darrin Qualman, May 8, 2018, https://www.darrinqualman.com/house -size/.

52. Brian Wansink, Robert J. Kent, and Stephen J. Hoch, "An Anchoring and Adjustment Model of Purchase Quantity Decisions," *Journal of Marketing Research* Vol. 35, No. 1 (February 1988): 71–81, https://doi.org/10.2307/3151931/.

53. Tim Vipond, "Anchoring Bias," Corporate Finance Institute, accessed on September 14, 2023, https://corporatefinanceinstitute.com/resources/capital-markets /anchoring-bias/.

54. "Why Do We Feel More Strongly about One Option after a Third One Is Added?" Decision Lab, last modified April 13, 2024, https://thedecisionlab.com/biases /decoy-effect/.

55. Sam Peltzman, "The Effects of Automobile Safety Regulation," *Journal of Political Economy* Vol. 83, No. 4 (August 1975), https://doi.org/10.1086/260352/.

56. "The Peltzman Effect," Decision Lab, last modified March 17, 2021, https://the decisionlab.com/reference-guide/psychology/the-peltzman-effect/.

7. IT'S NOT FAIR

1. Danielle McLeod, "More Than One Way to Skin a Cat," Grammarist, September 18, 2023, https://grammarist.com/phrase/more-than-one-way-to-skin-a-cat/.

2. Korin Miller, "As a Video about White Privilege Goes Viral Again, Experts Caution It Could Actually Cause More Damage," Yahoo, June 3, 2020 https://www .yahoo.com/lifestyle/as-a-video-about-white-privilege-goes-viral-again-experts -caution-it-could-actually-cause-more-damage-170528763.html.

3. Justin D. García, "Privilege (Social Inequality)," Salem Press Encyclopedia, 2018, https://guides.rider.edu/privilege/.

4. "Closing the Wage Gap between Workers and CEOs," Canadian Union of Public Employees, last modified June 12, 2023, https://cupe.ca/closing-wage-gap -between-workers-and-ceos/.

5. L. Taylor Phillips and Brian S. Lowery, "I Ain't No Fortunate One: On the Motivated Denial of Class Privilege," *Journal of Personality and Social Psychology* 119(6) (2020): 1403–22, https://doi.org/10.1037/pspi0000240/.

6.   Patrick J. Kiger, "Why People Who Have It Easy Claim They Had It Rough," Insights by Stanford Business, May 4, 2021 https://wwwgsb.stanford.edu/insights/why-people-who-have-it-easy-claim-they-had-it-rough/.

7.   "People and Ideas: Early American Groups," PBS, last modified August 1, 2019, https://www.pbs.org/wgbh/americanexperience/features/godinamerica-early-american-groups/.

8.   Max Weber, *The Protestant Ethic and the "Spirit" of Capitalism: and Other Writings* (New York: Penguin Classics, 2002).

9.   Richard D. Pancost, "Acknowledging Your Privilege Is an Act of Community," *University of Bristol—The Uncertain World*, September 24, 2022, https://richpancost.blogs.bristol.ac.uk/2022/09/24/acknowledging-your-privilege-is-an-act-of-community-and-love/.

10. TEDx Talks, "Understanding My Privilege," YouTube Video, 12:48, December 6, 2019, https://www.youtube.com/watch?v=XlRxqC0Sze4/.

11. Peggy McIntosh, "White Privilege: Unpacking the Invisible Knapsack" and "Some Notes for Facilitators," *Peace and Freedom Magazine*, July/August 1989, 10–12, https://www.nationalseedproject.org/key-seed-texts/white-privilege-unpacking-the-invisible-knapsack/.

12. Elizabeth Leiba, *I'm Not Yelling: A Black Woman's Guide to Navigating the Workplace* (Coral Gables: Mango Publishing, 2022), 32.

13. Leiba, *I'm Not Yelling*, 37.

14. Brian McGlashan, "Consequences of Having a Criminal Record in Canada," McGlashan Company Barristers and Solicitors, February 24, 2022, https:/mcglashanlaw.ca/2022/02/24/consequences-of-having-a-criminal-record-in-canada/.

15. John Gramlich, "Black Imprisonment Rate in the U.S. Has Fallen by a Third since 2006," Pew Research Center, May 6, 2020, https://www.pewresearch.org/short-reads/2020/05/06/share-of-black-white-hispanic-americans-in-prison-2018-vs-2006/.

16. Leah Wang, "The U.S. Criminal Justice System Disproportionately Hurts Native People: The Data, Visualized," Prison Policy Initiative, October 8, 2021, https://www.prisonpolicy.org/blog/2021/10/08/indigenouspeoplesday/.

17. Micah Guiao, "Black and Indigenous Prisoners Continue to Suffer from Poor Correctional Outcomes: Report," *Canadian Lawyer*, November 10, 2022, https://www.canadianlawyermag.com/practice-areas/criminal/black-and-indigenous-prisoners-continue-to-suffer-from-poor-correctional-outcomes-report/371402/.

18. Samuel R. Gross, Maurice Possley, et al., "Race and Wrongful Convictions in the United States 2022," University of Michigan Public Law Research Paper No. 22–051 (September 23, 2022), http://dx.doi.org/10.2139/ssrn.4245863/.

19. Christopher Ingraham, "Black Men Sentenced to More Time for Committing the Exact Same Crime as a White Person, Study Finds," *The Washington Post*, November 16, 2017, https://www.washingtonpost.com/news/wonk/wp/2017/11/16

/black-men-sentenced-to-more-time-for-committing-the-exact-same-crime-as
-a-white-person-study-finds/.

20. Jim Rankin, "Canadian Registry of Wrongful Convictions Shines Light on Cases
the Headlines Miss," *Toronto Star*, February 20, 2023, https://www.thestar.com
/news/gta/canadian-registry-of-wrongful-convictions-shines-light-on-cases
-the-headlines-miss/article_45fcf08c-dd73-5b6a-87/.

21. "Disaggregated Trends in Poverty from the 2021 Census of Population," Statistics
Canada, last modified November 8, 2022, https://www12.statcan.gc.ca/census
-recensement/2021/as-sa/98-200-X/2021009/98-200-X2021009-eng.cfm/.

22. John Creamer, "Poverty Rates for Blacks and Hispanics Reached Historic Lows in
2019," United States Census Bureau, September 15, 2020, https://www.census
.gov/library/stories/2020/09/poverty-rates-for-blacks-and-hispanics-reached
-historic-lows-in-2019.html/.

23. Dedrick Asante-Muhammad, Esha Kamra, et al., "Racial Wealth Snapshot: Native
Americans," National Community Reinvestment Coalition, February 14, 2022,
https://ncrc.org/racial-wealth-snapshot-native-americans/.

24. Leiba, *I'm Not Yelling*, 44.

25. *Sorry to Bother You*, Boots Riley (Annapurna Pictures, 2018).

26. *Insecure*, 2016, Season 1, Episode 3, "Racist as Fuck," directed by Melina Matsou-
kas, aired October 23, 2016.

27. Amina Dunn, "Younger, College-Educated Black Americans Are Most Likely to
Feel Need to 'Code-Switch,'" Pew Research Center, September 24, 2019, https://
www.pewresearch.org/short-reads/2019/09/24/younger-college-educated
-black-americans-are-most-likely-to-feel-need-to-code-switch/.

28. "The Mental Toll of Code-Switching," NeuroLeadership Institute, February 18,
2022, https://neuroleadership.com/your-brain-at-work/code-switching-mental
-toll/.

29. Courtney L. McCluney, Myles I. Durkee, et al., "To Be, or Not to Be . . . Black:
The Effects of Racial Codeswitching on Perceived Professionalism in the Workplace," *Journal of Experimental Social Psychology* Vol. 97 (November 2021): 104199,
https://doi.org/10.1016/j.jesp.2021.104199/.

30. Courtney L. McCluney, Kathrina Robotham, et al., "The Costs of Code-Switching,"
Harvard Business Review, November 15, 2019, https://hbr.org/2019/11/the-costs
-of-codeswitching.

31. Alan Henry, *Seen, Heard & Paid: The New Work Rules for the Marginalized* (New
York: Rodale Books, 2022), 50.

32. Madeline Will, "Teachers Are as Racially Biased as Everybody Else, Study
Shows," *EducationWeek*, June 9, 2020, https://www.edweek.org/teaching-learning
/teachers-are-as-racially-biased-as-everybody-else-study-shows/2020/06/.

33. Jon Marcus, "Racial Gaps in College Degrees Are Widening, Just When States
Need Them to Narrow," *Hechinger Report*, August 13, 2021, https://hechinger

report.org/racial-gaps-in-college-degrees-are-widening-just-when-states-need
-them-to-narrow/.

34. "Learning and Earning: The Payoffs of Higher Education," Bank of Canada, last
modified November 23, 2023, https://www.bankofcanada.ca/2020/10/learning
-and-earning/.

35. Rachel M. Cohen, "Stop Requiring College Degrees for Jobs That Don't Need
Them," *Vox*, March 19, 2023, https://www.vox.com/policy/23628627/degree
-inflation-college-bacheors-stars-labor-worker-paper-ceiling/.

36. Tori DeAngelis, "Unmasking 'Racial Micro Aggressions,'" *Monitor on Psychology*
Vol. 40, No. 2 (February 1, 2009): 42, https://www.apa.org/monitor/2009/02
/microaggression/.

37. Arelis Diaz and Carlos Rangel, "Racial Equity in Financial Services," McKinsey
& Company, September 10, 2020, https://www.mckinsey.com/industries
/financial-services/our-insights/racial-equity-in-financial-services/.

38. Rebecca Knight, "7 Practical Ways to Reduce Bias in Your Hiring Process," *Harvard Business Review*, June 12, 2017, https://hbr.org/2017/06/7-practical-ways
-to-reduce-bias-in-your-hiring-process/.

39. "2021 Edelman Trust Barometer Special Report: Addressing Racism in America's
Financial System," Edelman (2021), https://www.edelman.com/trust/2021-trust
-barometer/addressing-racism-america-financial-system/.

40. Maxwell Young and Lex Suvanto, "Financial Firms Are Still Falling Short at
Serving Communities of Color," *Fortune*, January 21, 2022, https://fortune
.com/2022/01/21/financial-firms-are-still-falling-short-at-serving-communities
-of-color-banks-diversity-edelman/.

41. Tamaryn Water, "Wells Fargo Bank Sued for Race Discrimination in Mortgage
Lending Practices," *USA Today*, April 26, 2022, https://www.usatoday.com
/story/money/2022/04/26/wells-fargo-being-sued-discriminating-against-black
-borrowers/7451521001/.

42. Ken Sweet, "Bank to Pay $31M for Avoiding Mortgages to Minorities, Largest Such
Settlement in U.S. History," Associated Press via PBS, January 12, 2023, https://
www.pbs.org/newshour/economy/bank-to-pay-31m-for-avoiding-mortgages
-to-minorities-largest-such-settlement-in-u-s-history.

43. Sylvia Novac, "Housing Discrimination in Canada: The State of Knowledge,"
Canada Mortgage and Housing Corporation, last modified April 3, 2013, https://
publications.gc.ca/collections/collection_2011/schl-cmhc/nh18-1/NII18-1
-273-2002-eng.pdf.

44. Falice Chin, "Banking Barriers: How the Canadian Financial Sector Excludes
Black Entrepreneurs, Stifling Innovation," CBC Radio, October 31, 2020, https://
www.cbc.ca/radio/costofliving/banking-while-black-1.5780927/.

45. "2022 Report on Firms Owned by People of Color: Based on the 2021 Small Business Credit Survey," Fed Small Business, last modified June 29, 2022, https://

www.fedsmallbusiness.org/survey/2022/2022-report-on-firms-owned-by -people-of-color/.

46. Maria Puente and Cara Kelly, "How Common Is Sexual Misconduct in Hollywood?" *USA Today*, February 23, 2018, https://www.usatoday.com/story/life/people /2018/02/20/how-common-sexual-misconduct-hollywood/1083964001/.

47. "Women in Male-Dominated Industries and Occupations," Catalyst, last modified May 31, 2023, https://www.catalyst.org/research/women-in-male-dominated -industries-and-occupations/.

48. Emily Liner, "A Dollar Short: What's Holding Women Back from Equal Pay?" Third Way, September 13, 2017, https://www.thirdway.org/report/a-dollar -short-whats-holding-women-back-from-equal-pay.

49. Rakesh Kochhar, "The Enduring Grip of the Gender Pay Gap," Pew Research Center, March 1, 2023, https://www.pewresearch.org/social-trends /2023/03/01/the-enduring-grip-of-the-gender-pay-gap/.

50. Asaf Levanon, Paula England, and Paul Allison, "Occupational Feminization and Pay: Assessing Causal Dynamics Using 1950–2000 U.S. Census Data," *Social Forces* Vol. 88, Issue 2 (December 2009): 865–91, https://doi.org/10.1353/sof .0.0264/.

51. Jorgen Harris, "Do Wages Fall When Women Enter an Occupation?" *Labour Economics* Vol. 74 (January 2022): 102102, https://doi.org/10.1016/j.labeco.2021 .102102/.

52. Claire Cain Miller, "As Women Take Over a Male-Dominated Field, the Pay Drops," *The New York Times*, March 18, 2016, https://www.nytimes.com/2016/03/20 /upshot/as-women-take-over-a-male-dominated-field-the-pay-drops.html.

53. "Coverture: The Word You Probably Don't Know But Should," National Women's History Museum, last modified September 4, 2012, https://www .womenshistory.org/articles/coverture-word-you-probably-dont-know-should.

54. Irene Mosca and Robert E. Wright, "Economics of Marriage Bars," Global Labor Organization, No. 933 (2021), https://hdl.handle.net/10419/240912/.

55. "Milestones to the Millennium: Serving the Public Good," Treasury Board of Canada, last modified January 1, 1997, https://www.tbs-sct.canada.ca/pubs_pol /partners/milemill01-eng.asp/.

56. "Canadian Women's History," Public Service Alliance of Canada, last modified April 13, 2024, https://psac-ncr.com/canadian-womens-history/.

57. Jamela Adam, "When Could Women Open a Bank Account?" *Forbes*, March 20, 2023, https://www.forbes.com/advisor/banking/when-could-women-open-a -bank-account/.

58. Karen A. Duncan, Kristyn Frank, and Anne Guèvremont, "Estimating Expenditures on Children by Families in Canada, 2014 to 2017," Statistics Canada (September 29, 2023), https://www.doi.org/10.25318/11f0019m2023007 -eng/.

59. "EI Maternity and Parental Benefits," Government of Canada, last modified December 29, 2023, https://www.canada.ca/en/services/benefits/ei/ei-maternity-parental.html/.

60. Ivona Hideg, Anja Krstic, et al., "The Unintended Consequences of Maternity Leaves: How Agency Interventions Mitigate the Negative Effects of Longer Legislated Maternity Leaves," *Journal of Applied Psychology* 103(10) (2018): 1155–64, https://doi.org/10.1037/apl0000327/.

61. Robin J. Ely and Irene Padavic, "What's Really Holding Women Back?" *Harvard Business Review*, March–April 2020 issue, https://hbr.org/2020/03/whats-really-holding-women-back.

62. "State of the World's Fathers 2019 Report Finds that 85 Percent of Fathers Say They Would Do Anything to Be Very Involved in Caring for Their New Child, but Are Still Taking on Far Less than Mothers," MenCare, last modified June 5, 2019, https://men-care.org/2019/06/05/state-of-the-worlds-fathers-2019-report-launch/.

63. "Gender Wage Gap," Conference Board of Canada, last modified April 5, 2023, https://www.conferenceboard.ca/hcp/gender-gap-aspx/.

64. Alexandra Fleischmann and Monika Sieverding, "Reactions toward Men Who Have Taken Parental Leave: Does the Length of Parental Leave Matter?" *Sex Roles: A Journal of Research* 72(9–10) (2015): 462–76, https://doi.org/10.1007/s11199-015-0469-x/.

65. Julie A. Kmec, Matt L. Huffman, and Andrew M. Penner, "Being a Parent or Having a Parent? The Perceived Employability of Men and Women Who Take Employment Leave," *American Behavioral Scientist* 58(3) (September 12, 2013): 453–72, https://doi.org/10.1177/0002764213503338/.

66. Morgan Smith, "Nobel Prize–Winning Harvard Economist Claudia Goldin: The Gender Pay Gap Will 'Never' Close Unless This Happens," CNBC, October 10, 2023, https://www.cnbc.com/2023/10/10/nobel-prize-winner-claudia-goldin-the-gender-pay-gap-will-never-close-unless-this-happens.html/.

67. Kochhar, "Gender Pay Gap."

68. Lise Dassieu, M. Gabrielle Pagé, et al., "Chronic Pain Experience and Health Inequities during the COVID-19 Pandemic in Canada: Qualitative Findings from the Chronic Pain & COVID-19 Pan-Canadian Study," *International Journal for Equity in Health* 20, 147 (2021), https://equityhealthj.biomedcentral.com/articles/10.1186/s12939-021-01496-1/.

69. "Reports on Disability and Accessibility in Canada," Statistics Canada, last modified February 14, 2024, https://www150.statcan.gc.ca/n1/en/catalogue/89-654-X/.

70. "Prevalence of Disability & Disability Types," Centers for Disease Control and Prevention, last modified October 27, 2021, https://www.cdc.gov/ncbddd/disabilityandhealth/features/disability-prevalence-rural-urban.html/.

71. Statistics Canada, "Reports on Disability."

72. Angela Kryhul, "Why Don't We Hire People with Disabilities?" Queen's University–Smith Business Insight, November 14, 2022, https://smith.queensu.ca /insight/content/Why-Dont-We-Hire-People-With-Disabilities.php.

73. H. Stephen Kaye, Lita H. Jans, and Erica C. Jones, "Why Don't Employers Hire and Retain Workers with Disabilities?" *Journal of Occupational Rehabilitation* 21(4) (March 13, 2011): 526–36, https://doi.org/10.1007%2Fs10926-011-9302-8/.

74. Michelle Maroto and David Pettinicchio, "Disability, Structural Inequality, and Work: The Influence of Occupational Segregation," *Research in Social Stratification and Mobility* Vol. 38 (2014): 76–92, https://doi.org/10.1016/j.rssm .2014.08.002/.

75. "Ontario Disability Support Program," Ontario.ca, last modified April 8, 2024, https://www.ontario.ca/page/ontario-disability-support-program.

76. "September 2023 Rentals.ca Report," Rentals.ca, October 13, 2023, https://rentals .ca/blog/september-2023-rentals-ca-report.

77. Andrew Pulrang, "Why Is the Employment Gap for People with Disabilities So Consistently Wide?" *Forbes*, October 31, 2022, https://www.forbes.com/sites /andrewpulrang/2022/10/31/why-is-the-employment-gap-for-people-with -disabilities-so-consistently-wide/.

78. "Study: Mental Disorders and Access to Mental Health Care," Statistics Canada, last modified September 22, 2023, https://www150.statcan.gc.ca/n1/daily -quotidien/230922/dq230922b-eng.htm/.

79. "The Facts: What You Need to Know," Money and Mental Health Policy Institute, last modified June 2, 2017, https://www.moneyandmentalhealth.org/money -and-mental-health-facts/.

8. A PATH FORWARD

1. Nicholas C. Coombs, Wyatt E. Meriwether, et al., "Barriers to Healthcare Access among U.S. Adults with Mental Health Challenges: A Population-Based Study," *SSM Population Health* 15 (June 15, 2021): 100847, https://doi.org/10.1016%2Fj .ssmph.2021.100847/.

2. "Mental Health Care Needs, 2018," Statistics Canada, last modified October 7, 2019, https://www150.statcan.gc.ca/n1/pub/82-625-x/2019001/article/00011 -eng.htm/.

3. Kathleen Rowan, Donna McAlpine, and Lynn Blewett, "Access and Cost Barriers to Mental Health Care by Insurance Status, 1999 to 2010," *Health Affairs (Millwood)* 32(10) (2013): 1723–30, https://doi.org/10.1377%2Fhlthaff.2013.0133/.

4. Mary Bartram, "Income-Based Inequities in Access to Mental Health Services in Canada," *Canadian Journal of Public Health* 110(4) (August 15, 2019): 395–403, https://doi.org/10.17269%2Fs41997-019-00204-5/.

5.   NICABM, "Treating Trauma: 2 Ways to Help Clients Feel Safe, with Peter Levine," YouTube Video, 6:33, June 2, 2017, https://www.youtube.com/watch?v=G7zA seaIyFA/.

6.   Andrew Huberman, "Reduce Anxiety & Stress with the Physiological Sigh," YouTube Video, 2:45, April 7, 2021, https://www.youtube.com/watch?v=rBdhqB GqiMc/.

7.   Melis Yilmaz Balban, Eric Neri, et al., "Brief Structured Respiration Practices Enhance Mood and Reduce Physiological Arousal," *Cell Reports Medicine* 4(1) (January 17, 2023): 100895, https://doi.org/10.1016%2Fj.xcrm.2022.100895/.

8.   Dana, *Anchored*, 91–92.

9.   Ellie Lisitsa, "Physiological Self-Soothing," Gottman Institute, March 4, 2024, https://www.gottman.com/blog/weekend-homework-assignment-physiological -self-soothing/.

10. Kendra Cherry, "13 Types of Common Cognitive Biases That Might Be Impairing Your Judgment," Verywell Mind, February 22, 2024, https://www.verywellmind .com/cognitive-biases-distort-thinking-2794763.

11. "One in Four Canadians Are Unable to Cover an Unexpected Expense of $500," Statistics Canada, last modified February 23, 2023, https://www150.statcan .gc.ca/n1/daily-quotidien/230213/dq230213b-eng.htm/.

12. Ivana Pino, "57% of Americans Can't Afford $1,000 Emergency Expense, Says New Report. A Look at Why Americans Are Saving Less and How You Can Boost Your Emergency Fund," *Fortune*, January 25, 2023, https://fortune.com/recommends /banking/57-percent-of-americans-cant-afford-a-1000-emergency-expense/.

13. Jiten Puri, "State of the Nation: Canadian Life Insurance Trends 2019," Policy Advisor, October 29, 2019, https://www.policyadvisor.com/life-insurance /canadian-life-insurance-trends-2019/.

14. New Study Shows Interest in Life Insurance at All-Time High in 2023," LIMRA News Releases, April 24, 2023, https://www.limra.com/en/newsroom/news -releases/2023/new-study-shows-interest-in-life-insurance-at-all-time-high-in-2023.

15. Keisha Blair, *Holistic Wealth: 32 Life Lessons to Help You Find Purpose, Prosperity, and Happiness* (Catalyst Books, 2019).

16. "Pheochromocytoma," Yale Medicine, last modified September 7, 2022, https:// www.yalemedicine.org/conditions/pheochromocytoma/.

17. "Estate Planning: Report Reveals Many Canadians Are Not Prepared," RBC Wealth Management Insights, last modified November 3, 2023, https://www .rbcwealthmanagement.com/en-ca/insights/estate-planning-report-reveals -many-canadians-are-not-prepared/.

18. Rachel Lustbader, "Caring.com's 2024 Wills Survey Finds that 40% of Americans Don't Think They Have Enough Assets to Create a Will," Caring.com, last modified January 16, 2024, https://www.caring.com/caregivers/estate-planning /wills-survey/.

19. Cristina Zarbo, Giorgio A. Tasca, et al., "Integrative Psychotherapy Works," *Frontiers in Psychology* 6 (January 11, 2016): 2021, https://doi.org/10.3389%2Ffpsyg.2015.02021/.

20. Daniel David, Ioana Cristea, and Stefan G. Hofmann, "Why Cognitive Behavioral Therapy Is the Current Gold Standard of Psychotherapy," *Frontiers in Psychiatry* 9 (January 29, 2018): 4, https://doi.org/10.3389%2Ffpsyt.2018.00004/.

21. *The Me You Can't See*, 2021 (RadicalMedia and Harpo Productions, 2021), Season 1, Episode 4, "We Need Each Other," directed by Asif Kapadia, aired May 21, 2021, on Apple TV+.

22. Danielle Beauvais, Elissa McCarthy, et al. "Eye Movement Desensitization and Reprocessing (EMDR) for PTSD," U.S. Department of Veterans Affairs, last modified July 18, 2023, https://www.ptsd.va.gov/professional/treat/txessentials/emdr_pro.asp/.

23. "Eye Movement Desensitization and Reprocessing (EMDR) Therapy," American Psychological Association, last modified July 31, 2017, https://www.apa.org/ptsd-guideline/treatments/eye-movement-reprocessing/.

24. Richard C. Schwartz, *No Bad Parts: Healing Trauma & Restoring Wholeness with the Internal Family Systems Model* (Boulder: Sounds True, 2021).

25. Voices of Esalen, "Dr. Richard Schwartz: Internal Family Systems," recorded May 15, 2020, https://soundcloud.com/voices-of-esalen/dr-richard-schwartz-internal-family-systems/.oi909ooooo/.

26. Internal Family Systems–IFS Institute, "Intro to Internal Family Systems (IFS) by Dr. Richard Schwartz," YouTube Video, 4:57, October 23, 2018, https://www.youtube.com/watch?v=6X45Y74blSg/.

27. Hope Gillette, "What Is Internal Family Systems Therapy?" PsychCentral, December 7, 2021, https://psychcentral.com/health/internal-family-systems-therapy.

28. Daniel Crosby, *The Laws of Wealth: Psychology and the Secret to Investing Success* (Hampshire: Harriman House, 2021), 122.

29. Crosby, *The Laws of Wealth*, 124.

30. David M. Blanchett, "Financially Sound Households Use Financial Planners, Not Transactional Advisers," *Journal of Financial Planning* Vol. 32, Issue 4 (2019): 30, https://openurl.ebsco.com/EPDB%3Agcd%3A3%3A25059/detailv2?sid=ebsco%3Aplink%3Ascholar&id=ebsco%3Agcd%3A135675645&crl=c/.

31. Jeremy Burke and Angela A. Hung, "Do Financial Advisers Influence Savings Behavior?" RAND Corporation (October 8, 2015), https://www.rand.org/pubs/research_reports/RR1289.html/.

9. AT THE HEART OF MONEY

1. Jason Vitug, *Happy Money Happy Life: A Multidimensional Approach to Health, Wealth, and Financial Freedom* (Hoboken: Wiley, 2023), xix.

2. Andrew T. Jebb, Louis Tay, et al., "Happiness, Income Satiation and Turning Points around the World," *Nature Human Behaviour* 2 (2018): 33–38, https://doi .org/10.1038/s41562-017-0277-0.

3. Amy Patterson Neubert, "Money Only Buys Happiness for a Certain Amount," *Purdue University News*, February 13, 2018, https://www.purdue.edu/newsroom /releases/2018/Q1/money-only-buys-happiness-for-a-certain-amount.html.

4. "Inflation Calculator," Bank of Canada, last modified April 11, 2024, https:// www.bankofcanada.ca/rates/related/inflation-calculator/.

5. Daniel Kahneman, "High Income Improves Evaluation of Life but Not Emotional Well-Being," *Proceedings of the National Academy of Sciences* Vol. 107, No. 38 (September 21, 2010), https://doi.org/10.1073/pnas.1011492107/.

6. Matthew A. Killingsworth, "Experienced Well-Being Rises with Income, Even above $75,000 per Year," *Proceedings of the National Academy of Sciences* Vol. 118, No. 4 (January 26, 2021), https://doi.org/10.1073/pnas.2016976118/.

7. Matthew A. Killingsworth, Daniel Kahneman, and Barbara Mellers, "Income and Emotional Well-Being: A Conflict Resolved," *Proceedings of the National Academy of Sciences* Vol. 120, No. 10 (March 7, 2023), https://doi.org/10.1073/pnas .2208661120/.

8. Michele W. Berger, "Does More Money Correlate with Great Happiness?" *Penn Today*, March 6, 2023, https://penntoday.upenn.edu/news/does-more-money -correlate-greater-happiness-Penn-Princeton-research.

9. *Friends*, Season 2, Episode 5, "The One with Five Steaks and an Eggplant," directed by Ellen Gittelsohn, aired October 19, 1995.

10. Vitug, *Happy Money Happy Life*, 6.

11. Laura Caseley, "1800s Quack Medicine People Used to Actually Take to Treat Illness," Little Things, September 19, 2016, https://littlethings.com/lifestyle /victorian-quack-medicine/2290431-2.

12. "Regrets of the Dying," Bronnie Ware, last modified February 25, 2022, https:// bronnieware.com/blog/regrets-of-the-dying/.

13. Melissa Madeson, "Seligman's PERMA+ Model Explained: A Theory of Wellbeing," PositivePsychology.com, February 24, 2017, https://positivepsychology.com /perma-model/.

14. Mihaly Csikszentmihalyi and Judith LeFevre, "Optimal Experience in Work and Leisure," *Journal of Personality and Social Psychology* 56(5) (1989): 815–22, https:// doi.org/10.1037/0022-3514.56.5.815/.

15. "Harvard Second Generation," Harvard Study of Adult Development, accessed January 13, 2024, https://www.adultdevelopmentstudy.org/.

16. Robert Waldinger and Marc Schulz, *The Good Life: Lessons from the World's Longest Scientific Study of Happiness* (New York: Simon & Schuster, 2023).

17. Rick Warren, *The Purpose Driven Life: What on Earth Am I Here For?* (Grand Rapids: Zondervan, 2013).

18. Madeson, "PERMA+."

19. Lewina O. Lee, Peter James, et al., "Optimism Is Associated with Exceptional Longevity in 2 Epidemiologic Cohorts of Men and Women," *Proceedings of the National Academy of Sciences* Vol. 116, No. 37 (August 26, 2019): 18357–62, https://doi.org/10.1073/pnas.1900712116.

20. Yu Tahara, Saneyuki Makino, et al., "Association between Irregular Meal Timing and the Mental Health of Japanese Workers," *Nutrients* 13(8) (2021): 2775, https://doi.org/10.3390/nu13082775/.

21. Deborah R. Wahl, Karoline Villinger, et al., "Healthy Food Choices Are Happy Food Choices: Evidence from a Real Life Sample Using Smartphone Based Assessments," *Scientific Reports* 7(1) (December 6, 2017): 17069, https://doi.org/10.1038%2Fs41598-017-17262-9/.

22. Felice N. Jacka, Adrienne O'Neil, et al., "A Randomised Controlled Trial of Dietary Improvement for Adults with Major Depression (the 'SMILES' trial)," *BMC Medicine* 15(23) (January 30, 2017), https://doi.org/10.1186/s12916-017-0791-y/.

23. Amanda Blackwelder, Mikhail Hoskins, and Larissa Huber, "Effect of Inadequate Sleep on Frequent Mental Distress," *Preventing Chronic Disease* Vol. 18 (June 17, 2021): 200573, http://dx.doi.org/10.5888/pcd18.200573/.

24. Vijay Kumar Chattu, Dilshad Manzar, et al., "The Global Problem of Insufficient Sleep and Its Serious Public Health Implications," *Healthcare (Basel)* 7(1) (December 20, 2018): 1, https://doi.org/10.3390%2Fhealthcare7010001/.

25. Cara A. Palmer, Joanne L. Bower, et al., "Sleep Loss and Emotion: A Systematic Review and Meta-analysis of over 50 Years of Experimental Research," *Psychological Bulletin* (December 21, 2023), https://doi.org/10.1037/bul0000410/.

26. "Canadian Health Measures Survey: Activity Monitor Data, 2018–2019," Statistics Canada, last modified September 1, 2021, https://www150.statcan.gc.ca/n1/daily-quotidien/210901/dq210901c-eng.htm/.

27. Nazik Elgaddal, Ellen A. Kramarow, and Cynthia Reuben, "Physical Activity among Adults Aged 18 and Over: United States, 2020," *National Center for Health Statistics* No. 443 (2022), https://dx.doi.org/10.15620/cdc:120213/.

28. "Health Benefits of Physical Activity: The Evidence," *Canadian Medical Association Journal* 174(6) (March 14, 2006): 801–9, https://doi.org/10.1503%2Fcmaj.051351/.

29. Hsin-Yu An, Wei Chen, et al., "The Relationships between Physical Activity and Life Satisfaction and Happiness among Young, Middle-Aged, and Older Adults," *International Journal of Environmental Research and Public Health* 17(13) (July 4, 2020): 4817, https://doi.org/10.3390%2Fijerph17134817/.

30. Mayuree Rao, Ashkan Afshin, et al., "Do Healthier Foods and Diet Patterns Cost More than Less Healthy Options? A Systematic Review and Meta-Analysis," *BMJ Open* Vol. 3, Issue 12 (2013), https://doi.org/10.1136/bmjopen-2013-004277/.

31. "How Much Sleep Is Enough?" National Heart, Lung, and Blood Institute, last modified March 24, 2022, https://www.nhlbi.nih.gov/health/sleep/how-much-sleep/.

32. Elizabeth Dunn and Michael Norton, *Happy Money: The Science of Happier Spending* (New York: Simon & Schuster Paperbacks, 2014), 136.

33. Aaron C. Weidman and Elizabeth W. Dunn, "The Unsung Benefits of Material Things: Material Purchases Provide More Frequent Momentary Happiness than Experiential Purchases," *Social Psychological and Personality Science* 7(4) (2016): 390–99, https://doi.org/10.1177/1948550615619761/.

34. "Living Happily in a Material World: Material Purchases Can Bring Happiness," ScienceDaily, December 21, 2015, https://www.sciencedaily.com/releases/2015/12/151221194128.htm/.

35. Amit Kumar, Matthew A. Killingsworth, and Thomas Gilovich, "Spending on Doing Promotes More Moment-to-Moment Happiness than Spending on Having," *Journal of Experimental Social Psychology* Vol. 88, Article 103985 (May 2020), https://doi.org/10.1016/j.jesp.2020.103971/.

36. Leaf Van Boven and Thomas Gilovich, "To Do or to Have? That Is the Question," *Journal of Personality and Social Psychology* 85(6) (2003): 1193–202, https://doi.org/10.1037/0022-3514.85.6.1193/.

37. Fred B. Bryant, Colette M. Smart, and Scott P. King, "Using the Past to Enhance the Present: Boosting Happiness through Positive Reminiscence," *Journal of Happiness Studies* Vol. 6 (September 2005): 227–60, https://doi.org/10.1007/s10902-005-3889-4/.

38. Dunn and Norton, *Happy Money*, 34.

39. Karon Liu, "Sriracha Is Once Again in Short Supply. Here Are Some Alternatives," *Toronto Star*, October 30, 2023, https://www.thestar.com/news/gta/sriracha-is-once-again-in-short-supply-here-are-some-alternatives/article_700ad28b-22cc-5eae-8e70-ebad4899bbd9.html.

40. Ashley V. Whillans, Elizabeth W. Dunn, et al., "Buying Time Promotes Happiness," *Proceedings of the National Academy of Sciences* 114(32) (August 8, 2017): 8523–27, https://doi.org/10.1073%2Fpnas.1706541114/.

41. Sean Clarke and Vincent Hardy, "Working from Home during the COVID-19 Pandemic: How Rates in Canada and the United States Compare," Statistics Canada, August 24, 2022, https://doi.org/10.25318/36280001202200800001-eng/.

42. "Remote Work Is Linked to Happiness: Study of 12,455 Respondents," Tracking Happiness, last modified March 23, 2024, https://www.trackinghappiness.com/remote-work-leads-to-happiness-study/.

43. Jessica Howington, "Losing Talent to Return-to-Office Mandates: Insights from the FlexJobs Survey," FlexJobs, last modified January 2017, https://www.flexjobs.com/blog/post/losing-talent-to-return-to-office-mandates-insights-from-the-flexjobs-survey/.

44. Elizabeth W. Dunn, Daniel T. Gilbert, and Timothy D. Wilson, "If Money Doesn't Make You Happy, Then You Probably Aren't Spending It Right," *Journal of Consumer Psychology* Vol. 21, Issue 2 (April 2011): 115–25, https://doi.org/10.1016/j.jcps.2011.02.002/.

45. Amit Kumar, Matthew A. Killingsworth, and Thomas Gilovich, "Waiting for Merlot: Anticipatory Consumption of Experiential and Material Purchases," *Psychological Science* 25(10) (2014): 1924–31, https://doi.org/10.1177/0956797614546556/.

46. Elizabeth W. Dunn, Lara B. Aknin, and Michael I. Norton, "Prosocial Spending and Happiness: Using Money to Benefit Others Pays Off," *Current Directions in Psychological Science* Vol. 23, No. 1 (February 2014): 41–47, https://www.hbs.edu/faculty/Pages/item.aspx?num=45753.

47. Jake Fuss, Nathaniel Li, and Grady Munro, "Generosity in Canada: The 2023 Generosity Index," Fraser Institute, December 12, 2023, https://www.fraserinstitute.org/studies/generosity-in-canada-the-2023-generosity-index.

48. Ivana Saric, "Americans Are Giving to Charity at Lowest Level in Nearly 3 Decades," Axios, June 22, 2023, https://www.axios.com/2023/06/22/charitable-giving-donations-income.

49. Kathleen Vohs, Nicole Mead, and Miranda Goode, "The Psychological Consequences of Money," *Science* 314(5802) (December 2006): 1154–56, http://dx.doi.org/10.1126/science.1132491/.

50. Vohs, "Psychological Consequences," 1154–56.

51. Dunn and Norton, *Happy Money*, 116–23.

52. "Currency," Online Etymology Dictionary, last modified June 8, 2018, https://www.etymonline.com/word/currency.

53. Lynne Twist, *The Soul of Money: Reclaiming the Wealth of Our Inner Resources* (New York: Norton, 2017), 102–3.